D1187101

6·21·98

HAPPY FATHER'S DAY,
DAD!
LOVE, RICH

DOUBLEDAY
CELEBRATES
100 YEARS OF
EXCELLENCE

BUTKUS

FLESH AND BLOOD

DICK BUTKUS

AND

PAT SMITH

DOUBLEDAY

NEW YORK
LONDON
TORONTO
SYDNEY
AUCKLAND

PUBLISHED BY DOUBLEDAY

a division of Bantam Doubleday Dell Publishing Group, Inc.
1540 Broadway, New York, New York 10036

DOUBLEDAY and the portrayal of an anchor with a dolphin are trademarks of
Doubleday, a division of Bantam Doubleday Dell Publishing Group, Inc.

Library of Congress Cataloging-in-Publication Data

Butkus, Dick.
    Butkus : flesh and blood : how I played the game / Dick Butkus and
Pat Smith. — 1st ed.
       p.   cm.
    1. Butkus, Dick.   2. Football players—United States—Biography.
3. Chicago Bears (Football team)   I. Smith, Pat, 1937–   .
II. Title.
GV939.B88A3   1997
796.332'092—dc21
    [B]   97-30738
                                                             CIP

ISBN 0-385-48648-0
Copyright © 1997 by Dick Butkus and Pat Smith
All Rights Reserved
Printed in the United States of America
November 1997

Text design by Stanley S. Drate/Folio Graphics Co., Inc.

10   9   8   7   6   5   4   3   2

To my parents, Emma and John Butkus

BUTKUS

C H A P T E R

1

I'm feeding my pet koi fish a pellet at a time and watching them swarm like fire on each one. Behind me are a few features of California success: sun deck, hot tub, and the modern glass-and-wood home. In the grass over by the eucalyptus tree is a football left by my son Matt, who played for USC. And beyond the tree, leaning against a stone bench, is a surfboard belonging to Rick, my oldest son. It's December in Malibu, Sunday, seventy-five degrees under a sky as big and blue as the Pacific, which is spread out like a picnic tablecloth 200 feet below me.

I hear a vehicle pull up to my front door on the other side of the bushes. I turn around and peer through the jacaranda. It's my wife Helen and our daughter Nikki, home from shopping. I turn back to my koi fish, my ears following their progress through the house until they come out onto the deck and sit down, talking away like old friends—something about going to Chicago. I listen for a bit. Helen's exuberant voice sounds just as it did a million years ago when she took a ride on a motor scooter with me, a bashful high school kid.

I look over the far edge of the fish pond, down to the Pacific, and watch the easy progress of a sailboat, its canvas gleaming, tiny in the distance—and I think how easy and peaceful all of this feels. Then I think about how far we have come, and like a hang glider, my memory lifts off, makes a big turn over the sailboat, and swings back over L.A., floating briefly above the Coliseum and the Rose Bowl in Pasadena, then back across the years and beyond the seasons, before hundreds of games and thousands of practices, back to a blue-collar neighborhood of frame houses on Chicago's South Side.

To a place called Roseland.

Maybe it's October, and in my mind I see a boy of seven or eight. He mounts an old, scarred football on an empty Skippy jar, steps back three paces, brings his oversized feet together, and glances at the freshly painted picket fence some twenty yards away. Lowering his eyes to the ball, he focuses on a spot just below its center. Then, holding his breath, he steps lightly forward, his arms lifting out from his sides, his head down, he cocks his right leg behind him and swings it forward.

Thump!

The ball lifts into the crisp autumn air, revolving backward as it flies forward, climbing against the backdrop of the house across the street, the late-afternoon sunlight glancing off the hard, smooth leather. It lands on the pavement beyond the fence.

The boy does not shout or raise a fist in triumph. Nor does he look to see if anyone is watching. He seems almost not to care as he walks out through the fence gate and onto the dead-end street. He picks up the ball and takes it back across the lawn to the passageway between the house and the garage where the chickens are kept and tees it up again.

Over and over, until the light thins and his mother calls

him into the house, the boy kicks the ball toward the white picket fence. He's got it down now, he's found the rhythm—and with each successful flight onto Lowe Avenue, he drives the process deeper and deeper into his memory.

"Dickie! Come in and eat!"

He sits at the small kitchen table with his three older brothers. They don't say much—certainly not to him. Ron is sixteen and already a man of the world. He calls Dickie "Duke a'Sandwich" because of the boy's affinity for putting anything edible between two pieces of bread. Don, fifteen, is long, slim, and silent: He sits with the lower half of his six-foot-three frame folded like easel sticks under the Formica table. Dave is closest in age, but at eleven he's trying to make the grade with his older brothers. So he too ignores "the Kid." And Dickie, or Duke a'Sandwich, or the Kid—the one they ditch whenever he tries to tag along—well, he might just as well be invisible.

Their mother keeps bringing plates heaped high with food, and the boy eats with his head down, his thoughts elsewhere, perhaps on the flight of a football. When the feeding is over, the brothers scrape their chairs back from the table and go their separate ways, each finding a private spot in the tiny house to do his homework or listen to the radio.

If it is Friday or Saturday, then maybe Ron and Don, with their windbreaker collars high against their necks and their hair slicked back with Wildroot Cream Oil, slip out into the night beyond the scope of the boy's imagination, so he sits alone on the front porch and gazes dreamily at the white picket fence glowing in the gathering dark.

Maybe his father comes shambling along the sidewalk, wearing bib overalls and carrying a black lunch pail from his electrician's job at Pullman Standard, makers of luxury railroad sleeping cars. Maybe the father and son nod at each other, or maybe they issue short hellos. But always their eyes meet, and that's enough. The boy loves his father, but he doesn't really know him. His father is a quiet man from another country.

Night is falling rapidly now and the boy listens to the last songs of the birds coming from the trees across the street. Through the window behind him, he can hear his mother talking in a steady stream of Lithuanian and occasionally his father stems the flow with an agreeable syllable or two. The boy doesn't understand a word because his parents only speak the hard, guttural language between themselves. Perhaps it is a code for them, a means of sharing secrets.

One of his sisters—Dolly or Babe—might arrive, carrying a big bag of groceries and maybe some sausages and bread from a Lithuanian delicatessen. She smiles at him and gives him a little wave before disappearing into the house. He likes his sisters. But they're so much older. Both were married and gone before he was born. They're more like aunts than sisters. Maybe the phone rings, shrill like they used to, and from the altered pitch of his mother's voice the boy knows it's Dolly, wanting to know when she and her husband should come by on Sunday. Or maybe it's John, calling from his Army post far away in a place called Bardot, France. The boy hardly knows John. There are thirteen years between them. John's more like an uncle than a brother.

So, alone with his thoughts, the boy sits on the little porch until the birds stop singing altogether and night presses in on the dead-end street and the inevitable call comes from within the house.

''Bedtime, Dickie!''

In the eight-by-ten room he shares with his brothers, the boy pulls off Dave's hand-me-down dungarees and ripped PF Flyers and climbs into the upper bunk across from the window. He pulls the thin covers up to his chin and closes his eyes. And there, in the dark quiet of the narrow room, the show begins: A football lifts slowly and silently into the air, tumbling and turning as if it were alive, climbing higher and higher, going farther and farther.

As good as he was at dreaming, the boy could not have imagined, not at eight years old, that the game of football would be the thing that would drive him, fill him up, and make him whole for the next twenty-three years. Yet the act of kicking that ball over the white picket fence onto Lowe Avenue stands out in my memory today as a defining moment. It was as though the boy had discovered a form of magic, a secret skill all his own. Little Dickie Butkus had learned how to make a football fly.

Weighing in at thirteen pounds, six ounces, at Roseland Community Hospital on December 9, 1942, I was the first Butkus child to have been born outside the little house at 10324 South Lowe Avenue. I spent my first week in an incubator, the first—and last—private bedroom I ever had. I was a "blue baby"—a term describing newborns who suffer from a lack of oxygen due either to a lesion on the heart or inadequate lung expansion—and like my brother Le Roy, who had been born dead of the affliction eleven years earlier, I was not supposed to make it.

I was also not supposed to have been a boy. After producing four males in a row, my mother was looking forward to the company of a baby girl. My two oldest sisters, Babe and Dolly, were married and living in their own homes, leaving only Rita, who was fourteen. Babe once told me that our mother refused to cut my hair until well after my third birthday. I don't remember those locks, but I've preferred flattops ever since I've had anything to say about it.

I was christened Richard Marvin Butkus at St. Helena's Roman Catholic Church, and about all I recall of my first half dozen years is taking an occasional trip with my mother to a three-story apartment building called a "three-flat" and climbing the stairs to the top floor, where I would sit on the back porch while she spoke Lithuanian to a sickly woman friend.

I also remember sitting on a cart as it was towed through the back alleys of our neighborhood by an old black ragman who would sing out, "Rag-o-li-i-ine!" Once I must have decided to sign on for the full tour of Roseland, because I didn't get home until well after dark. My little adventure threw a big scare into everyone. This would have been in 1948 or so, a decade and a half since the Lindbergh baby had been snatched from his bedroom in Hopewell, New Jersey, but the heinous crime of kidnapping was still fresh in the national fear bin.

But Roseland was not Hopewell, and no self-respecting kidnapper would have remotely considered our family ripe for a ransom. One look at our house would have told you that. Even by Roseland standards, it was modest. It sat in midblock, squeezed between much larger two- and three-story homes that fronted right on the sidewalk, and it looked more like a converted garage than a house. But it was always clean and neat, and every year it got a fresh coat of paint.

It had two small bedrooms, a dining area, a miniature living room, and a kitchen. The entire structure could not have covered more than 900 square feet. A few years before I was born, my father built a small basement with a furnace and some living space for my three sisters. They'd all reached ages when they needed some privacy. Ten members of the Butkus family lived under that little slattern roof at one time or another.

Unremarkable though it was, our little homestead had some interesting, even unique features. A deep front yard glowed with thick grass in the summer, and that white picket fence always seemed newly painted. In front of the garage was a garden that gave us fresh corn and tomatoes in season. Next to the garden was a coop where my father raised chickens, ducks, and geese. At one point we even had a couple of pigs, compliments of my oldest brother John, who brought them home one day from his job in the stockyards.

Chicago was still growing then, still filling out, and Roseland was a relatively new community. It got its name honestly. Once the area was covered with acre upon acre of commercial rose fields. Old-timers recall how on certain days the scent of the flowers mixed with the burning smells from the steel mills. John and Babe remember an unpaved Lowe Avenue with wooden sidewalks. Babe says that in heavy downpours she and John and Dolly sometimes had to chase the sidewalks as they floated down the street so that Pa could anchor them back in place.

Scattered across the gridded sprawl of working-class two-story homes that had replaced the rose fields were dozens of vacant lots, some of them a block or two square, called "prairies." During our grammar school years, they were the preferred playgrounds. Hell, other than a park or two, the prairies were our *only* playgrounds. We'd build huts and dig tunnels in the prairies and we'd play "war" in them, hiding like Marines in the high grass. Later, when demolition derbies became popular on TV, we would clear an oval in one of the prairies and race our bikes, crashing into each other and twisting the handlebars, the wheels, and the spokes. At night we'd build bonfires, transforming the prairies into places of mystery and danger. In the mornings we would use them as shortcuts to school. I probably logged a thousand miles running through the prairies of Roseland.

From May until November, Roseland had the feel and smell and color of a small town, even as it sat on the edge of what was then the second-largest city in America.

In the winter it was just cold.

Most backyards had gardens, some with little vineyards and stands of apple trees. Those yards often told you the nationality of their owners. White grapes and apples were raised by the Germans, red grapes and plums by the Italians. The Hungarians grew cabbages, and the Dutch cultivated the most beautiful flowers. My brother John remembers a Lithuanian guy over on 105th who kept a pair of cows and sold us two gallons of milk daily. But only the Butkus family had livestock in their front yard.

Most residents of Roseland saw themselves as simple and hardworking, with no false airs, no unrealistic expectations. The women had a couple of fancy dresses and the men each had a suit and maybe a couple of pairs of "good" shoes. Some families even owned a car. In 1948, when Uncle Miltie hit the airwaves, some of the folks on my block could watch him in their living rooms. But there was no television in the Butkus house that year. My mother didn't have any fancy dresses and my father never had more than one pair of dress shoes. If there was lots of good healthy food on the table, there was nothing extra.

When I'm asked to describe the circumstances of my childhood, I have to swallow hard and say we were poor, maybe dirt poor. On bitter cold winter nights when the furnace needed feeding, my older brothers and sometimes my sisters would wheel a big iron cart a mile or so along 103rd Street to the railroad tracks. They'd wrestle the cart down the gravel slope to a fenced-in coal yard. If they couldn't find enough stray pieces outside, someone climbed over the fence and threw chunks out to the others. If a guard was on duty, they'd stand by the tracks and wait for the lights of a locomotive to appear. Then they'd wave and yell to the fireman and point at the cart, hoping that he'd throw some coal to them as he rolled by.

Every member of the family worked. Ron, Don, and Dave had after-school jobs, and although Babe, Dolly, and John were on their own as far back as I could remember, they always helped out. Not many days went by that one of them didn't show up at the house with a bag of groceries. I got my first job when I was eight, in a bakery on 103rd. I ran errands, carried out the trash, swept up, cleaned the big metal bread pans, and washed the windows. I was paid with fresh rolls and bread, which was better than money to me. I was proud to carry those big warm bags home and put them on the kitchen table.

Even Ma worked a fifty-hour week at the Monarch Laundry. How she managed it I'll never know. She cooked every meal, kept the house spotless, did our laundry, and got Dave and me off to school on time. Hell, just cooking for the Butkus boys was a full-time job. Babe recalls the place was more like a restaurant than a house, and according to Dave, the weekly food consumption was staggering: twenty dozen eggs, twenty-eight loaves of bread, seven gallons of milk, ten pounds of bacon—and that was just breakfast!

Dinner resembled feeding time at a Western ranch—or maybe a zoo. Although table manners were not my mother's speciality, she did try to keep us from eating like cattle. Mom wisely ate first, sitting by herself, savoring the quiet time before the storm. She would clear the table, put down two loaves of bread, a pound of butter, four glasses, four plates, four knives, four forks, and a gallon of milk. Then she'd yell, "Okay!"—and we'd materialize, coming through the back door and in from the living room. Amid sounds of scraping chairs and heavy breathing, we'd take up our positions around the little table.

The milk and bread would disappear in a blur. Then a platter piled high with the meat of the day would arrive: pork chops, hamburgers, or lots of garage-raised chicken. Don had the longest reach, but Ron was older and tougher. Dave and I tried to compete, but we were puppies by comparison. Meanwhile, a mountain of mashed potatoes and a forest of vegetables would be set down—cauliflower, lima beans, corn, tomatoes—whatever was ripe in the garden.

In the winter jars of pickled vegetables and bowls of homemade sauerkraut were brought up from the cellar. In either season the feeding frenzy would be over in minutes. Not a word would be exchanged, except perhaps a snarl or two at whoever drank the last drop of milk or ate the last slice of bread. Then we'd each go our own way, and the little kitchen would look as if an army had been through there.

Everything was carefully budgeted. We gave each other haircuts. Clothes were handed down, brother to brother, and I don't think I had a new pair of sneakers until I was in college. Due to my wide feet, which would eventually grow into size EEE, I was always coming out of my shoes, like extra cargo on a Mississippi barge. This wasn't a big deal except in the winter, when I'd come home from the park with no feeling in my feet. My jackets were thin, my underwear frayed, and my socks were full of holes. And despite my mother's late-night efforts with needle and thread, my shirts and pants were always ripped.

Maybe our clothes were shabby, but we weren't a bad-looking bunch. Certainly there was nothing small about any of us. At six-foot-three and 250 pounds, I would be hard to spot if my brothers formed a tight circle and I stood in the middle. Don, for example, stands six-foot-six and Ron is just two inches shorter. John is lanky, like my father, and Dave is stocky, like my mother. Taken together, the four of us were the answer to any football coach's dreams. Growing up, my sisters were easy enough to look at. Babe and Dolly were tall and quite attractive, each with her share of suitors. But Rita, the youngest of the three, was a stunner: a natural blonde, with sky-blue eyes and a great figure. Babe remembers her as ''a lovely cross between Marilyn Monroe and Mother Teresa. Almost too good to be true, really.''

One autumn afternoon in 1946, Rita came home early from her job at the Campbell Soup Company with a sore throat. Three days later, she was diagnosed with diphtheria and admitted to the Hospital for Contagious Diseases. Even though I was very young, I remember watching my mother worry as the days, weeks, and months went by. Diphtheria was a known killer in those days. Then came news that Rita had beaten the disease and would be coming home soon. But she never made it, dying early one morning in March after having contracted pneumonia. Rita was just nineteen. I will always remember the deep quiet that settled over our house after Rita died. It stayed that way for a long time.

No matter how strong my mother was—or how hard she worked—she always seemed to be getting sick. Over the years, she was stricken with hepatitis, had her gall bladder removed, and even had a mastectomy. One June day when I was about nine, I saw her collapse in the living room. I still carry the image of her falling to her knees, and the ambulance coming and taking her away, and I remember being frightened for the first time in my life. She was taken to Augustana's Hospital, far away on the North Side. When we went to visit her, I was told I was too young to go up to the room, so I stood out in the sunlit street and waved to her as she stood at the window, thinking everything was going to be okay. Years later, I learned that she had nearly died from a ruptured appendix.

I don't know where I'd be if my mother had died then. I certainly wouldn't be here in Malibu. There would have been just too many rivers to cross alone. My mother was my friend and confidante. She was the one I told my thoughts to. When I was ten, I told her about my plans to play football. Most mothers would try to talk their son out of such a notion, but Mom encouraged me. Ronnie played defensive end at Tilden Tech—and the college scholarship offers were beginning to roll in. Mom didn't know anything about football, but she believed that college degrees were like money in the bank. And she saw football as perhaps the only available means to that end.

Our happiest times together took place on the porch, during those frequent summer showers that blow in off Lake Michigan—when the prairie heat would break and she would visibly relax, the lines in her face seeming to disappear, and we would talk, sharing our hopes and dreams. I can still see her sitting in that rocker, her hazel eyes sleepy, her hands resting peacefully in her lap. She would listen to me talk about football and smile softly.

Even today the sound of rain on a roof calms me.

I may or may not have been my mother's favorite son. But once football took hold of me, I believe I became her fondest hope. From my first game in high school until my last game for the Bears, she never missed an opportunity to be in the stands.

Family legend has it that my mother was born "on a pile of coal." Not true. But she only missed that distinction by a few minutes. On the afternoon of September 5, 1904, my grandmother was working in one of the mines that burrow through the hillsides of Spring Valley, Illinois, when the contractions began. She barely made it to the little house outside the company gate before my mother arrived. Afterward, according to the story, my grandmother washed up, drank a cup of coffee, and returned to her station in the mine, leaving Emma Ramona Goodoff in the care of a midwife.

The circumstances of my mother's birth help to explain her energy and toughness. She was a natural-born leader, her authority unchallenged in our house. She was equal parts majordomo, chief confessor, mother superior, and grand inquisitor. She only stood five-foot-six, but she parented like a giant.

Her husband was one of the kindest, sweetest men Roseland had ever seen. He stood six-foot-two and weighed about 180. As my sister Dolly says, "Pa was Lincoln-thin." He walked pigeon-toed, with long strides, his head down. I would eventually grow larger than my father, but we shared the same physical makeup: long arms, long trunk, big between the shoulders. His hands were huge, the callused palms permanently crisscrossed with black electrical burns from all the hot wires he'd held.

I never saw anyone work harder and expect less. After putting in ten- and twelve-hour days, half of that time spent on his water-puffed knees in "the shops" at Pullman Standard, he typically did odd jobs around the neighborhood. He was called upon to wire people's homes, fix their appliances, even repair the faulty coils of a local bootlegger's still, which was always on the fritz. Pa once set up a still of his own down in the cellar, but Ma found out and promptly confiscated it. He was a good electrician, but because he couldn't speak English all that well, he never got a union card.

Ma and the girls badgered him into taking a night course in English at Fenger High and eventually he became a citizen. I think he did it more to please Ma than anything else. I never noticed any difference between the immigrant who was my father and the citizen they had him become. He was still Pa, shy as a rabbit and always smiling at adversity. When a customer told Pa he couldn't pay him right away, my father would just bow his head and say, "Oh, don't worry about it." Most of the time, they didn't worry about it and my father didn't get paid. But I never heard him complain.

In 1893 in Kaunas, Lithuania, John Butkus came into a world where complaints weighed even less than the dead leaves that flew on the Baltic winds. For more than three decades, the Russians had been conducting a policy of ethnic cleansing and the Roman Catholics were the main targets. Although my father loved to talk about his days in the lumber camps of Minnesota, he seldom mentioned his earlier life in Lithuania. In 1903 my grandparents quietly arranged for their children's escape across the southwestern border into Poland. The plan was for the parents to soon follow, and together the family would make their way to America. John, his brother, and his sister made it into Poland. And there they waited until one day they learned that their parents would never come out.

I often think about my father, especially about him never complaining. Maybe getting stiffed for a few bucks was almost pleasant after what he'd been through. I believe he was just happy to be in America and to have a woman like my mother to care for him. Though to hear her sometimes, you'd wonder. She could ride him pretty hard. At night in my bed, I'd hear her urging him in no uncertain terms to demand payment from the "dirty, no-good deadbeats" that he worked for, and if he wasn't going to be more aggressive in his future dealings, then perhaps he should spend more time "fixing up *our* home, since that's where charity begins." But to my mother's great regret and frustration, my father was simply unable or unwilling to change.

No matter how many stories she'd heard from her parents about how bad it was in the old country, my mother never really knew what it was like to live in mortal fear. It's a little like the difference between playing pro football and watching it. Until you've felt those hits, until you've struggled through an injury on a frozen field, you can't really take the measure of a player's inner worth. For my mother, the American dream was making enough money so you never had to worry about paying the bills. For my father, it meant being able to breathe.

After I'd retired from the Bears and Pa was gone, my mother and I would sit on her porch in Florida and we'd remember the days back at 10324 South Lowe. We'd retell all the stories, laughing a lot and skipping over the rough spots. Eventually our shared memory would land on Pa, and my mother would slap her thigh, still angry at his easy attitude toward those who cheated him. "All they had to do was buy him a beer and your father was theirs." But then her face would soften at the memory of Sunday mornings when my father would lead us all to Catholic Mass at St. Helena's.

It wasn't long before I was kicking the football clear across Lowe Avenue and bouncing it off the front porch across the way. This feat was not greatly appreciated by the man who owned the porch. After he'd complained to my mother once too often, I was forcibly graduated to Fernwood Park, which began just six houses down the street from our house. Fernwood was a stage large enough for even *my* dreams.

Four blocks square, Fernwood in the summer shimmered as you approached it. Huge elms and oaks overhung the baseball and football fields, casting cool shadows in the heat. In the fall Fernwood blazed good-bye to baseball choose-ups and said hello to pickup football, and in the winter it lay still as a Currier and Ives etching, white-mantled except for the wet black of the tree trunks and the ice on the hockey pond that we'd create with our neighbors' garden hoses each Christmas season.

Fernwood was the green heart of Roseland and the center of my life beyond the white picket fence. But at first it was not all that easy fitting in because the park "belonged" to my older brothers and their friends. None of those older guys adhered to a policy of inclusion, at least not as it might have applied to my brother Dave and me. In their estimation, our presence was totally unnecessary. John, who came over to Fernwood and played on weekends even after he was married, once told me: "You and Dave were always whining that we wouldn't let you play with us. You'd hang around, grousing and kicking the grass. We had all the equipment—what there was of it. But you'd complain to Ma, and she'd buy you a bat or a ball just to shut you up. Then we'd steal it from you." He laughed.

So instead of footballs or baseballs or bats, Dave and I usually carried water. Occasionally someone would get hurt or maybe there wouldn't be enough players available and we'd be picked to fill out a team. We were the backups, the stand-ins eagerly waiting for somebody to go down with an injury.

My brothers were all good athletes, but Ron was a standout. He was big, strong, and fast, the perfect prototype of a defensive tackle. And he had heart. He might have had a damn good pro career if it hadn't been for that primary occupational hazard of football players: the fucked-up knee. Ron's injury always hovered just beneath the surface and eventually drove him off the playing fields of three colleges and one NFL team, the old Chicago Cardinals. After trying to hook up with a pro team in Canada, Ron finally gave up the ghost and came home and got a real job at Jensen's Movers, where we all worked at one time or another.

Ron was the brother I always watched on the football field and it is from him that some of my ideas about the game first took root. Observing Ron play in pickup games at Fernwood and later in high school educated me in some of the game's subtler ways. I always had a sharp eye for detail. I noticed the little things, and watching how he set himself during the count, how he moved laterally, and how he used his hands and shifted his feet provided me with some valuable lessons.

But perhaps Ron's greatest gift to me was his sense of adventure. City neighborhoods can be traps. They're like small towns. If you're not paying attention, most of your life can go by before you realize you never really went anywhere, never saw anything. Remember, this was back in the 1950s, before air travel was common, and I knew lots of folks who never went anywhere. I mean *nowhere*.

When Ron boarded that Greyhound for Tulsa, Oklahoma, part of me went with him, down the two-laners into August 1952. The rest of me stayed home and waited to see what happened to him. Somehow I knew that whatever happened to him didn't matter, because he'd already done something special. He'd played football so well, that a college was willing to feed, house, and educate him in return for the use of his talent, and I was determined to follow in his footsteps.

Thinking back on my life, I realize it wasn't so much that I wanted out of Roseland. I was happy enough there, despite its limitations. But I wanted something more. I wanted to hear other voices, see other places and faces—but I only wanted to do it while playing football. Years later, Mrs. Rose Bertetto, who watched me grow up alongside her son Rick, remarked that football was my ticket out of myself, out of that bashful, tongue-tied, very private boy.

———

Two friends who came earliest and stayed latest were Rick Bertetto and Rick Richards. We met in the first grade at Fernwood Grammar School, and due to a common interest in sports, mischief, and mayhem, we bonded like lemmings.

I have never had many close friends. Real friends. But the ones I do have I try to keep. The two Ricks—Bertetto and Richards—formed the base of my social life.

We did all the usual things and a few more. We committed light terrorism against neighbors, merchants, classmates, and faculty. We spent many hours on the "punishment bench" in front of the principal's office. According to Rick Bertetto, I was always the instigator. "You could get a classroom riled up just by looking a certain way," Rick told me recently. "Richards and I just went along for the ride. You started things, and we usually got blamed."

He may be more right than wrong, because I certainly loved to fool around. But I remember one classic incident for which Bertetto must claim full responsibility. Because Fernwood was a public school, and we were Catholic, Bertetto and I were "release-time" students, which meant that every Wednesday afternoon we went to St. Helena's for religious instruction from the nuns. Bertetto loved those sisters and he loved to make fun of them behind their backs. One Wednesday during the fourth grade, Rick demonstrated his ardor by lifting one of the sister's habits to see what was underneath. The poor sister went ballistic—and I, of course, went into hysterics.

Our behavior was promptly reported to the Fernwood faculty and Rick and I were suspended for a week. But Bertetto's fascination with nuns didn't end there. Years later, Rick married a former mother superior.

In time our interests turned to larceny. We swiped cases of Canfield's root beer from the storage room of a banquet hall called Craple's, on 103rd and Wallace, and hid them in a sewer under the trees in a nearby prairie. Those cool amber bottles were worth their weight in gold when we came off the baseball field in the midsummer heat. We raided the neighborhood gardens at least once a day during the growing season, filching fruits and vegetables whenever we felt like it. Which was often, since there was never any food available between meals in my house. I particularly enjoyed the succulent, semisweet Concord grapes that hung from our German neighbors' backyard trellises in the fall.

Sometimes we commandeered major items. We always needed bicycles, because our demolition derbies could ruin a bike in an afternoon. But the biggest job we pulled was the procurement of a first-rate basket and backboard. Roseland was without an adequate outdoor basketball court, so Richards, Bertetto, and I conspired to produce one for the betterment of our community. One winter night we set off for Beverly Hills, a wealthy neighborhood about six miles away, packing a set of wrenches we'd "borrowed" from Bertetto's father.

We jumped the fence into a newly constructed public playground. Apparently the city fathers felt the residents of Beverly Hills, with its two-acre zoning, needed such a facility more than the folks of Roseland. Since Bertetto could climb like an orangutan, Richards and I sent him up the pole to the back of the half-moon basket, where he loosened a couple of nuts and the whole thing nearly killed us as it fell resoundingly to the icy court.

I'll never know how we managed to get it to Roseland

without getting caught. We slid that backboard and rim over snow-packed hill and dale for some six miles to the backyard of Bertetto's house, where we stashed it. The next morning Bertetto's father woke up, looked out the back window, and discovered the metal monster. I forget the cockamamie story we told him, but I remember he accepted it with the expression of someone eating a lemon.

Now the question was: Where to put it? There was a brickyard behind Bertetto's house, and the owner had recently paved a loading area. It was perfect for basketball, so we decided to put the backboard there. While Bertetto went to speak with the owner, Richards and I borrowed a couple of sledgehammers from his tool shed, and before very long we had broken a hole in his new cement and driven an appropriate length of pipe into the ground. By the time Bertetto returned with the owner, who knew us all too well from earlier incidents, the basket and backboard were firmly in place.

At first, the brickyard owner did not appreciate our presumption of his goodwill. But after considerable pleading—or what my brother John calls whining—we convinced him of the merits of his cooperation. From then on, every Saturday morning, outdoor basketball games were played in Roseland. By late spring, kids from all over Roseland and Fernwood came to play at the brickyard court, sometimes with their girlfriends in tow. Eventually the brickyard owner got so involved he even bought us navy blue T-shirts with THE BRICK-YARD BUMS on the backs.

But for all our community work, we played our best pranks against each other. Maybe it's because I grew up with a bunch of older brothers, but playing pranks came naturally to me. Once I almost went too far. On a snowy day in January, Rick Bertetto and I had stolen a couple of sleds from our friends over in Beverly Hills and were sledding on 110th and

Longwood Drive, a two-block-long grade that offered the fastest and wildest ride in the neighborhood. The strategy called for one of us to stand at the intersection at the bottom of the hill and signal when the coast was clear.

That day was cold and I was bored and probably hungry, and there was Rick at the top of the hill with his stolen sled at the ready, and here was this car coming along the intersecting thoroughfare. I guess I just couldn't help myself. I gave Rick the go-ahead. Down the hill he came, right into the path of the oncoming car—and when Rick, the driver, and I saw what was about to happen, our hearts jumped into our throats. Both drivers put on the breaks and Rick's hot Flexible Flyer bounced off the car's left front tire. Rick was unhurt. But for a moment there, I thought I'd lost my best friend.

One lazy summer afternoon Rick Richards and I were playing a little pastime that predated guerrilla theater. We'd stand on the corner of, say, 103rd Street, and when a car or truck came along, one of us would go into a big-time windup and make an exaggerated throwing motion at the oncoming vehicle. We thought it was hilarious when the cars bobbed and weaved by, the drivers' heads often ducking below the dashboard to avoid our imagined projectiles.

So one day here comes this poor, unsuspecting car, and I crank up nice and slow so the driver will be able to see me, and just as I follow through like Bob Feller—*BAM!*—I hear something actually hit the car. I look at my hand, which of course is empty. Then I turn and spot Rick running away, looking back at me and laughing like a maniac.

With the paint can he threw still spinning along the street, the car screeches to a halt and four very large guys with serious looks on their faces pile out and start coming toward me. I take off after Rick, thinking of the many ways I'm going to kill him. After a long, stressful, back-alley, through-the-park escape, I arrive at my father's garage, where Rick Richards is scaring the chickens half to death with his insane laughter.

"I got you," he said, all doubled over. "I got you good this time." The more Rick laughed, the less mad I got—until finally I began to laugh with him while the chickens clucked and fussed and shed feathers all around us.

We always had sports. In the schoolyard the three of us played handball, dodgeball, and buck-buck. My favorite was buck-buck, or Johnny-on-the-pony, as it is called in Eastern cities. Eight or so guys would form a human chain, one behind the other, each bending over and grabbing the guy in front of him around the waist, with the first "link" holding on to a pole. The competing team of four would try to break the chain by hopping, one by one, onto their backs. By virtue of my size and weight, I was the undisputed champ of buck-buck.

But Fernwood Park was the true center of my early sporting life. It was pickup football in the fall, baseball in the spring and summer, and ice skating in the winter. We never had the proper equipment, so in addition to making the ice and the goals, we devised an interesting version of the game— using our bodies as the puck. Actually, the made-up game had more in common with football than hockey.

Three times a week, beginning in fifth grade, Rick Bertetto and I would go directly from school to an indoor pool known as "the tank," which was located on 104th Street near the railroad tracks. We made the swimming team and got our first taste of organized sports. We practiced in the evening, after the general public had gone home, swimming naked. Rick and I went on to become productive team members and junior lifeguards. In the meets I swam well enough, placing consistently in the distance events, but Rick Bertetto was unbeatable in the sprints.

Two of our instructors, the Kooastra brothers—Bill and Sam—made the Olympic swimming team. We always felt they represented "the tank."

My older brothers also swam in "the tank." Ron, Don, and Dave were on the water polo team and I don't think they ever lost a match. Rick Bertetto and I would sometimes scrimmage against them. Those sessions were brutal, but they toughened me and built up my stamina, which I am sure helped me later when I played football. Water polo is the most strenuous sport I have ever played.

Of the two Ricks and myself, Bertetto was the best all-around athlete. He could run the fastest and had the best balance and the quickest reflexes: It seemed as though he developed earlier than Richards and me. But each of us had a specialty. Richards was the best basketball player, and I had the edge in football. The fact that I didn't dominate in all sports as a kid probably helped fuel a competitive nature that in coming years would be the hallmark of my career and the subject of endless analysis.

I wasn't particularly fast, nor was I much bigger than other kids my age. But I had big hands and long arms and most of me was upper body. At physical maturity, my inseam measured thirty-two inches, while my cuff length was thirty-seven inches. If the short legs helped me to kick the football with consistent accuracy, they also provided me with the extra leverage that results from a lower center of gravity. This physical feature, when combined with the long torso and arms, gave me the basic tools to excel on the downfield side of the game.

I realized I had the physical edge when Bertetto, Richards, and I used to wrestle in a room filled with floor mats at the gym where we played basketball on weekday nights. After getting beat pretty bad by Richards in roundball, I'd convince them to go into the room and we'd wrestle with the lights out. They'd try to gang up on me, but I'd always prevail.

On those nights when we watched high school football games at nearby Gateley Stadium, I'd insist we go home the long way, through a neighborhood that had lots of nice lawns where we'd play our own version of night football to the detriment of the lush grass. We called it "goal line stand." We played the game on our knees, using someone's cap as the ball, each in turn trying to "score" by getting past the others. I think it was on my knees that I learned to tackle high, which is the way I always preferred to bring a runner down. Through the years that were to follow, Bertetto and Richards and I stayed in close touch. We'd call one another whenever the mood hit us, and we'd see each other whenever we had a chance. And the pranks, which were the medium of our affection, never stopped. One time I invited Richards down to Florida for a little cruise aboard Bob Irsay's yacht—a sleek seventy-footer straight out of a James Bond thriller.

It was summer, hot as hell, and Richards's skin was the color of a bedsheet; he worked in the steel mills, where, as they say, the sun don't shine. I was as brown as Jon Hall in *South of Pago Pago*, having been lying around on the beach outside our condo on Marco Island for a month.

As we cruised through Biscayne Bay, I started ragging Richards about how sickly he looked, urging him to take off his shirt so he could get a little color. I told him it would be a damn shame to come all the way down to the Sunshine State and not get a tan. On and on, as Coral Gables and Key Biscayne slipped by, I kept after him. Finally, to shut me up, Rick took off his shirt. By the time we reached the Ocean Reef Club at the top of the Keys, he was a strip of cooked bacon.

By nightfall, he was more than uncomfortable. But like a good soldier, Rick went out on the town with us, standing next to an air conditioner all night, his teeth chattering, smiling and drinking and wincing, and having a good time with his buddy, despite the rotten joke I'd played on him.

I'm not suggesting that we were closer than family. But I did experience a sense of freedom with the two Ricks that wasn't there with my brothers. We were friends, companions by choice, not blood, and in 1995, when Richards died of a heart attack in a little music store he'd managed to open a few years earlier, he left at least two friends who would always remember him.

I don't recall exactly when I gave him the black Greek sailor's cap with the shallow peak and the filagree across the front. He must have liked it a lot though, because he wore one just like it at the wake and still had it on when they put him in the ground.

When Bertetto and I arrived at the funeral, we were surprised to see more than 150 people in the church, and afterward, over drinks and cold cuts at a local hall, some of them told us how much Richards meant to them, how he had helped them out. Quietly, with no fanfare. Some had tears in their eyes. I know I did.

In a life overrun by an unholy procession of business partners, lawyers, agents, actors, teammates, coaches, hangers-on, and members of the media, the value of real friendship cannot be overstated. And if friendship, like good wine, improves with age, as I believe it does, then it's important to keep the ones from childhood when the party is still fresh and full of good cheer.

The only organized sport other than swimming that was available to us during our grammar school days was baseball. The Roseland Little League had recently been formed and I made the roster of the Olds Rockets. I caught, pitched, and played third. I was pretty good. When I was fourteen, I played in the Babe Ruth League and made the all-star team representing the South Side in the citywide playoffs. There was a kid on our team who didn't like me for some reason, and one day he spit on me because I'd put a hard tag on one of his friends. He was older than me, probably sixteen, and because his father was one of the coaches, the situation was not right for me to respond, so I filed away the incident for future referral, marking it "payback" in my mind.

We played the big game in Wrigley Field and my second time at bat I connected with a high, hard one and bounced it off the 368-foot sign in right center. Watching that white pill grow smaller on its way to the ivy was exhilarating, but it was nothing compared to the maiden flight of that football over the white picket fence in front of my house. There was another, more practical reason why baseball would not be in my future: The curveball proved an insoluble mystery.

Baseball and all other sports were just things to do while I waited for the leaves to fly. In those years before high school, when Ron was bouncing around three colleges, I thought of nothing else. Caught in the web of my fantasies, my imaginings gained in complexity as my knowledge of the game expanded almost day by day. Perhaps my first glimpse of gridiron greatness came when I was eleven, sitting before our brand-new television set with my father.

It was a Saturday night game, on the long-darkened Du-Mont Network, the Baltimore Colts against somebody, and I remember just two things: the white football used briefly in the NFL to compensate for the comparatively soft lighting available at the time and Chicago-born and -bred Buddy Young—all five-foot-five of him—running like a jackrabbit, dipping, dodging, and delivering the white parcel around, under, and over everybody in his way.

It was a performance that went beyond anything I had ever thought possible. Suddenly I wanted to one day be able to do what Buddy was doing, to perform astounding acts for my team and have people react to me the way the fans and the announcers were reacting to Buddy's brilliance. I was shocked, delighted, and inspired. This was a warm-blooded Disney cartoon, art come to life in living black-and-white, scatback Buddy Young at play in the land of the giants.

Years later, over a drink following a Bears home game, my father recalled my excitement on that autumn night. He said it was the first time he clearly understood how much football meant to me. As for Buddy Young, well, he became a recurring character in my future dreams, and when I played for Illinois, Buddy's greatness as an Illini was held up for our instruction by coach Pete Elliott, alongside Ray Nitschke and the incomparable Red Grange.

When I went to New York for the NFL draft, I finally met Buddy in the flesh. He was baby-sitting the gifted Gale Sayers, my future teammate. Buddy was a godsend during that first year in the pros, guiding Gale and me with sound, brotherly advice. Buddy and I stayed close throughout my pro career. Although he's gone now, the memory of Buddy Young on the football field will never fade from this battle-scarred head.

By the fall of my thirteenth year, I was regularly splitting the uprights down at Fernwood Park. This was before the soccer kick had been introduced to American football and the straight-ahead "toe" kick was the standard technique. It was even more difficult for me, since I didn't own the type of squared-off shoe that was used in organized competition. Every day I'd follow a strict solo regimen. After knocking a few dozen extra points through the uprights, I'd practice my punting, launching high spirals up and down the field, then running flat-out and falling on the ball as though it were a fumble. As it began to get dark, I would run through the wooded parts of Fernwood, dodging the trees as though they were players looming into my sight out of the gathering shadows.

Those one-man drills never failed to fire my imagination. I'd be out there with twenty-one other guys, crowds pressing the sidelines, umpires and referees and maybe a band playing in the background, and thousands of voices would flood my head as I charged downfield, running under the ball, up there twisting and wobbling. And just as it came down into the arms of the receiver, I'd hit him so hard that the ball would pop free and I'd snatch it off the bounce and cross the goal line under a roaring avalanche of approval.

I'll never know why I craved approval. Nor am I likely to locate the precise source of my loneliness as a boy. But for all my loneliness and shyness, I was ahead of the game in at least one respect. I had found something that very few little boys ever find in the long course of their lives. I found the thing I could do best, and perhaps fueled by my father's quiet, immigrant pride, my mother's aggressiveness, and something else that came from nobody—something nameless—I was ready not only to test my talent out on the high school gridirons of Chicago's South Side, I was ready to beat the world at this game I had already come to love.

C H A P T E R
2

*I*n those days, the Chicago city buses were built for guys like Bertetto and me. The rear bumper was set a good three inches out from the back of the bus and there were lots of grooves to grip with your fingertips. That's how we went to our first day at Chicago Vocational High School (CVS), clinging like human flies to the back of the 103rd Street bus.

You might ask why we traveled that way. The standard answer—that we both saved fifteen cents every time—would only be partly true. The real reason was that nobody else did it that way, and Bertetto and I loved to be different.

It had been our trademark throughout grammar school. When one teacher signed our eighth-grade yearbooks, he wrote the same message in both: "To two guys who definitely walk to a different drummer. You were both a lot of trouble and a lot of fun. Here's to the future, where I am sure I'll be reading about both of you in the newspapers." Bertetto and I thought the teacher's remarks referred to football: TWO RICKS SIGN WITH THE BEARS. But as I read those words today, I'm not so sure he didn't envision another kind of headline: TWO RICKS ENTER JOLIET.

Choosing CVS was a no-brainer for me. I wanted to do one thing for the next four years, and of all the high schools on the South Side, CVS offered football in greatest quantity and quality. Fenger High, where Ronnie had starred, would have been my first choice, but the head coach had recently left after many winning seasons.

From my parents' point of view, CVS must have made sense in two important ways: One, their son would get the best possible training at the thing he loved; and two, if he got hurt or if he didn't develop into as good a player as his brother Ron and wasn't offered a college scholarship, well, he'd still have a trade, a way to make a living.

So when I hopped on the back of the bus at 103rd Street that first Monday morning after Labor Day in 1956, I started to stretch the geography of my life beyond the boundaries of Roseland. Very soon now I'd be crossing over into an organized world of men in striped shirts with whistles, of grandstands and scoreboards, of raucous locker rooms and those hard-driving, flinty-eyed coaches who seemed to love the game with as much passion as I did.

I should say "we." Besides my buddy Rick Bertetto, many other guys carried their football dreams to CVS that day. We came from all points on the South Side, from Roseland to Beverly Hills, from Calumet to Morgan Park. We were Irish, Italian, Slovak, German, Dutch, Mexican, African American, Jewish—everything you can think of. We were the athletic picks of our neighborhood litters, brought together by a particular passion that separated us from the other students.

Thousands of years ago, we would have been given breastplates, iron helmets, and swords and told to go out and slay the enemy, or die trying, for the greater glory of the empire. In the 1950s, we got shoulder pads, cleats, and fiberglass helmets, and if the price of defeat wasn't as great, we certainly felt like warriors nonetheless, the shapers of Saturday's dream, the embodiment of school pride and of the half a million working-class people who lived on the South Side of Chicago. People who didn't win all that often, who were always struggling to raise themselves up. In many ways, we carried their hopes on our backs for a few hours each weekend in the fall.

If you have ever driven into Chicago on the Chicago Skyway from Gary, Indiana, you might remember an area where the highway runs about thirty feet off the ground, curving through dozens of long brick buildings with black smokestacks. In the background, above and beyond the roofs of the buildings, you can see Lake Michigan. On clear days, the view can be beautiful—the deep reds of the aged brick, the sunspashed windows, the black perpendicular stacks, and the biting blue of the lake.

This is not far from where I was born. It's right about where we used to scrounge for coal on winter nights, where Rick Bertetto and I swam in "the tank." Talk about mean streets. It might be beautiful from a distance when you're traveling at fifty-five miles an hour on your way to the Pump Room. But when you're down there in the dark between the buildings, it's not so pretty.

This is where Cliff Bowles grew up.

Rick Bertetto and I met Bowles during the first week of school. He was interviewing each and every wide-eyed football wanna-be. Short, stocky, and military to the bone, Bowles looked tougher than all of my brothers put together. He was the kind of guy who eats buckshot for breakfast and sleeps out in the rain. By the way he talked when Rick and I went into his office to sign up for freshman football, I began to think maybe even *I* wasn't dedicated enough—and if *I* wasn't, I don't know who the hell would have been. Looking us up and down as though we were modeling dresses, Bowles told us that CVS freshman football was no cakewalk, and if we were just looking for a way to beat some classes and become paper lions on campus, it might be better if we didn't waste anybody's time.

We would suffer and learn under the varsity coaching staff soon enough, but for our first season our coach was a soft-spoken Irishman named George Moran. There were times, of course, when Moran would lose it (and then watch out!), but for most of our "kindergarten" days, Coach Moran taught us the basics of the game with a kind of magical blend that was three parts milk and one part kick-ass home brew.

Under the direction of George Moran, we began our journey into gridiron enlightenment. I loved every moment of it. This is what I had waited for, why I dodged trees in Fernwood, practiced solo until long after dark, and studied every move Ronnie made in his high school games. Throughout the preseason practices, my concentration was so intense that I remembered every nuance of every lesson. Going home on the bus, throughout dinner, and lying exhausted in my bed, I reviewed every drill over and over until I'd drift off to sleep.

But I wasn't alone in my commitment. Angelo Valasquez, Ray Scott, Jim Cline, Andy Kracik, Frank Wellever, Bill Glass, and Rick Bertetto were all equally devoted to football. One afternoon early in the season, Wellever, who played offensive guard, asked me if I wanted to stay after practice and work on some drills. Since I was also playing offensive guard, I was excited at the prospect of putting in some extra hours. Wellever was of French descent, from the neighboring blue-collar community of Calumet. He was as tough as they come and already had a full beard. I felt that if I could hold my own against him, I'd be able to kick some ass in real competition.

Day after day following our regular practice, Wellever

and I would work out together, knocking the hell out of each other, critiqueing each other's moves, suggesting alternatives, and experimenting. It was the most fun I'd ever had, and it must have showed results because pretty soon the other guys were out there with us, staying each day until darkness forced us off the field.

We had a winning season that freshman year. But perhaps even more important, we learned the complex routine of team sports. Under Coach Moran's guidance, we learned how to win with grace and how to mine the gold from defeat if we lost. We learned how to arrive someplace on time and be ready to play, how to stay fit and eat the right foods, how to *think* before, during, and after a game.

Each of us had his own way of getting up for combat. My method should probably be studied by psychiatrists interested in the dynamics of the obsessive personality. As I look back today, I'm not so sure we all weren't a little crazy. But certainly I was different—and the other players knew it.

My obsession with football seemed to grow by the day. I learned not only what I was supposed to do on every play, but what everyone else was supposed to do, too. Playing offensive guard was not exactly the fulfillment of my dream. But I worked hard at it, and over the next summer, as I grew taller and stronger and faster, my dream grew closer to reality. My dream, of course, was to dominate the game: to lead the offense by carrying the ball, throwing it, and kicking it, then to lead the defense by making every tackle and forcing every fumble. That first year I joined a second family, known as the CVS Cavaliers, where I had a voice and a role considerably larger than the one accorded me in the caboose of the Butkus train.

In our second year, Bertetto and I made the varsity squad and played under head coach Bernie O'Brien. Unfortunately—or maybe fortunately—Cliff Bowles had left CVS to coach at another school. Rick landed one of the defensive corners, while I secured another piece of my dream. In addition to my duties as offensive guard, I was given a critical role on defense: "nose" guard.

In the "nose" position, I had to take care of the middle and always be ready to go left or right. As quick off the ball as I was, I usually made my presence felt. If the play turned out to be a pass, I'd shoot the gaps on either side of the center and create some havoc in the backfield. Bernie let me operate like an actual linebacker, and the results spoke for themselves. That season the CVS Cavaliers were runners-up in the playoffs of the Chicago Public School League. In eight regular season contests, the defense allowed just 55 points. I averaged one fumble recovery per game.

They began writing stories about me in the Chicago papers, comparing me with my brother Ronnie, who had starred as a defensive tackle with Fenger High. By now Ronnie had been hired away from a local semipro team by the Chicago Cardinals of the National Football League.

One afternoon my brother Don took me out to the Lake Forest College campus just north of the city to watch Ronnie practice with the Cardinals. The team was spread out over two fields and I remember how impressed I was with their size. You could tell right off that these guys were pros. And then I saw one man, a cornerback, who stood out from the others. Dressed in the old institutional gray sweatshirt, gym pants, and the new cutoff cleats, he moved with a special grace and purpose. There was something about him, a sense of pride maybe, and I asked Donnie who he was.

"Oh, that's Night Train Lane," Donnie said.

"He looks pretty good," I said.

"Pretty good? He's *great*," said Donnie.

Ronnie might have been great, too. But he would never play a minute in the NFL. His knee, damaged from all the college gridiron wars, finally gave way during the exhibition season. Meanwhile, his little brother, who at fifteen weighed in at 210 pounds and counting, had picked up the family torch and was establishing a rep of his own.

Inevitably the reporters would ask me if I thought I could ever be as good a player as my big brother. Didn't they realize what a difficult question that is for a kid? Even simple answers created problems. A "no" would be a lie, and a "yes" would make me sound like a smart-ass. So I usually shrugged and said, "Maybe." But when the *Chicago Sun-Times* published its 1958 All-City lineup and I was given an honorable mention, coach Bernie O'Brien described me as a "very fine high school player with a nose for the football," adding that the idea of me becoming a pro "was not far-fetched."

Nothing positive that has been written about me since has meant quite so much. Whether Bernie actually believed his words, I'll never know. Certainly, as my coach and the sensitive man I knew him to be, he wasn't about to throw cold water on my dreams. Anyway, those words mattered: They gave my dream wings.

―――――

On holidays the Butkus family would gather at 10324 South Lowe. Everybody would come: Dolly, Babe, and John, all married, would bring their kids. After spending an appropriate period upstairs with the women and children, the males would drift off one by one to gather around a table in the basement for an extended game of poker. As the cards were dealt, the beer and the jokes and the stories would flow through the afternoon into the evening.

My father had to be one of the worst poker players I've ever seen. Sometimes we'd sneak a mirror behind him and read his cards. But it wasn't really necessary because everything registered on his face. If his hand was unpromising, he'd scowl like Churchill. But if he held good cards, he'd morph into Santa Claus. Whenever Pa would start to get jolly, we'd all drop our cards on the table and get out of the hand, leaving him a slim pot to collect. Once in a while we'd let him win, but then one of us would sneak upstairs and tell Ma about it, and she'd come down and take it all from him.

Once in a while, Pa would get a great hand dealt to him. When he did, his face would light up like a Christmas tree. Then he'd rake in the chips and say, "The baby needs a new pair of shoes." It was his favorite poker-playing line, and we'd all wait for him to say it. When he finally did, we would all crack up.

After a few beers, John, Ron, and Don would begin to tease my father about the women he knew before my mother, prompting him to tell us about his days as a cook at a Minnesota lumber camp. One tale was about some girls in the local town who knew how shy he was. Whenever he went shopping for food, they'd call out to him in the street, "Oh, *Johnny*! Your *mommy's* callin' ya!" Whenever Pa told that story, my brothers would laugh and my father's face would glow like a traffic light. Once he said to us, "You could all have been half-Indian." When we asked him to expand on that remark, he just laughed, waving us away.

Babe recalls how my father would sometimes say, "Ma's mad at me."

"Why is Ma mad at you, Pa?" she'd ask, each time thinking he was serious. Looking very somber, my father would say, "She's not telling me what to do."

But if my mother ran the Butkus show successfully, it

was because my father was there to enforce her authority. It took a lot for him to summon sternness from that sweet nature of his. But when he did, it was memorable. Only once do I recall him using a belt on me. It was down in the basement. I was about eleven and scared. But when I looked into his eyes and saw how much he hated what he was about to do, the fear left me and I realized how much I loved him. But the belt burned anyway.

I guess my father and I were alike, both shy and reluctant to call somebody on something. Even today I let people take advantage of me—but only up to a point. Then I sometimes tend to overreact. I didn't realize it while I was growing up, but the balance between my mother and father made them both better individuals. I think the same is true between Helen and me, each making the other better, creating a whole that is larger than the sum of its parts.

I still remember the day when Rick Richards pulled the old Cushman motor scooter we had bought on "credit" from Bertetto up to the curb where these two cuties were standing. And I also remember wanting to pound his head down through his shoulders.

Helen was dressed in white—boots, Levi's, a soft blouse with a rounded collar, and a puffy sweater—and she flashed one of the brightest smiles I'd ever seen. I noticed her eyes were hazel, the same color as my mother's, but a little darker and just as strong and intense. Richards knew the girls from Fenger High, where he played on the basketball team.

Rick took the other girl for a ride on the scooter, which meant that I had to wait for him to come back. There we stood, Helen and I, marooned on one of the South Side's busiest avenues. I don't remember saying a single word to her. After what seemed like a week, Rick brought the other girl back. In order to escape further humiliation in front of my smart-ass friend, I offered to take Helen for a ride, fully expecting her to decline. But she climbed on the back of the scooter, put her arms around me, and hasn't let go since. Helen became my first girlfriend, the mother of my children, my wife forever, and my closest confidante.

The long version of how Helen and I got together is a little more complicated. The next day, while playing pickup baseball in Fernwood Park, Richards told me that Helen had let it be known that she wanted me to call her. Knowing that Richards was constitutionally incapable of telling the truth in such matters and also knowing that I had barely spoken to Helen on that first meeting, I shrugged him off. But Rick wouldn't let it go. All day long, whenever our team was at bat, he'd sit next to me on the bench and insist he was being straight. When he saw I was not buying it, Rick said, "Maybe you should forget the whole thing. What the hell do I care anyway? It's none of my business. I'm just the messenger."

This reverse psychology brought me back to the bait, and after the game I borrowed a dime and called Helen from a public telephone booth. While we were talking, I could see Richards doubled over with laughter. He'd gotten me again, the SOB. Even though Helen agreed to see me, I would have killed Richards if I'd caught him that day.

Now, of course, I wish I could kiss him.

That fall Helen transferred from Fenger High to CVS and when I wasn't playing football, we were together, usually with Richards tagging along. Sometimes Bertetto was with us, too, but he was usually preoccupied with his own love life. Make that love *lives*. Bertetto was almost a year older than Richards and me, and he already had a car. The wheels, combined with his good looks, transformed him into Roseland's Elvis.

Richards, Helen, and I didn't have a car. But Jimmy

Brink, a cousin of Rick's from Fenger and a neighbor of Helen's, had an old four-door Chevy and we often went out with him, the four of us cruising the avenues, hanging out at soda fountains, and watching outdoor movies at the local drive-in, where Richards and I would often sneak in by hiding in the trunk.

Richards and I continued to dabble in petty crime well into our junior year of high school. Beyond raiding the local gardens and enhancing Roseland's recreational facilities, we managed to keep Jimmy Brink's fuel gauge needle out of the red by siphoning gas from unsuspecting donors who'd had the misfortune to park their cars in certain out-of-the-way lots.

You might ask if stealing bothered me. I suppose it should have, but it really didn't. I felt that the things I stole were mine for the taking—maybe because I had so little when I was growing up. I never had more than a few coins in my pocket and I hardly ever experienced the feel of a new shirt or pair of pants, unless it was Easter or some other special occasion. I wasn't all that concerned about the legitimacy of what I was doing. Taking a few gallons of gas from someone's tank or some fruit from a neighbor's tree seemed small payback for those nights my brothers collected coal or when I came home from Fernwood Park with frozen feet because all I had to wear were ripped sneakers or busted-up hand-me-down shoes. But the danger of stealing is that it's a kick—and, like most kicks, it's hard to stop once it gets going.

I was well aware that some of my contemporaries were disappearing from the neighborhood and going to state reform schools and even to the state penitentiary. The specter of such a consequence never really entered my mind. Nor do I believe it occurred to Richards. We considered ourselves enterprising young men of the streets, closing the socioeconomic gap between Roseland and Beverly Hills.

Then one Saturday evening our life of petty larceny ended in disgrace. Richards had gotten permission to take out his father's new car, and we were happily cruising through the neighboring community of Morgan Park when I spotted a canary yellow 1956 Ford all spiffed out with a chopped hood and customized rear fender skirts. It was parked under a tree in a lot behind a bowling alley. The cash register in my head instantly began ringing. I'd heard on good underworld authority that I could get good money for those fender skirts. I was out of the door before Rick even knew what was going on, and I had the first skirt off that Ford when the patrol cars closed in on us like we were Bonnie and Clyde.

There had been a rash of robberies in Morgan Park and the cops decided Rick and I were the perps. Who was to say they were wrong? With one hot skirt in my hand, I was in no position to argue the point. So after hauling us into the Morgan Park police station, where they grilled us pretty good in an unsuccessful effort to make us confess to the other robberies, the cops told us we would be held at the juvenile detention home until we could go before the judge for sentencing on Monday morning.

Sentencing?

That word fell on me like a load of bricks. Jail time was definitely not in my plans. Nightmarish possibilities began to flood my brain: newspaper stories, suspension from school, maybe even expulsion—and worst of all, a ban on football. Bad as those thoughts were, they didn't compare to how I felt when the cops took me to my parents' house and told them what I had done and where I was going. Thank God none of my brothers were around, especially Ronnie. It was bad enough without them getting all over me. I will never forget the expressions on my parents' faces. I had disappointed them, but their eyes said I'd done a good deal more: I had hurt them.

Then the cops put us back in the paddy wagon and we headed downtown on Michigan Avenue. All the way I kept trying to push back the reality of what I had done to myself, my parents, and to Rick by insisting that the cops were not serious about putting us in the juvenile detention home. "They're just scaring us," I said, my confidence slowly disintegrating. "They'll let us go."

Well, they scared us all right.

They put us right into the detention home, just as they said they would, and if I felt bad for myself, I felt worse for Rick. He hadn't done a damn thing, and here he was, in the cooler with his friend Butkus, Roseland's not-so-Teflon don of mischief and mayhem. They took our clothes and gave us something to wear that amounted to a sheet with a hole in the middle and some numbers on it. Our fellow inmates were scruffy, hard-bitten, and, of course, innocent.

That first night at the detention home was the longest of my life. Sleep was impossible. I never felt more alone, lying there in the half-darkness. But I was learning something the hard way. I was learning how quickly everything in life can change. I thought about Ronnie, how he too had done some pretty stupid things, but at least he'd made it through high school and had gotten his shot at making it in the NFL. I thought to myself, *Am I going to get my shot?* Suddenly I didn't know anymore. As Rick and I lay there among a bunch of losers, I thought, *Am I a loser, too?*

For the first time, I understood the fragility of my good fortune, how I could waste my talent if I wasn't careful. It was something that I would have to protect. One stupid act could erase everything I'd worked for, and right then I promised God that if He threw a couple of blocks for me I'd clean up my act.

Sunday was a little better, but not much. Sitting on those

narrow bunks with our heads sticking through those sheets, we must have looked like ghosts. By Monday morning, when we and the other reprobates shuffled into Criminal Court, Rick and I no longer had any illusions about the seriousness of our situation. We'd heard enough stories from our fellow inmates to know that the judge could drop the dime on us if he felt like it.

While we waited, Richards and I played a game that had gotten us through a lot of tight moments in the past. When we didn't think anyone was watching, we made faces at each other, and when we thought no one could hear, we made funny sounds. This somehow reassured us, kept us in touch, right up until the moment my name was called by the bailiff and I stepped forward. The judge had gotten hold of my most recent report card, which—fortunately for me—did not bear any F's. So on the basis of my passing grades, a perfect attendance record, and a promise to give up my life of crime, he sentenced me to a year of probation.

Then the judge turned his attention to Richards. "As for you, young man," he said, waving Richards's report card. "How do you explain a failing grade in American history?"

In the swollen silence that followed, I cut a sideways glance at Richards. He looked sad as hell, as if his life were over. And just like the time I waved Bertetto down the hill on that sled and into the path of the oncoming car, a devilish feeling came over me. I cleared my throat. This caused Richards to break into a bizarre series of facial expressions, which the judge did not find amusing.

If Rick didn't get the whole book thrown at him, he certainly was slapped with a chapter or two. In addition to a year of probation, the judge sentenced him to a similar period of hard labor: Rick was ordered to get a job! The judge said he hoped that some extra work might calm Rick's nervous manner, cure his facial tics, and improve his study habits.

Rick was not pleased. Since he played basketball for Fenger High, he would have to start work late. For the rest of that school year, Helen and I often visited Rick on his night shift—washing Chicago real estate off several dozen United Parcel trucks.

The repercussions at school were comparatively light, no doubt due to the intercession of coach Bernie O'Brien, who explained to me in practical, no-nonsense terms the importance of my off-field behavior. "The good colleges," he said, "the ones with the best football coaches, don't recruit players with jail records, no matter how good they are." With firmness and clarity, Coach O'Brien, God bless him, made the point in such a way that it stuck.

———

Looking back on my high school years, I don't necessarily like everything I see. My dedication to football certainly remains a source of inner pride, but there were other parts of me I could have done without. One that will remain regrettable until the day I die is the lack of regard I sometimes exhibited toward my parents during those teenage years.

If you grew up in a big city like Chicago or New York, chances are you have heard the expression "dumb immigrant." You don't hear it that much today, but it was a common, everyday reference when I was a kid. It probably goes back to when the first non-English speakers arrived in the United States. Most of them came from Western Europe: the Dutch and the Germans, then the Irish and the Italians after that. The thing that marked you back then was how you spoke; if you didn't know the language, you qualified as a "dumb immigrant." The phrase instantly put you in a social box. Difficult as it was for those early arrivals, English was not completely foreign to Western Europeans, given its common Latin roots. They could master the language soon enough with hard work.

But if you were Slovak or Russian or Polish or from any Eastern European country, the sounds of English were as far from your ear as Mars is from Venus, and no matter how hard you tried, it was impossible to hide the sounds of your native tongue. My father must have known that because even though he'd passed that night course in English, he never learned to speak it well. Never learned to think freely in it. For many of our neighbors, including some who had only recently stepped up from similar circumstances, my father remained a "dumb immigrant" until the day he died. Maybe that's why Polish jokes still ring unpleasantly in my ears. We weren't Polish, of course, but I always felt the jokes were aimed at Slavs in general, Lithuanians included.

I have a deep love for Chicago, but no one ever said it was the most comfortable place to be a minority. A city churning with people of varying nationalities, Chicago bubbles constantly, and whoever is the last one "off the boat" feels its heat and sting, at least until the next wave arrives. I never cared for the humor of initiations in college or in the pros, because I can't ever forget my father's initiation into America. There was nothing funny about it.

Yet at some point in high school, I became a little self-conscious of my parents and stopped telling them where I'd be playing my next game. But they found out anyway and came to cheer me on from the stands whenever they could. Was it simply a classic case of a son not wanting people to know that his father was an immigrant? Sure, I suppose so. His shy manner and halting English made him slightly different than some of the other fathers who attended our football games. My father was a working man, and his clothes didn't exactly have a Brooks Brothers label. In those bib overalls, he might not have appeared as successful as some of the other fathers in the stands or as I was out on the field. But I know now that he was a bigger success than I will ever be, because the odds he faced were a hell of a lot longer.

Through the lens of history, it's easy to see that America was verging on major change in the 1950s. Soon to come were a whole raft of wrenching social adjustments. But from my limited Roseland view, life moved with a slow predictability—except maybe in the movies. TV was in our lives by then, but the movies were still our biggest window on that world outside the South Side.

I remember the two Ricks and I discussing the latest flicks and arguing about who were the coolest actors. We all admired John Wayne, but there was an almost visceral response to a new guy on the cinematic block: James Dean. There was something about him, something about the characters he created that got to the three of us. Wayne was our ideal, but Dean sometimes said the things that were in our hearts. I liked him a lot in *Giant*, where he played a poor boy, angry at his poverty, but damned if he'd let anybody see it, damned if he'd let anybody push him around, and damned if he wouldn't change his circumstances.

If that Dean character played football, we'd say he was hungry. I guess I was hungry, too, but I didn't begin to realize *how* hungry until I jumped on the back of that bus on 103rd and headed for CVS. From that moment forward, I entered a wider ring of society and realized just how little I really had in the way of material things. But thanks to my gridiron talent, I started to receive a new respect and protection, perhaps even to the point where a judge went a little easier on me than he might have on another kid.

J unior year, 1959, was the official coming-out of Rich Butkus. During spring practice, we all learned that a kid named
Lamus Rush, our star fullback, would be marching to a different band that fall—one playing *Anchors Aweigh*. He'd
joined the Navy to see the world, and without him the Cavaliers probably would not be seeing much in the way of postseason play, much less the All-City championship. Someone
would have to step into the void. I knew Bernie would give
me the middle linebacker role, so that spring I suggested to
him that maybe I could also handle the heavy hauling at fullback.

He smiled tolerantly and shrugged.

"Maybe," he said.

That summer I grew up—and out—reaching six-foot-
two and 220 pounds by the time I reported for preseason
practice in mid-August. I'd been lifting cases of tile eight
hours a day on my summer job, and I was ready to throw
my new weight and strength around the football field.
Throughout the summer, I had practiced running the ball;
each evening after work, Bertetto and I and some of the other
players would work out at Palmer Park, which had better
facilities than Fernwood. Before the preseason was over, I'd
changed Bernie's springtime "maybe" to a "perhaps." By the
time the leaves flew, Bernie gave me an official "yes" via a
rare wink and grateful tap on the top of my helmet.

That season the full force of my football talents and the
promise of things to come emerged. In addition to playing
both sides of the ball—offense and defense—I did all the foot-
work: punts, extra points, and kickoffs. I threw long passes,
caught short ones on circle routes, ran the ball into the middle, plunging for first downs and scores, often carrying several opponents into the end zone, and, on defense, I ran the
show, calling the formations and making 70 percent of all the

tackles. That season I established myself as somebody to be reckoned with, maybe even feared. With my buddy Bertetto playing the left corner of our defensive unit, and my relentless, sometimes obsessive leadership, we just got better and better.

When everything is working right out there on the field, when all the drills and hard work have paid off in an actual game, football becomes a display of creative precision unmatched in any other sport. Basketball and hockey have it to a lesser degree—and so does baseball in its own way. But a football team cannot succeed without teamwork.

And when it happens on the defensive side, when all eleven guys begin to click in some kind of mysterious dynamic, each man doing exactly the right thing, reacting in exactly the right way, the sound and the sight of it alone often carried me to an emotional high that is the closest thing I've ever known to pure happiness.

We were eleven highly athletic adolescents, each bursting with his recently acquired manhood, each carrying a little bit of James Dean's confusion, frustration, and anger, each finding reasons to express himself physically in a highly prescribed scheme. In all my dreams, I hadn't known it could get that good. The thrill of it lifted me higher than I'd ever been before.

One time I tried to describe this feeling to a friend who had been a Marine Corps drill instructor. He said that the best recruits were kids like me, kids who came from large families who for one reason or another never felt completely at home. It was those kids who sought the disciplines of precision marching, the sound of a single footfall from a thirty-five-man platoon on the parade ground. He said those are the young men you want to lead into battle. You'd be willing to die for them because you knew they'd do the same for you.

====

Remember the kid who spit at me during my illustrious Babe Ruth career before I discovered the evils of the curveball? It just so happened that he became the quarterback for Fenger High the same year that I became the middle linebacker for CVS. When I learned of this development, I thought about how life can sometimes be as sweet as stolen grapes.

Revenge would take place at Eckersall Stadium on September 26, when Fenger and CVS would meet for the season opener of the Red Division of the Chicago Public School League. This might sound a little rough to people who don't like to admit that they take pleasure in getting even, but I built myself up, day by day, practice by practice, minute by minute, for that game, my big chance to pay the kid back on a level playing field, which made it even sweeter.

September 26, 1959, began dark and rainy. A fitting atmosphere for the afternoon's agenda. It was D-Day for a certain Fenger quarterback. Never had the motivational fires blazed higher than when we arrived that morning at Eckersall in the misting rain. Our brotherhood would have been strong in any case; after all, this was Fenger High, an archrival of CVS and the school where most of Rick Bertetto's and my grammar school friends had gone. But my memory of being spat upon became my teammates' memory as well, and together we drove the Fenger spirit deep into the mud, 19–0— and in the process claimed vengeance for one of our own.

I got to the quarterback frequently and each time I hit him as hard as I could, causing him to fumble at least twice and make I don't know how many mistakes. After the first hit, I noticed something had changed in his eyes. They got a little glassy, and for the rest of the game I could see him looking for me on every play. And I could almost hear his thoughts: *What's that crazy Butkus doing?* and *Where is he* now? and *What the hell's wrong with him anyway?* He was a pretty good player, but he was less than half of what he would have been if he hadn't had to worry about me.

By then I was aware of the benefits of intimidation, but in that game against Fenger, I expanded the possibilities of the tactic and turned it into an art form. Over the years I would develop it the same way a good actor finds new depths to a character he keeps playing in a TV series or a Broadway show. I knew that motivation was the key to performance, so I began searching for ways to bring new energy to my role.

To find that fire, I began to fantasize. I had been fantasizing since I was a little kid, only now the dreams were not only about doing marvelous things with the football. Now I was making up stories to stoke my anger, creating images from somewhere deep inside me, calling up stuff from my memory and twisting it to work in my favor. An easy exercise was to pretend a star offensive player on the other team had done something to me or a member of my family.

By game time I was usually volcanic. My emotions had built steadily all week, bubbling like hot tar, and when I saw the opposing team come out on the field, I looked for the guy who could hurt us most, and if I had never seen him before, I studied him, measured him. Now I had a face and a number—a *most wanted* poster—to focus all my anger on. It didn't matter that my seek-and-destroy mission had been fabricated, nurtured like a rattler's venom, or even that the poor guy had never really said anything about my mother. To me, he was the enemy, and if I could turn him into roadkill, I would do it with enthusiasm and a sense of righteousness that sometimes shocked me.

Yes, football *is* a game. But it's serious, too—in a way that badminton and yachting are not. If football is played the way I was taught to play it, there is no pretense at good man-

ners. As the sport closest to war, football is at its core an expression of physical violence. On defense, the object is to stop
the other team from pushing the ball down the field and scoring. You do it however you can—inside or outside the rules.
Just don't get caught by the guys in striped shirts.

On either side of the ball, you look for every edge. Nothing is too small to take into account. Connie Mack said that
baseball is a game of inches. Well, so is football. A yard is
thirty-six inches, not thirty-five or thirty-four—and I've been
in games that were decided by as little as that. Knock the man
down. Hit him high, hit him low, but hit him—and hit him
hard, as hard as you can, so hard that next time he'll be
thinking about you instead of what he's supposed to be
doing. This became my M.O., my modus operandi. I could
throw it, I could kick it, I could run the ball better than a lot
of guys. But the thing that emerged above all else was the
ease with which I played the middle linebacker position.

I had always been a watcher. As the youngest Butkus, I
closely observed my brothers, sisters, and parents, spotting
small actions and mannerisms that gave away their moods
and, perhaps most important to a little kid, their intentions.
Picture yourself as a little squirt in a tiny house filled with
giants, then add to the mix a major lack of communication.
It was like living in a silent film, in which the trick was to
figure out what someone was going to do before they did it.
The clues to their intent were often found in the details of the
movements, and I learned to read those details as part of my
survival.

It was these people-reading skills that I applied to football. Between plays, while my teammates were scratching
their asses or looking for their girlfriends in the stands, I was
looking into the other team's huddle, trying to read the quarterback's lips. I got pretty good at it, too. He might say, "Red,

right, thirty-five, on *two*." Then everyone would clap their hands and break out of the huddle. Well, by that time, if I'd read the quarterback accurately, I knew a few important things. "Red" meant a particular formation, could be the T or the single wing, "right" meant a run to *my left*, and "thirty-five" meant the three back, or fullback, to the five hole, or between the tackle and guard. The last number, "two," meant that the snap would come on the second *hut* called. Certainly there were variations, but calling plays is done pretty much the same way everywhere, and after a possession or two I could usually figure the signals out and act accordingly. Chalk it up to fear. Sometimes quarterbacks would look directly at me as they called the count.

Perhaps you could excuse such an oversight in high school football, but you would expect college men to know better than to give their plans away so openly. However, as I was to learn at Illinois—and even later with the Bears—many quarterbacks seemed to operate as though they were in a void, unaware that a spy with a sharp eye for detail and serious designs on the football was watching their every move. I'm laughing now as I write this: I had so damn much fun playing Sherlock out there.

If the quarterback had the presence of mind to cover his face when he called the play, I'd turn my attention to the running backs as they broke from the huddle. Running backs operate almost exclusively on adrenaline—a natural stimulant that sometimes produces a telltale effect on the body. An obvious giveaway were the eyes, which on some players light up as though somebody has thrown a switch. Then there were the ones who actually tried to be cute by acting bored, their posture saying, *I really am not part of this nonsense*, which of course told me they were getting the ball.

Others would give themselves away during the countdown: They'd hold their arms differently, or lean a little and press one foot more firmly into the turf, or turn their shoulders an inch or two in the direction they planned to go. If they did none of these things and carried off the deception perfectly, they almost invariably would sneak a peek at the spot in the line they intended to hit—and I'd usually be there to meet them.

If the quarterback went to the sidelines during a timeout to talk with the coach, I'd watch them out of the corner of my eye and, often as not, I'd pick up a valuable piece of recon. It seems too easy to be true, too obvious—but it happened over and over. The most obvious sign is still the way the offensive linemen set up in their three-point stance. If they're back on their heels, it's a pass. If their shoulders are down, it's a run. Count on it.

Football players will tell you that they are aware of all this, but their state of mind changes when the game begins. They become so intent on doing the right thing when the ball is snapped, they forget that their behavior before the action can reveal their plan.

That season, my junior year, I was unanimously voted Chicago's High School Player of the Year and Bernie O'Brien paid me the ultimate compliment on my defensive skills. He said I was a "heady" player, who seemed to "smell out" the opposition's play. "It's like an added sense," said Bernie. "He seems to *feel* a play coming and he moves into the spot to stop it."

There really wasn't anything prescient about what I did. Anyone could have done it, and many others did then—and do so today—to one degree or another. But as I look back, I know that what gave me the edge, what gave me such a sharp sense of "smell," was my obsession with the game. Almost every moment of my conscious life—and probably my

dream life as well—I thought about these things. From draw-
ing up plays in class to dodging leaves on the sidewalk to
dreaming in my bed, I was immersed in the warm bath of my
imagination, creating highly specific game situations from
which I always emerged victorious.

Here is an example:

It's late afternoon at Soldier Field, fourth quarter of the
Chicago Public School League championship game: CVS vs.
Lane. The score is tied, 0–0. Lane is threatening, deep in our
territory; it's third and three.

I watch the quarterback in the huddle, reading his lips. He
says, "Green, right, thirty-six, on *three*," meaning fullback to
the six hole. As they break the huddle, I stay positioned over
the center, about three yards from the quarterback. I think to
myself, *Don't want to give myself away. I'll move to the six hole*
after *he starts the count—when it's too late for him to change
the play. Damn it! Look at his eyes. He smells something. Shit! An
audible. He's changing the call. What's he saying? "Blue lookie."
What the hell's "blue lookie"?*

"Hut, hut . . . *hut!*"

As the ball is snapped, the tight end cuts left across my
zone and the QB tosses a pop pass to him. I swing around to
my left, knowing he's already got the three yards for the first
down. All this happens in a single piece. But I see it in minute
detail, making mental adjustments. I've got to create a fumble, so I try something different. Instead of just tackling him
hard, which is what he expects me to do, I grab the back of
his shoulder pads, right behind the neck where there is a good
handhold. Stopping him cold, I start pulling him back. Football players are like everyone else: They don't like to fall down
backward. So while he is thinking about hitting his head on
the frozen field, he relaxes his death grip on the ball at the
precise instant my right fist hits it with a good uppercut.

The ball floats in the air long enough for the safety, who has come up from his deep spot, to snatch it and pass through the oncoming crowd, heading for home like a commuter in the off hours. With a sense of something close to splendor, I watch my teammate cross the goal line, giving CVS the championship. Victory music plays. Fans are tearing down the goal posts. The safety and I are carried off the field on the shoulders of our exultant—and deeply grateful—teammates. Beaming from the packed stands are my mother, father, and Helen.

Well, the reality almost matched the dream. CVS *did* go undefeated that season, and yes, we played for the championship against Lane High, from the North Side, at Soldier Field, and the score *was* tied late in the game. Some 14,000 faithful watched the teams beat each other almost to death, and when the gun sounded in the late-November afternoon, the score was still tied, 6–6.

Lane had a big, strong team, with a line that averaged about 220, while ours I'm sure didn't go above 200. But we played our hearts out, and Bernie O'Brien was damn proud of us, saying in the *Chicago Tribune*, "Our boys played like real champions."

But we were only half-champions at best. Because Lane's game statistics were a little better than ours, they were selected to play against the best of the Catholic League for the All-City title, which they won handily. It was the only championship I ever won sitting on my ass. We all joked about it and took it graciously, but in our hearts we knew we hadn't won a damn thing.

The night after the tie I sat alone in the bedroom back at 10324 South Lowe, running over the key plays of the game, searching for a lesson to be learned, one small nugget of wisdom I could carry away from the experience and apply to a

similar situation at a later date. My mother walked in, sat
down next to me, and I asked her why we had to lose after all
our hard work. She told me to review the game in my head
because that's where the answer was. Somewhere something
could have been done differently perhaps. But, she added, if I
could find nothing to criticize, then I should put the game
behind me and chalk the final score up to God's will. Some
things just have to be forgotten.

The next day I discovered in the *Tribune* that I had made
quite an impression on at least one member of the opposition.
"That Dick Butkus is tremendous," said Lane High tackle and
cocaptain Jerry Mroczek, who weighed in at 248. "He was
everywhere. I never saw anything like it. You just couldn't
stop him. He's a team all by himself."

Even as I read those words today, I feel an unsettling mix
of emotions, equal parts red-faced embarrassment and hidden
pride. I was raised to follow a certain Catholic, blue-collar
ethic. The one that prohibits even the slightest show of self-
satisfaction, the idea that the greater your accomplishments,
the softer you go. I believe in that ethic, though sometimes it
is very hard to follow. Whenever the adulation gets too high
to handle gracefully, I remember my father going softly
through a life of service to his family, and I usually get quiet,
too. But it can be a struggle, this thing called fame.

━━━━

There's a well inside me, and I don't know what is down
there. Even today, in a settled life that brims with the joys of
middle age, with three great kids doing well, with friends and
health, there are times when this little kid comes climbing out
of that well and demands to be heard. I never know when he
might show himself and sometimes I don't even know what
the hell his problem is. But there he'll be, making a fuss, and

then he'll go away as quickly—and mysteriously—as he showed up.

Back in high school, it seemed as though the little kid was never very far away. One afternoon in my senior year, he threw his biggest tantrum. I had bought a '49 Plymouth for $50, a green two-door coupé with white sidewalls and a big rip in the cloth roof. Helen and I were grateful for the privacy after a year in the constant company of Rick Richards and Jimmy Brink. During football season, she would wait in the car and do her homework while I was at practice.

Helen was my one and only girlfriend, then and now, and I guess I could be a little possessive of her. One day I happened to look across the field and out onto 87th Street where my car was always parked, and there was Helen sitting in the passenger's seat, talking to some guys in another car, guys I didn't recognize. Ordinarily this would not have been a major concern. But it was late in the season and I was going through my mental gymnastics in preparation for the playoffs.

I started walking toward the car. As I got closer, I could see these guys were definitely not my type. Something about their manner, maybe the way they laughed, rang in my head. I started yelling at them as I headed across the street, un-mindful of the steady stream of traffic—horns honking, wheels screeching, a pissed-off driver or two yelling at me—and the closer I got to them, the angrier I became. I was like John Wayne in *Red River*, walking through a bawling herd of longhorns on his way to kill Montgomery Clift. I was in full uniform, cleats and helmet included, and when they finally saw me coming toward them, the driver began to pull away. But this hurried exit was not good enough for me. I ran after them, and just as they were about to make a left turn, I dove through the rolled-down window on the passenger side.

The rest was pure craziness. The car zigzagged down

87th Street. Inside I was a wild animal, a bear caught in a snare, grabbing the wheel and kicking the guys in back with my cleats. I must have made quite an impression as we passed the front steps of CVS, where half of the students in the school were waiting for buses that would take them home. The driver hit the brakes and I delivered some choice words of warning, underscored by several memorable shots to mouths and noses, while from down the street, the entire football team came to see what had happened to their buddy.

There would be hell to pay. I thought Bernie O'Brien was going to have a heart attack. He roasted, boiled, and deep-fried me. They say Irish anger can cause permanent injury, but not Bernie's, because his was stoked in the heart. Bernie was worried, not so much for the team, but for me. He knew my football talents were special—hell, he'd shaped and honed them himself—and he wanted to see his favorite pupil, the kid who hung out in his office between classes, go on in life and make something of himself. Perhaps more than anyone except my mother, Bernie knew that if the fire in my belly was not channeled onto the football field, it could consume my future before the train ever left the station.

My last season at CVS would require all my physical ability, dedication, and heart if I was to maintain the standard I'd set when I became the first junior ever to be awarded Player of the Year by the *Chicago Sun-Times*. Every game in my senior year was harder—on both sides of the ball. As high school sportswriter Emil Stubits said in a preseason piece in the *Sun-Times*, "Rich Butkus of Vocational will be a marked man in public school football this season."

Stubits was right. But I had been preparing myself for the challenge. I had always expected that one day I'd look across the line and see my double—or worse, my superior—and I also knew that such a confrontation would be my greatest

test. I never actually met that player in high school. Instead, gangs of doom came at me that year, and playing the game became less like football and more like the kind of thing that happens in the back alleys on the South Side. When I carried the ball, it seemed as though *everyone* keyed on me. Where one or two guys tried to stop me the previous season, there were now three and four players assigned the task. Hell, I was getting gang-tackled on every play.

I bore up pretty well. Not because I was some sort of superman, but because I had been preparing one particular muscle for this challenge: my heart. I knew other bodies would catch up to mine, and many did that year, some exceeding my six-foot-three, 225-pound frame, but I seriously doubted there was another player anywhere who *cared* as much as I did. And that caring, that passion, I hoped would see me through. I brought the full force of my heart to every play. But something else began to happen, something that I had never included in all my daydreams. My body, the thing I had always taken for granted, began to show some cracks.

The shoulder injury came early in the season. I can't recall exactly when it happened, certainly not the play or even the game. Maybe that's because I tend to forget negative things, or maybe it's because I am blessed with a high threshold of pain. The biggest reason I didn't remember the injury was my pride. I didn't want any member of the opposition to know he had hurt me. I was like the batter who won't rub the spot where the 100 mile-an-hour fastball has just struck him, even though later he'll take off his shirt and see the league logo clearly tattooed on his skin. But in football, with so many bodies flying around, injuries happen all the time without anyone but the player in question being aware of it, and sometimes even he isn't aware of it until after the game. There was a practical side to this secrecy, too: If an opposing player sees that you are hurt, he'll tell his buddies and they'll come after you even harder. While this wolf pack philosophy was not prevalent in high school or even in college, it was standard operating procedure in the pros. But it was my philosophy from the very beginning.

To practically everybody in the league, except the student body at CVS, I wore the black hat. At every away game, I would hear the boos. It was a response that would continue throughout my career. I took this particular form of disapproval as a compliment, a motivator to play even harder. But now nicknames began to follow me, names like "Ox" and "Animal"—the usual insults slapped on the backs of strong men by those who themselves lack a certain something inside. I haven't lied yet in this book, so I won't start now. The names didn't stop me; in fact, I hit all the harder when I heard them. But they stung.

Anyway, the injury hurt so much that Bernie decided to play me only on the defensive side for a few games. Rick Bertetto was having a great season at halfback, breaking away time and again for long gains; often I'd throw an especially good block for my buddy, then sit back on my ass or just stand there and watch him go. God, I love to watch a good running back. Passes are fun, but watching a nifty back like Bertetto—and later, the greatest innovator I ever saw, Gale Sayers—is high entertainment. I guess my appreciation of the running game dates back to that afternoon when my father and I watched Buddy Young run wild on TV.

Time helped to heal my injury and soon I was healthy enough to contribute on both sides of the ball. We continued our victorious march through the season, giving up a grand total of 6 points to the opposition and, of particular delight to me, crushing Fenger, 40–0. Then, in the semifinals of the league playoffs, a second crack in my armor developed. I hurt my right knee, somehow pulling a ligament, and the next week we lost to Taft High, 14–6, in the finals at Soldier Field. Before the game, Bernie, who also acted as our trainer, taped my leg from hip to ankle and told me I would only be playing defense. I couldn't kick and I couldn't run, and the fact is I couldn't play much defense either. Despite Bernie's taping job, the knee just couldn't respond to the pressure of a quick lateral move, and Taft had their way on a lot of plays up the middle that I would have stopped easily if I had been healthy.

But this salient point didn't deter Taft coach Joe Kupcinet, a man deeply ignorant of blue-collar ethics, from crowing to the press after the game that he *knew* CVS could be beat. Employing the first-person singular at every opportunity, much the way his brother Irv did for years as the Bears' radio announcer, Joe explained in glowing detail his ingenious strategy—when everyone knew it was his kids who won the game. Finally Kupcinet boasted, "We would have won even if Butkus had been healthy and played on both sides the whole game."

Meanwhile, in the losing locker room, Bernie's comments were classy and subtle. Never mentioning my injury and the injuries to two other key backs, Ron Craig and Harry Reidel, Coach O'Brien simply said: "Taft's a good team, the best we played this year. We couldn't stop them up the middle. That was the difference." Bernie's words, when decoded, meant: If Butkus was healthy, Taft wouldn't have scored a point—and CVS would have been the champs, undefeated in two seasons.

———

November 1960.

With my high school playing days behind me, my focus shifted to college. Each week dozens of "letters of offering" with postmarks from around the country appeared in Bernie

O'Brien's letter box at school. Sports observers based in the Midwest—writers, coaches, athletic directors, boosters—were calling me the most sought-after high school player in the country. Whether or not that was true, the attention I was getting was almost overwhelming. For the first time in my life, I actually had more of something than I needed, and the choice of where I would play was not an easy one for the kid from Roseland.

To make matters even more pressing, I felt as though I had to make my choice in a hurry. Due to the CVS split schedule, I graduated with my class in January and I wanted to enter college right away so that I would benefit from spring practice. I didn't know what I'd be up against, didn't know how good the other players would be, and I wanted to take advantage of the headstart that my early graduation offered.

The golden dome of South Bend, Indiana, beckoned. Notre Dame. What a name to a Catholic kid in those days. It rang in the spirit and swelled the soul, fact mixed with myth. It was heroism unbounded and sanctified to our neighbors in Roseland. The Gipper, Knute Rockne, Frank Leahy, Johnny Lujack. Names that swaggered through the best of America's sports history to a fight song that seemed to transcend sports. It's what I thought I wanted. Bernie O'Brien had played there, and there was no man I respected more. If he picked up some of his magic from that institution, then I wanted to go there, too.

But when I attended a postseason banquet arranged for all prospective players in South Bend, I heard a couple of things that turned me off. Well, actually it was what I *didn't* hear that made me think twice. Joe Kuharich, the varsity coach then, in his after-dinner speech, was summoning the ghost of coaches past through the cigar smoke, kindling the famous Notre Dame fever. He was going pretty good, too, until he got to the point where he said, "And in the locker room before every game I gather my boys around me and I say . . ." Then he stopped dead in his words, and we waited . . . and waited.

This temporary loss of memory did not impress me. Later, I was taken on a tour of the campus by one of the assistant coaches and a senior player. When we were done, one of them asked me if I had any questions. Feeling out of myself in the presence of all these high-powered, professional college types, I asked if I could see the living quarters for married undergraduates. The assistant coach looked at me as though my nose had just fallen off. "Oh," he answered from somewhere on the mountain, "we don't get married at Notre Dame before we graduate."

Oh yeah? Well, between a coach who couldn't remember his standard pregame line to his players and a school policy against marriage, the golden dome began to lose some of its glitter. Helen and I had no set plan to marry before I graduated from college, but I didn't appreciate being told that we couldn't if we wanted to, and anyway I already had been down to the University of Illinois and asked the same question of coach Pete Elliott and assistant coach Bill Taylor and their answer was an enthusiastic "yes, by all means," and they showed me where we would live, even offered to assist Helen in her search for a job.

So as I visited a number of other Midwest schools— Purdue and Iowa among them—Illinois kept coming up bigger and bigger, due mainly to the salesmanship of the Elliott–Taylor combo. They struck me as nice guys and I believed them when they said that Illinois, then at the bottom of the Big Ten, was going to flex its muscles for the first time in years. Another factor in the Butkus–Illinois equation was my brother Ronnie. He had gone to Illinois and knew it to be the right place for his kid brother; but, not entirely relying on his filial powers over me, he enlisted the one-and-only Ray Nitschke, ex-Illini and all-everything linebacker for the Green Bay Packers, and after a weekend of those two beating the Illini war drum in my ear, I was so fired up that I signed a letter of intent with Illinois, which bound me to accept no other offer from a Big Ten school.

But I still had a little time to kill before I left for the elm-shaded streets of Champaign, Illinois, which were under a foot of snow at the time, so I took advantage of two free trips to Florida. Naturally, I had never been to Florida and I wanted to see what all the hoopla was about. Hell, I hadn't been any-where outside the state, except for an uncle's farm in Wiscon-sin. My first trip was to Tallahassee, the hometown of Florida State. The coach met me at the plane and took me straight to a party where I was surprised to see the assistant coach hus-tling girls for the players. This dazzled me a bit, not alto-gether unpleasantly. But my senses spiraled even higher the next day when running back Tucker Frederickson blew in from Fort Lauderdale and immediately asked the coach if he had lined up some "dates." I soon realized they were not talk-ing about game dates, and I began to wonder if we were ever going to be shown the training facilities—the gym, the fields, the weight room. Stuff like that. You know, football stuff.

That night we all went out on the town. I thought Tucker was a pretty good guy, and four years later, when he was a running back for the Giants and we were vying, along with my buddy Gale Sayers, for Rookie of the Year honors, I hit him hard and often in the one game we faced each other, rag-ging him after each hit about the candy-ass school he went to. Anyway, when I got on the plane for home the next day, I realized I never did see those damn training facilities.

If I hadn't been so serious about Helen, I might have

thought about going to Florida. I may not have checked out their facilities, but I did see another reason to consider the school. Some of the girls I saw on that trip would have caused riots in Roseland.

My second trip to Florida was less enlightening than it was infuriating. I had been invited to look over the University of Miami by head coach Andy Gustasen, who must have been busy the day I arrived because I was met by some asshole halfback whose name I don't remember, fortunately for him. I call him an asshole because when I told him I had signed a letter of intent with Illinois, he reported it to Gustasen, who hot-boxed me for half an hour, chewing me out and threatening to call Pete Elliott and tell him I had freeloaded a trip down South with no intention of going to the school.

I hate snitches.

———

So it was back to Chicago, but I felt wiser for having made the trip. Not all coaches are as kind and caring as Bernie O'Brien, and not all players are automatically your buddies. Life beyond the South Side was proving to be very different. If the game was the same, the rules outside the lines changed all too easily. At no time was this more clearly demonstrated than one December night when I walked home from Helen's house and saw a man sitting alone in a car on South Lowe, his cigarette a hot point in the dark.

When I got to the gate, the man called over to me. He asked me if I was Dick Butkus. I said I was, looking around and wondering why this guy was waiting for me outside my house at ten o'clock at night. As he began to speak, I looked toward my house and saw Ronnie and my mother sitting at the table, and now I could hear the guy telling me that he was "connected" with the athletic department at the University of Indiana and that he and others of influence admired the way I played. Would I consider coming to Bloomington?

When I told him I had signed a letter of intent with Illinois, he sucked meditatively on his cigarette, looking up at me from under the brim of his hat. Then he shrugged and quickly looked away, and as little bits of smoke escaped with each word, he said that I shouldn't let that worry me. His associates would take care of the details. While the man talked on, his voice a monotone, his eyes seldom on me as I stood by his long shiny Caddy, I looked again into the house through the window, where I knew Ronnie and my mother *must* have seen by now. Now the man was asking me about my car, the old Plymouth with the hole in the roof and the flat tire, and we agreed that it had seen better days.

Sucking again on his smoke, which by now had burned down to his fingertips, the man asked me what kind of car I would choose if money were not a problem. I can't say I didn't know what the man was doing, because I did, and yet somehow, I don't know, maybe it was the tone of his voice, so calm and confident, or the cut of his clothes, or the Cadillac he was driving, but he made me feel important. I said I'd choose a Corvette. After acknowledging my good taste, the man suggested that perhaps a new Corvette might be waiting for me in Bloomington.

I was suddenly interested. After all, none of the other recruiters had offered me anything to go to their school, so when the man suggested that I come in out of the cold, I climbed into the passenger's seat, liking the feel and the smell of the leather upholstery, and the green and red glow of the famous Caddy dashboard. We talked about life at the University of Indiana and how much I would enjoy it.

After a bit, we shook hands, and the man gave me his card and said I should call him in a day or two if I decided I wanted to take a look at the school. I thanked him and walked into the house, feeling pretty tall, a state of mind that was about to undergo a serious revision. As I told Ronnie and my mother (my sister Dolly may also have been there) what the man had said, they started shaking their heads as though I shouldn't be let out after sundown, and all of a sudden I began to feel like that little kid who'd stayed out too late on the cart pulled by the man who sang, "Rag-o-li-i-ine!"

My mother reminded me that I'd made a commitment to Pete Elliott and Bill Taylor and that no lousy car was going to change that. "What if you get injured? Would Indiana do what Illinois promised to do? Keep your scholarship in place for four years?" And Ronnie was asking me what kind of an athletic program would have a recruiter who worked at night from his car. Why didn't the guy come into the house and talk with them, Ronnie and my mother wondered, and now I was wondering, too. By the end of the discussion, the man in the Cadillac was history, and I was back on track, heading south to Illinois.

But this was 1960, and although few of us knew it then, the American code of ethics was already undergoing a heavy rewrite, and in the years to come, I would meet more men who preferred to operate in the dark.

———

One day a few weeks later, as my mother was giving my shirts a few last-minute touches with the iron, I stood in the bedroom that I had shared for so many years with three of my brothers, putting some toiletries into an already tightly packed suitcase. Then I picked up the CVS yearbook and turned to the page where the varsity football team smiled proudly and innocently out into the coming years, and after scanning the faces of my friends and wondering how many of them I would ever see again, I read the longest of the messages, one that had been written without my knowledge, one that I hadn't seen before:

> To a son who will never know how much it
> meant to his dad and myself to see him go
> through his high school days—and the honors
> he got by doing what he always said he would like
> to do someday—playing football . . . And the day did
> arrive when he was chosen the star of football. Our
> hearts were overflowed. May God look out—and
> take care of you.
>
> > Love,
> > Mom and Dad.

A little later I would head south to Champaign. But first I stopped by CVS to say good-bye to the man who had done so much for me over the last three years.

I will always remember that meeting: Bernie O'Brien sitting behind his desk, his wise eyes resting easily on me. One look at him told me he wasn't upset that I didn't go to his alma mater. We talked small stuff for a few minutes and then he became silent, as though he were deep in thought or maybe prayer.

After a few moments, he lifted his head and looked at me. He said I was the best player he had ever coached. He thanked me for going to CVS and working so hard for him. Then we shook hands.

In just a few choice words, Bernie O'Brien had prepared me for college. I left his office walking on air. Little Dickie had done good—so far.

I remember it as a Rube Goldberg type of contraption, too big and complex for the simple job it performed. It was made of something light, maybe tubular steel or aluminum, and painted in Illini blue and orange. With the afternoon sun illuminating the various pieces, all angled every which way, it resembled the skeletal remains of a dinosaur. It had seven openings, or chutes, each about three feet long and four feet high, through which the offensive linemen were supposed to run, staying low until they came out of the other end and smacked into padded dummies held by teammates.

This was my first spring practice, and as I crouched in my three-point stance I was determined to impress everyone by hitting that dummy at the other end of the chute with every ounce of force I could muster, hoping to knock the teammate holding it flat on his ass. So when someone called the signals, I exploded forward on the appropriate *hut* and— *BAM!*—I promptly whacked my nose on a four-foot-high bar at the entrance to the chute. Blood spouted all over my jersey. But being the number-one tough guy from the South Side of Chicago, I acted as though I'd nicked myself shaving. Inside, however, I felt humiliated, and outside I not only had trouble seeing for the rest of the day, I had permanently altered a perfectly good nose.

I mention the incident because it is an apt metaphor for my introduction to college life. In addition to my embarrassment at practice, I was blindsided by Illinois academics. In high school I never did much homework, but in college I was expected to carry a full academic load. The burden of this new responsibility became clear to me during my first week of classes. Even though my major was physical education, there was one course—rhetoric—that could have put my scholarship in jeopardy if I had failed it. The required reading alone took three and four hours a night. I was a pretty good reader, but the subject matter—sports pages, magazines, and so on—had always been user-friendly. Now I was asked to read essays and study grammar and I found the going very rough. When I told Bill Taylor, he smiled and said that short of contracting a communicable disease, "we" should make every class, explaining that if there were any grading problems "our" attendance record could be a valuable bargaining tool with "our" teacher, Emily Watts.

I particularly liked his liberal use of the words "we" and "our."

So on Monday, Wednesday, and Friday mornings, I showed up at Miss Watts's rhetoric class, and each week she would have us write a "theme." Well, hell, I'd never even heard the word before. But I wrote themes for Miss Watts—always on football, of course. During our first "progress meeting," she looked at my records, laughed, and shook her head. Then she said that she didn't know how I got into Illinois, but if I was willing to do my part, she would do what she could to help me get through.

If my freshman year was a trial in the classroom, it was

even more difficult outside of it. With no wheels—the '49 Plymouth had all but died during the winter—and no money to buy a few beers or call home, I felt pretty isolated. I kept in touch with my mother and Helen by writing a letter every day, and to keep my bargain with Miss Watts I read, read, read. But I was lonely, so lonely that sometimes I could feel it in my throat. I missed Helen and the two Ricks, and I missed the quiet talks with my mother. I even missed my brothers. And although the campus was beautiful, I missed our little house on South Lowe and Fernwood Park down the block and everything else about Roseland.

Other Chicago high school players had been recruited by Illinois, even a few I played against. But most of them would not be arriving in Champaign until August when training camp began. That seemed like an eternity to me. Anyway, every one of those recruits came from the North Side; they might as well have been from the moon as far as I was concerned.

I told myself it was best not to get too close to anyone. Illini football was my superhighway to the NFL and the complications of friendships might slow me down. Or that's what I told myself. What is probably closer to the truth is that I was a very shy young man—and maybe a little spoiled, too. I'd been allowed to do nothing but play football for the last four years. Without any interference by my teachers—or even my family. My mother and Helen were my biggest fans, and very few demands were made of me because I did so well on the football field.

But now I was alone in a new environment. I had a roommate at Snyder Hall, but we had nothing in common. Football had always been my outlet, but in those days freshmen were not eligible to play varsity ball. They were generally viewed by the older players as so much extra baggage. So when spring practice began, I didn't have a place to relax and let my mind out of its cage. I was emotionally homeless, lost. The glory of my high school years was gone, and I didn't know if I would ever get it back. Later, beginning in my sophomore year, whenever I got the blues, I would go and hang out with the trainers and listen to them tell stories. But as a first-year player I didn't feel I rated that privilege.

Across the way from my room in Snyder Hall was the stadium, Memorial Stadium, looming above the flat Midwestern terrain, big and dark and empty. Sometimes in that first, bleak semester I would walk over there, climb the fence if the gate was closed, and go inside. But even there, within the silent confines of the stadium, I wasn't completely at rest. One day, in a February rain, I found myself sitting alone in the stands, looking down on the field, hearing the rainwater sluice through a hundred drains, watching it sift in curtains across the backdrop of the grandstands. And I wondered if I would make it at Illinois, wondered if I was good enough—and the emptiness I felt inside seemed to grow.

But then I would think about the dreary consequences of dropping out of Illinois. My parents' disappointment, my altered future with Helen, and the generally silent response by Roseland to a favorite son not making the grade all swirled turbulently in my head. But the heaviest consideration was the fear of my own disapproval. That's when I would think of Ron transferring from one college to the next with his bad knee. Somehow I knew as I sat alone in the rain that wherever I went in this life I'd meet myself. As a linebacker, I also knew that lost ground was very difficult to regain.

There was one guy on campus who took an interest in me. Although his behavior did not exactly qualify him for student of the year honors, he was a good friend to this displaced South Side kid. Ed O'Bradovich had gotten on the wrong side of Pete Elliott and a number of the faculty and it was determined that he and the university might do better outside each other's company. Ed was strictly Chicago and blue-collar all the way. He was the kind of guy who would show up at ROTC marching drills wearing white sneakers when everyone else was wearing black leather boots.

O'Bradovich was always getting his girlfriends to write his school papers. He was famous for this, even envied—until the day he handed in a paper that was supposed to have been done in class. His girlfriend was late with the goods, delivering the folded document to Ed through an open window while the rest of class penned their tomes. The clue that Ed may not have been the author of the paper surfaced when the teacher noticed that Ed's paper was typewritten.

Since there wasn't a typewriter within sight, Ed was collared.

Because of that incident and many others, Ed was on his way out when I was entering Illinois. Fortunately for me, he stuck around for most of that spring semester, living off campus with another player. And with nothing better to do, Ed took me under his big wing. His style of mentorship could hardly be compared to that of Mr. Chips, but he helped me survive those early months. When Ed left in May to play pro ball in Canada, I knew I'd be all right. What I didn't know was that O'Bradovich would end up on the Bears a year later, brought south by George Allen, and that we would be roommates in my third year in the pros.

Besides Ed, there were two other standbys on the Butkus watch: Pete Elliott and Bill Taylor. As head coach, Pete wisely stayed in the background, letting Bill Taylor do most of the close communicating. Bill usually found the right words to fit the moment. The message was always the same: ''Hang in there. Life will get better next year when you join the big boys on the varsity.''

Meanwhile, Miss Watts and I were tiptoeing through the mine fields of rhetoric. Her patience and sense of humor were endless, both of which must have come in handy when she read my essays. Still, I worried about failing. On the night before the final, I sat in my room praying more than studying, my mind frozen in a kind of helpless panic. I didn't even know where to begin. I sat there staring at my textbook. Then, like an angel from on high, in walked Bill Taylor. Over the next two or three hours, we devised a solid game plan for the exam.

The next morning I woke up feeling I had a reasonable chance. A week later, the grades were posted. Miss Watts gave me a passing grade. I felt happy—and very relieved. We had done it together, Miss Watts and I—with a special last-minute strategy provided by Bill Taylor. When I returned to Illinois many years later to have my number retired, there she was, looking just the same with her short hair and horn-rimmed glasses. Emily was wearing the biggest smile at the banquet. When I thanked her for what she had done for me, Emily whispered, "You earned it."

I learned later that night that she had become a member on the board of athletics, with specific responsibilities toward guiding scholarship athletes through their academic trials. I don't know if I was her first charge, but I do know that without Emily's help, an Illini football shirt with 50 on it might not be hanging in the field house—and I might still be working on my retirement at Pullman Standard.

I consider myself very lucky.

Given today's widespread awareness of athletic departments' coddling of star players, you might suspect that my experience was simply a matter of form, a charade—that I was going to pass no matter how I did on the final. Well, I didn't believe that then—and I don't believe it now. I lived in real fear of flunking out that first year, and I can still remember the despair I felt when things seemed very bleak. Yet somehow I found the will to weather those months.

Did I receive special help? Of course I did, but I had to cooperate, pull my own oar. This is also the way it was financially. Bill Taylor got me a summer construction job, but I did the rest, busting my ass every day for that paycheck. One of my jobs was to carry loads of bricks, and I intentionally carried them out from my body to build up my arm strength. Pete Elliott also got Helen a job at a bank in Champaign after we were married and living on campus, but it was Helen who won the praise and affection of her fellow workers. As for direct financial assistance, there wasn't any—no cash at all—except once. In my junior year, I had to go to Chicago for Anson Mount's *Playboy* preseason All-American team. An alumni friend slipped me $60 to buy a suit so I wouldn't look like a bum. I took it and bought the first suit I ever owned—one of those light seersucker jobs with the skinny blue lines. Otherwise, not so much as a nickel crossed my palm.

Nor did any cash or checks bearing boosters' signatures—or those of the treasurers of their companies—ever arrive in the mailbox at 10324 South Lowe. And there was no new car, no free airline tickets, no paid-for vacations, no perks of any kind. Other athletes at other colleges may have gotten some things, but I really don't know. You'd have to ask them.

I'm not sure how I would have reacted if someone had offered me something. I do know that I didn't want anything to interfere with my scholarship at Illinois, so I wouldn't have even considered such an offer. But my mother and father could have used some help, especially with me off playing ball instead of contributing to the family like most South Side high school graduates did in those days. Eventually, of course, I was able to repay part of my parents' enormous generosity when I made the pros. But as a freshman I knew that three long years loomed ahead, three football seasons in which I would either prove myself worthy of the next level or . . . what? I didn't know, I didn't *want* to know. I never let myself think of an alternative. I had chosen a goal and the notion of not reaching it was unthinkable.

My sophomore year broke clear and bright—and no one was more bullish about my future than my head coach, Pete Elliott. I hadn't even played a college game yet, and Pete was already calling me the best player he'd ever coached. "If Butkus is not a Heisman Trophy winner, then I've never seen one," he told his friend Ed O'Neil, a columnist at the *Champaign News-Gazette*. From O'Neil's column the quote multiplied a hundred times across the country, finally appearing in a story by a guy named Dan Jenkins in a relatively young national magazine called *Sports Illustrated*.

Such a statement was uncharacteristic of Coach Elliott, but having just presided over the only winless season in Illinois history, he was probably anxious to put the best face on the immediate future, which he decided was me rather than the team. There was no question that we were going to get better. Pete and Bill Taylor had recruited some very good players, most of them in-state and many straight out of Chicago. It was as though Pete had tapped directly into the Windy City's well of high school talent.

So the question was not if but when this new infusion of talent would reverse the historic misfortunes at Illinois. We were riding a ten-game losing streak that had begun two seasons earlier, and although Pete, who was in his second year

as head coach, proclaimed the 1962 season as "Operation Rebound," the sportswriters were a good deal less visionary.
They warned us that while the future looked good for the
Illini, we should not move our furniture out of the Big Ten's
cellar just yet.

It turned out they were right.

Our struggles began in Seattle against the highly ranked
team from the University of Washington. The Huskies were
not very big, but they were fast, deep in talent, and considerably more experienced. They were also out for revenge. The
previous week Purdue had tied them, 7–7, and the Huskies
wanted to send a message back to the Big Ten by beating us
convincingly. We held our own through the first half, but our
lack of depth showed itself after intermission and we lost,
28–7. What surprised me was just how quick and crisp the
Huskies were off the ball. Since this was my first exposure to
actual college game conditions, I wasn't quite ready for the
Huskies. They broke the huddle and came right after us with
quick snaps, confidence, and high precision. But I did okay,
leading our team with eleven tackles and assisting on six
more.

Ara Parseghian, who was then the coach of our next opponent, Northwestern, remarked to the press that I appeared
to be a little slow against Washington. Well, I'm sure I did.
Due to a hip-pointer injury, I hadn't practiced in ten days. By
the end of the third quarter, I was so tired that I was sucking
air. Poor Pete and Bill tried to hide their disappointment. But
we were family now and there would be no secrets. I had gotten to like them so much that I felt their regret as well as my
own, and I remember thinking, as our chartered DC-3 prop
job lifted off the runway at *Sea Tac* Airport and headed east
over the World's Fair Grounds spiked by the newly erected
Space Needle, that the worst was over. We had received our

cold-water shock of baptism, and now we would build on this experience.

Wrong again. The next week Parseghian's Wildcats pounded us into the turf at Dyche Stadium, 45–0, extending our winless streak to twelve and dropping Pete Elliott's hopes so low on that humiliating Saturday, his thirty-sixth birthday, that he had no answers for the press. "I don't know what's wrong," he told O'Neil. "But we'll get better." But over the next three games—against Minnesota, Ohio State, and USC—our notices did anything but improve. I had been out with a knee injury for two of those games, but the scores by which we lost left no doubt that I would not have made the difference between defeat and victory.

In the wake of the losses, the sportswriters were beginning to smell blood. Newspaper stories, sparked by earlier ones in the *Chicago Sun-Times*, began questioning Pete Elliott's coaching abilities. I could see the worry and strain root itself deeper on his face with each loss. Watching Pete fight his own private demons game after game, practice after practice, damn near made me crazy. This was the man who made me want to go to Illinois, the man who had sung my praises to the press. He'd promised that the team's fortunes would change in 1962. Well, they hadn't changed, and now, losers of fifteen straight, we prepared for our game against Purdue.

Although I had managed to play the week before— against Southern California—my right knee still hampered me. But around midweek, I woke up and discovered the pain had left. That afternoon during practice, I felt reborn. For the first time in over a month, I could put all my weight on the knee. Later that day, Pete Elliott was also reborn. In a rare display of solidarity, the Illinois Athletic Department voted unanimously to reappoint Pete as head coach for another season. The good news picked up the team and the coaching staff and carried us like a refreshing sea breeze into the Boilmakers' stadium that Saturday. Despite a pregame line that put us 23 points down, we prevailed, 14–10.

When we arrived back on campus, the student body greeted us as though we had defeated the Axis. During the rally that night, with the ghost of Red Grange swirling among the cigarette and cigar smoke in the rafters of the field house, the quiet kid from the South Side grabbed the microphone and, in a hoarse voice, spoke to his fellow students from the heart, proclaiming Pete's "Operation Rebound" alive and well, and then he issued a warning to the rest of the Big Ten. "The beatings are over!" he whispered fervently. The Illini were back on the Rock Island Line and headed for the Rose Bowl in 1963—just as Coach Elliott had predicted.

In his column the next day, Ed O'Neil, who had stuck by Coach Elliott through the long siege, remarked, "There will be no more talk of a changing of the Illinois guard for a long, long time." Reading the words, I could almost hear Ed's gloating tone and see his Irish sneer. Little did I know that Pete, Bill Taylor, and the entire coaching staff would be blindsided from within their ranks less than three years down the road.

We won only one more game that year, but it was a big one. We knocked off Michigan State, 7–6. The victory stood tall among the hats in the press box—and they wrote glowingly of the new kids on the block, pulling out all the shopworn adjectives of their trade. Pete Elliott was suddenly Knute Rockne, I was Superman, and the Illini had changed from the Big Ten's doormat to its prodigy. We had hung in through the long, eventful season. We had faced the fire of criticism together, bore up under the stings of humiliation together—and, most important, we had learned how to pull together.

I learned not only that I could play in the Big Ten, but

that I could dominate. Despite my injury, I had played well, sometimes very well. In seven games, my abilities to defend had multiplied almost incrementally. By the season's end, I had made ninety-seven tackles, and I was beginning to hear the drumbeats of national recognition. Butkus, said the writers, was next year's All-American.

My first two years in college had been a roller-coaster ride. I had passed through those painful early freshman days, so often filled with downright loneliness and a desperate fear of failure in the classroom. But I had learned how to study. By the end of my sophomore year, I was maintaining a 3.6 grade-point average. As for my football abilities, I needn't have worried.

I could see my future more clearly than ever. Only one shadow fell across the way, the same shadow that once blotted out Ronnie's football career. If the significance of a knee injury had not impressed me in high school, it certainly had by now, underlining the frailty of my chosen life, forging the knowledge that a single play could end my career. This ugly, unavoidable truth somehow took me outside myself for perhaps the first time. No longer did I sit alone in the empty stands, listening to the rain and wondering whether I was good enough to play at the college level. I knew now that I *was* good enough, maybe more than good enough, and my longtime dream of playing in the NFL was being articulated by others as more than a possibility. It had become an expectation. I felt it, too, but I also saw the shadow.

It was as a junior that the full measure of collegiate glory surrounded me. I was recognized by the student body and by the faculty, and the campus was as much mine to walk on as anyone else's. It's funny that I had to be a star to feel accepted. But even more than public recognition, there was the interior feel of the team itself that filled me with satisfaction and peace. From the big-time stadium across the way from Snyder Hall to the practice fields, from the players to the coaches and the trainers, the whole thing was a world unto itself. It embraced me, defined me, and kept me safe.

No one has ever loved the camaraderie of a football team more than Dick Butkus. The shared commitment—the brotherhood of battle—still runs like a bright river through my daydreams. It is what I miss most. When I think about my playing days at Illinois, I remember that functional family of players, coaches, and trainers most vividly.

Certainly the games were of primary importance. They were the fire dances, the celebrations of athletic manhood so vital to the self-image of a Big Ten university. On the field I battled for the honor of my school. But what I loved most was the intensity of sixty men working together. The well-run practices, the team meetings, and the workouts left me drained but somehow euphoric.

Between our last practice of the week and every home game Illinois had a unique ritual. On Friday after practice, we would board buses and travel fifteen miles west across some of the country's richest farmlands. Then we would turn onto a secondary road and finally follow a dirt lane into a dark stretch of woods. Passing under a large stone gate, we would enter a world of tranquillity: the Allerton Estate.

Donated to the university in the 1940s by the Allerton family of Chicago, the Allerton Estate covered hundreds of acres of ponds and streams and woodlands. At its center was an imported slice of aristocratic England, a precious plot painstakingly designed in the grand style of the late nineteenth century. It had a rambling manor house with dozens of rooms, most with huge fireplaces, high ceilings, and ornately carved woodwork. The kitchen was bigger than the house I grew up in. Outside were acres and acres of gardens and greenhouses and pathways bordered by twelve-foot hedgerows.

In this silent, well-ordered place, away from campus Delilahs and late-night beer joints, we underwent the final phase of our pregame purification: eating a healthy dinner, then watching a movie that was invariably picked by Coach Elliott for its theme of personal courage, and, if you were a Catholic, telling your sins to Father Duncan, the team chaplain. We shared rooms according to our respective positions: the linemen together, the backs together, and so on. In such an intimate setting, I got to see how my teammates mentally prepared for the game. Some got very quiet, a few seeming to slip into trances, while others talked a blue streak or played pranks.

Lights went out at eleven and came on again at seven, in time for morning Mass and Communion. Before our breakfast of steak and eggs, we had maybe half an hour to ourselves. I would slip away and walk alone in the gardens, feeling whole and ready for whatever awaited me that day. I was usually quiet now. Not exactly calm, but ready, all the pieces in place, focused. I remember one particular Saturday morning when a heavy fog hung over the countryside, and I walked a graveled path in the enclosed gray silence of the gardens, feeling suddenly overwhelmed by my good fortune as the idea behind the reality of my life welled up inside me. I was in one of the most beautiful places I had ever seen. I had been forgiven for my sins and received Holy Communion. In just a few minutes, I would break bread with my comrades before going to the stadium to do what I loved before tens of thousands in the stands. In that moment, out there in the garden with the mist bathing my face, I suspected—hell, I knew—that I would never feel better about anything.

What added to my sense of completeness that junior year was the presence of Helen on the Illinois campus. We had married the previous July and had settled into our digs at Orchard Downs, a newly constructed campus compound for married students. No longer would I feel lonely after a home game, watching my mother and father and other members of my family drive out of the stadium parking lot. It had always seemed they left too early as I stood there with a lump in my throat. Now I had Helen, the love of my life, to go home with. Now, it seemed, I could study better, even sleep better. Things were looking up. In fact, things couldn't have been better.

On the football front, my life was right on schedule. National magazines and big-city newspapers were running their preseason All-American picks. I was selected as middle linebacker on practically every one, and seemingly overnight my name started to precede me wherever I went. Then *Playboy* magazine, the nation's new social bible, published its preseason team, and most of its 20 million readers—which included a lot of guys in a lot of barber shops—saw me in living color and read the hyperbole about my "primitive" ferocity.

This was the early fall of 1963. Ahead lay a season that would carry me on its shoulders, high above the crowd.

———

We'd showed up at preseason practice with fire in our bellies. At the weigh-in, just about everyone was at or below the weight head trainer Bob Nicollette had assigned us the previous spring. The spring practice had not ended on a happy note. Coach Elliott had delivered a blistering speech on the last day. He was not happy with our performance there, especially after a season in which we had been thoroughly outplayed in all but two games. Pete called us soft, mollycoddled, girlish. He suspected we liked losing, accused us of not knowing what a team effort really meant, and wondered if we would ever reach manhood. Never had I suffered such a barrage, each word carrying a sting.

But that August, when we had all returned in near-peak form, Pete couldn't have been more optimistic. At the preseason photo op—a special day set aside for the media—he turned on the full wattage of his considerable charm. Speaking with thick orange-and-blue fervor about our prospects for the upcoming season, Pete even suggested that there might be a Rose Bowl in our immediate future. He was even higher on my talents than a year ago, going so far as to predict I would someday be called "the greatest linebacker of all time."

Local sportswriter Ed O'Neil, who had accurately divined that we would win two games the year before, projected seven wins for the Illini in 1963. Impressed by his accurate forecast in 1962, we all wondered who we were supposed to lose to. We were still wondering after stopping coach Marv Levy's California team, 10–0, in our season opener under a sparkling sun in a half-filled Memorial Stadium.

Our defense was damn near flawless, stifling quarterback Craig Morton's troops at every turn. On the other side of the ball, our new fullback, sophomore Jim Grabowski, displayed outstanding skills. He would become a national sensation before the season was over. My stats were pretty good, too, leading the team with seven solo tackles and assisting on four others. Six of those stops came in the first quarter, forcing Morton to stay in the air or run wide for the rest of the game. The victory had an added sweetness. It was the first Illini season opener shutout in fifteen years and it came on the eve of Pete Elliott's thirty-seventh birthday. Just a year earlier he was going on ninety-nine.

But our real present to him came the next Saturday.

Fourth-ranked Northwestern, under head coach Ara Parseghian, barged into our stadium, bristling with confidence. They had beaten us, 45–0, the year before. Despite our victory over California, the press box prognosticators were predicting a repeat of last year's performance against Northwestern. Illinois was better this year, they said—but not *that* much better. But I foresaw a different outcome: Illinois would win. It seems that I had now developed a sixth sense about upcoming opponents. I would sit in the darkness with my teammates and coaches and watch the game films, concentrating on the *flow* of the opposition's offense. My concentration would get sky-high. As I watched the films, I would imagine myself up there on the screen, my black-and-white self shooting the gap into the backfield or plugging a hole in the line and stopping the runner in his tracks. Afterward the images would stay in my head and I would run the plays over and over in my mind. It was really weird, almost spooky. Before I fell asleep, I would piece together the future, finally imagining it in the form of a headline on the sports page of the morning edition of the *Chicago Tribune*.

That Saturday we arrived by bus from our purification at the Allerton Estate and noticed that the stands at Memorial Stadium looked heavier with humanity than usual. The attendance turned out to be 51,246. I was glad that so many fans had come, for I knew how the game would go that day, just as I knew that Helen and my parents would be watching from their seats. After the pregame warmups, after I had done my motivational exercises on the backs, including quarterback Tommy Myers, casting them in bad-guy roles, I stood with my teammates, helmet on my hip, while the Illini band played the national anthem.

Then we went out and shocked the Big Ten by beating Northwestern, 10–9, just as I knew we would. I led the team in tackles once again, seven solo and twelve assists, which just may have convinced Parseghian that I wasn't as slow as he thought when he watched me against Washington the year before. The whole team played that game with their guts on the line. We were tough for sixty minutes, rushing Myers and forcing him to throw short. Maybe it wasn't pretty, but we won our Big Ten opener against a team that had humiliated us the season before. Later, in the locker room, I responded heatedly to a newspaperman who implied we were lucky. "There was nothing lucky about it," I said. "We earned it. We started earning it last year when Northwestern stepped on our collective head and pushed it into the mud."

Now we were 2–0, and the next week we faced another fearsome Big Ten dragon: Ohio State. The Buckeyes of Woody Hayes had buried us the year before, 51–15, gaining over 500 yards on the ground for a conference record. Due to an ankle injury, I had not played in that game, and now, as Saturday approached, the poets in the press box began spinning yarns about me that recalled *Casey at the Bat*. I hoped my performance would be different than Casey's. He struck out. Well, this time we were ready for them. The coaches had made some minor adjustments in our defense, and I played my best game as a collegiate, making twenty-three tackles and otherwise acting as the linchpin to our defense.

On the other side of the ball, the great Paul Warfield was playing halfback. Paul was the genuine article: fast, sure-handed, and with the guts of a burglar. He was so sneaky that I even kept an eye on him during timeouts. Ten minutes into the first quarter, the quarterback checked Warfield twice, which was once too often. I dropped back and stepped in front of Paul to catch a deflected pass on the Ohio State twenty-eight. Six plays later, on fourth and goal, our halfback, Sam Price, took it over left tackle for our first touchdown before a stunned crowd of 84,712 Buckeye wackos. Again, in the third period, as Paul sliced across left tackle and headed for daylight, I relieved him of the ball, knocking it free for defensive back Mike Dundy to recover on the Buckeye twenty-six. Several plays later, Illini quarterback Mike Taliaferro connected on a pass to Ed Russell in the end zone.

Sports Illustrated was the only national publication to have predicted we would win the game. They were almost right. In the end, it took a record-breaking field goal in the waning moments to tie us, and when the gun sounded, Illinois had kissed its sister, 20–20. We were unhappy warriors in the locker room, but the word was spreading across the country: Pete Elliott's Illini troops were real and so was Butkus. We were beginning to smell, ever so faintly, the scent of roses in the crisp fall air.

Next up was Minnesota, home of All-American candidate Carl Eller. During the week, Ara Parseghian managed to stuff his foot in his mouth again, predicting that we were ripe to be picked. We won, 16–6. We forced the sure-handed Gophers to fumble five times, four of which we recovered and two of which led directly to the winning ten-point margin. We were 3–0–1 over all, three wins and a tie. That Wednesday, as we prepared to play UCLA, the Associated Press ranked us fourth in the nation.

But the national recognition nearly cost us a victory in Los Angeles. We figured the Bruins—with a record of 1–4— were easy pickings. All we were looking for was to get out of the Coliseum with a victory and no serious injuries. And that's the way it went—at first. Fullback Jim Grabowski and halfback Sam Price ran like I knew they could, alternating five-yard punches all the way to the UCLA twenty-one. Price took it in from there on a pitchout by Taliaferro. Then I knocked the ball loose from quarterback Larry Zeno on the

Bruins' next possession and lineman Ed Washington recovered for Illinois. A few plays later, Jim Plankenhorn booted a field goal. We were up 10–0, and the 30,000 fans rattling around in the Coliseum sank into deep silence.

Suddenly it was all too easy. But we were ranked fourth in the country, weren't we? No big deal. This was the way it was supposed to be, wasn't it? But we managed to make it a big deal. After blowing one opportunity after another, we ended the first half no better off, and by the end of the third quarter, we were losing 12–10. In the fourth quarter, it took a sustained seventy-nine-yard touchdown drive, highlighted by some great ground work by Grabowski and Price and a miracle tackle by Taliaferro, who was the last man between the runner and the goal line on a UCLA punt return, to preserve the victory.

I don't recall Pete Elliott saying a word in the locker room or on the chartered plane as it winged eastward toward more familiar turf. Sitting by the window, I privately assessed the game. It spoke volumes to me, shouting in my ear, *Never, ever, let up!* The difference between one football team and another can often be measured by a single word: effort. But we had our win, extending our undefeated streak to five. Even though our pride was shaken, our fourth-place ranking was intact.

On Sunday the *St. Louis Post-Dispatch* ran a four-page color spread of me, entitled "Gang of One." The writer called me the best linebacker in the nation, noting that I had made seventy-eight tackles in five games, intercepted three passes, and forced six fumbles, three of which I had recovered. There were still four games to go before the Big Ten title would be ours, and Purdue, our next opponent, would be looking to avenge last year's humiliating loss to us. At 2–1 in the conference, the Boilermakers could generate the steam to do it. I threw away the paper with the story about me and silently vowed never to take another team lightly.

I made fifteen tackles the next Saturday against Purdue. In our first kickoff-to-gunshot display of real offensive power, we hammered the Boilermakers, 41–21, leaving no doubts as to our authenticity among the 61,000 home fans at Memorial Stadium. In that Sunday's back pages across the nation, we were being compared with the best. On Wednesday the AP poll ranked us second to Texas. But back in the Big Ten we shared first place with two other schools: Michigan State and Ohio State. With three games still to play—against Michigan, Wisconsin, and Michigan State—it was clear to all of us that there would be no letup in the run for the roses.

So far my psychic peeks into the future had been dead-on. Each week I had accurately visualized how we would do on the football field, including the tie with Ohio State. But in the days before we played Michigan, a funny feeling came over me as I watched the game films. Something about Michigan's offensive flow disturbed me. I kept my doubts private throughout the weekday practices, hoping that my feeling would change. But it didn't. During pregame warmups at Memorial Stadium, Greg Schumacher ran up to me and said, "Okay, Dick, what does it look like?"

"Play hard, buddy," I said.

I don't know what happened that day. Bert Bertine of the *Champaign News-Gazette* wrote that we didn't hit as hard as the Wolverines. Supporting this thesis is the fact that we lost four fumbles, while Michigan never turned it over. But numbers are results, not reasons. Certainly the Wolverines— winners of just one conference game—were better than Illinois on that particular Saturday, November 9, 1963. *But why? I wondered after the game. Was it because we relaxed after last week's drubbing of Purdue and the news that we were*

Believe it or not, that's me when I was one year old. I wasn't supposed to make it. BUTKUS FAMILY PHOTO

At the age of ten, before I discovered the crew cut. BUTKUS FAMILY PHOTO

I looked good in the uniform, but I couldn't hit a curveball. BUTKUS FAMILY PHOTO

My parents. As my sister Dolly says, "Pa was Lincoln-thin." BUTKUS FAMILY PHOTO

The Brothers Butkus at my wedding. From left to right: Don, John, me, Dad, Dave, and Ronnie. We were every football coach's dream. BUTKUS FAMILY PHOTO

On the sidelines during a CVS game. BUTKUS FAMILY PHOTO

My University of Illinois
photograph. GLIESSMAN STUDIOS,
CHAMPAIGN, ILLINOIS

With Bill Taylor on my
right and Pete Elliott on
my left—years later.
BUTKUS FAMILY PHOTO

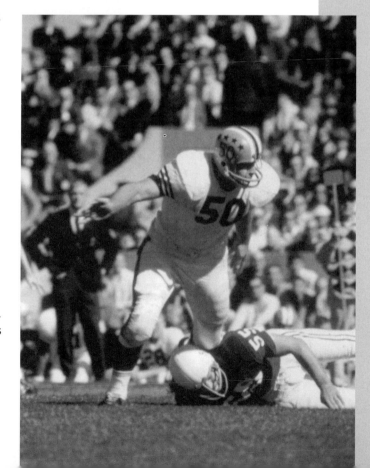

In action for the Illini.
UNIVERSITY OF ILLINOIS

That's me on the right with Otto Graham and Roger Staubach, the Offensive Player of the Year. AP/WIDE WORLD PHOTO

Mike Reilly and I listen to George Allen, the Bears' defensive coach. PHOTO BY BILL EPPRIDGE/LIFE MAGAZINE, © TIME INC.

Papa Bear checking my cleats. PHOTO BY BILL EPPRIDGE/LIFE MAGAZINE, © TIME INC.

Calling the shots against
Johnny Unitas and the
Colts. WILLIAM H. BIELSKIS

The amazing Gale Sayers
running for a TD against
the Packers.
WILLIAM H. BIELSKIS

Helen, who was expecting at the time, and I with Joy and Brian Piccolo. PHOTO BY JOSEPH JEDD.

Doing my mental aerobics before my first game at Wrigle
WILLIAM H. BIELSKIS

One Halloween Helen and I dressed up as Peter Pan and Tinkerbell for a costume party. We won the $5 first prize. BUTKUS FAMILY PHOTO

Closing in on Viking quarterback Fran Tarkenton, one of the best scramblers ever, with Doug Atkins, number 81.
WILLIAM H. BIELSKIS

Smothering the ball carrier at Kezar Stadium in San
Francisco, but I'm getting clipped at the same time.
PHOTO BY BILL EPPRIDGE/LIFE MAGAZINE, © TIME INC.

number two in the nation? Did we forget the close call of two weeks ago? Did we suddenly think we were invincible? Well, if that's so, I don't get it. You'd think we'd have played better, buoyed by the recognition. Hell, if we were number two, why couldn't we be number one?

Maybe that's just the way I am. I loved football, loved it more than anything else in the world. I loved playing it, practicing it, talking about it, and thinking about it. I even loved dreaming about it. When people said I was pretty good, I just played harder. And if another player decided to challenge me, I would gather all the fury that was in me, pack it tight, and launch it at him in a full frontal assault. Maybe it's because I never had very much of anything—whether it was money, clothes, or whatever—but I'll tell you now that I wanted to hurt anyone who tried to take anything away from me on the football field.

The Wolverines showed us no respect because we didn't pay them any. Winners of just one game in the conference, they came into our stadium and beat us, 14–8, knocking us back to third place in the Big Ten and down two notches in the national rankings. Now we had two games left. If we won both, we might still have a shot at the Rose Bowl. The next week we took out our frustration at being upset the week before on Wisconsin, beating them by a score of 17–7. The victory left only Michigan State between us and a trip to the big New Year's Day dance in Pasadena, California.

On the morning of November 22, 1963, we took off from Champaign–Urbana Airport in a chartered plane for the short flight to East Lansing, Michigan, and the most important football game of our lives. What we couldn't have known when we boarded the plane was that in less than an hour President John F. Kennedy would be murdered in Dallas, Texas.

When I heard what had happened, I felt personally hurt. Maybe it was because he was Catholic. I felt a closeness to him that I have never felt for another public figure, and when he was struck down it seemed as though the entire country had been blindsided.

In those frozen seconds at Dealey Plaza, the America I knew—or thought I knew—began to change. I was to learn of this slowly, hear it in the music of our times, see it in the faces that have come along since. It really *was* different then. There was a sense of duty that came with the honor of being American. I know this will seem corny to some of you younger readers. It was in the faces of players like Buddy Young and Ray Nitschke and Mike Ditka. In families, it was in the silent strength of the father, the commitment of the mother. And it used to walk the streets of Roseland. I'm not talking sainthood here, just pride. Where once it grew like milkweed, it's mostly gone.

The Michigan State game was postponed until Thursday, the day after President Kennedy was buried. We won, 13–0. I made fifteen tackles and forced two fumbles. Everyone played well. We took the treads off the Spartans' celebrated "Sherman Tank"—a terrific running back named Sherman Lewis. He would place third in the Heisman race. Sherman was short and fast, and—like Buddy Young and little Joe Morris of the 1986 Super Bowl Giants—his favorite ploy was to slip behind his blockers and disappear for a split second, only to reemerge in the open.

I realized after watching the game films over and over that in order to stop Lewis I would have to commit sooner on every running play. Instead of grabbing the offensive lineman and throwing him away when I saw which way the runner was going, I would have to commit off the snap—or even earlier if I could get away with it—and make Lewis commit sooner. Well, it worked beautifully most of the time, mainly because Michigan State never altered its running game. Over and over, we smacked Lewis at the line of scrimmage or behind it. Meanwhile, Grabowski had a big day carrying the ball for us. When the game was over, when the gun cracked in the crisp Michigan air, even we couldn't believe what we had accomplished: going from *Rags to Riches*, as Tony Bennett had sung a decade earlier, the last time the Illini had won a piece of the Big Ten title. The championship was all ours, and now we would go home to Champaign and prepare for New Year's Day and the Rose Bowl. An era of dismal gridiron defeat had ended for Illinois.

———

In the thirty-two-day interim, a blizzard of accolades and awards came down on me. I was on every All-America team, from the wire services to the coaches' polls to the national magazines. *Playboy*, *Look*, and *Sports Illustrated* called me the best linebacker in years. The Midwest writers voted me Most Valuable Player in the Big Ten. My teammates agreed, honoring me with a similar plaudit limited to just us, Pete's family. I appeared on *The Ed Sullivan Show* and *The Bob Hope Show*. I glared out of a thousand sports pages across the country. Helen was proud, my family was proud, Pete Elliott and Bernie O'Brien were proud, and I was happy for them all.

But between the holiday season and the banquet circuit, where I was getting stuffed nightly with baked chicken and still more honors, I gained a few pounds in the gut. On the day after Christmas, it was back to business as I landed with the team in Pasadena. Our Rose Bowl opponent would be the Washington Huskies, the same team that had doused our premature hopes with icewater, 28–7, the previous year in my first college game. In the heady postseason atmosphere generated by national television and the newspapers, we all got a little edgy. It had been five weeks since any of us had felt the pop of a real-time block or made a hard tackle. In addition, we were met with the partisan hoopla of a city that in those days was louder and brasher than Chicago and New York put together.

To many of the Los Angeles folks, football seemed a small part of the Rose Bowl. We were on display every afternoon and evening: going to Disneyland, posing with Mickey Mouse, and on to Knott's Berry Farms. This was all fine and good, except that we were supposed to be getting ready for the biggest football game of the year. What really bothered me was having to pose for pictures with the Washington players. I was trying to work myself up to hate those guys, and sharing photos with them rubbed me the wrong way.

Two nights before the game, the whole team went to Lawry's famous restaurant for a delicious prime rib dinner. This was a long way from the secluded gardens of the Allerton Estate.

On one practice day, the temperature reached into the nineties and the smog was so thick that our eyes and even our lungs were burning. We had just finished a particularly brutal practice—Pete and Bill were running the Christmas Day fat off us—and I climbed, hot and exhausted, into one of several school buses waiting to take us back to the locker rooms. The bus was sweltering. All I wanted was to get into a cold shower. As I waited for the bus to fill up with players, I could feel myself getting angrier by the second. I just wasn't ready for what happened next.

With the bus filled and ready to go, teammate Don Saunders stepped halfway through the door and decided to have a discussion with somebody outside. I let it go on for a few minutes and then I made a suggestion. "Hey, asshole! Get in here so we can get back to the locker room."

Well, Saunders said something, and I said something else—and the next thing anyone remembers is the two of us were locked in mortal combat. We were separated quickly by other players. Later that day, after hitting a bar with a few buddies, I arrived back at the hotel and found Bill Taylor and Pete Elliott waiting for me. They informed me that I would have to apologize to Saunders. Half-tanked and still pissed off, I refused. Pete suggested that it might be best if I were to return to Champaign, since I was so unhappy in California. At a team meeting the next morning, I issued what passed for an apology to Saunders. To this day, Pete swears that he would have sent me home if I had not apologized.

On the afternoon before the game, we checked out of the old Huntington Beach Hotel, climbed aboard the school buses, and rode into the hills outside Pasadena. We arrived at a Franciscan monastery that was to serve as our Allerton-away-from-home. And there was Father Duncan, ready to hear Confession and to say Mass. It was New Year's Eve—the quietest one of my whole life. We went about the business of gathering ourselves, each of us reaching inside and finding the "on" switch. As we watched the films of Washington for the last time that night, I had a good feeling. Yes, they were exceptionally quick and they were good, maybe better than the year before. But my inner voice told me we would be better.

At 1:05 P.M. the next day, we ran out into the huge maw of the Rose Bowl and 98,000 people cheered while millions more watched on TV. The sound and color and sun assaulted our senses. It's impossible for me to relate the feeling adequately. But it felt like a dream, unrelated to anything I was familiar with. You know that you and your mates are at the epicenter of something so raw and powerful that it seems as though the sky could fall at any moment or the ground could split open under your feet. To my way of thinking, you can go two ways with it. You either let the experience overwhelm you, or you use it to lift yourself above yourself. You either scream at it from deep inside, or you feel diminished. I screamed at it.

Just before the coin toss, Pete Elliott came up to me and shouted into my ear above the din. "On their first offensive play, just before the snap, I want every one of our guys to knock one of those Huskies on his ass! Got it? We'll take the penalty. But they'll get the message." I nodded happily. Nothing like a little intimidation to get things off on the right foot.

The Huskies won the coin toss and elected to receive. After they returned the kickoff to about their twenty-four, I informed the guys of Pete's wishes, and, I must tell you, I was deeply gratified by the malicious gleam in their eyes.

The Huskies broke the huddle and set up. But damned if the quarterback didn't call a fast count. By the time I called, "Hut," the ball had been snapped. The way it worked out, though, our timing couldn't have been better. We threw the runner for a short loss without incurring a penalty, and from then on we were in charge, eventually winning the game by a score of 17–7. Grabowski was the Most Valuable Player, running for big yardage. I didn't have a particularly outstanding game, certainly not like the regular season when I averaged over fifteen stops per game.

Our Rose Bowl effort was the culmination of all the hard work done by Pete and Bill and the rest of the coaching staff. It was a beautiful thing to be a part of. Everybody contributed, not just Grabowski on offense and me on defense. Lineman Ed Washington was the leading tackler. It seemed as though everybody had a great game.

Back then the prevailing West Coast opinion of the Big Ten was that we were big, fat, and slow. Needless to say, we did not agree with this assessment. At some point in the second half, when it became clear that the Huskies would not be able to mount a comeback, Jim Plankenhorn suggested that the entire team run laps around the field after the game to show just how out of shape we weren't. But we were so elated when the gun sounded that we decided to let the reserves take the tour around the field, which they did with great enthusiasm.

After the game, I joined Helen and my family. They had all come out on a special Rose Bowl train. My father was so excited that he could hardly speak. Most of his excitement was about our success, but I can still remember the look on his face when he saw all those orange groves, running on and on. To a man with such a great love of the land, California must have seemed like some sort of a miracle.

C H A P T E R

4

*I*t had been a great year. Of course, I had no idea at the time that the seeds of what would grow into the Butkus myth had been planted from coast to coast, but my dream of playing in the pros was gaining shape and substance with each passing day. The press coverage had already grown beyond anything I had ever imagined.

Long after the season was over, I was still being written about in newspapers and magazines. In fact, my name was beginning to be used as a metaphor for destruction. And the awards were still being offered in bunches. One award that came in January 1964 was the Defensive Player of the Year by the Washington Touchdown Club. I had to travel to Washington, D.C. That weekend changed the way I would feel about some politicians for the rest of my life.

The award ceremony was held in a hotel somewhere near the Capitol. The place was loaded with newspaper guys and politicians and some military types. An admiral from Annapolis presented the Offensive Player of the Year award to quarterback Roger Staubach, whose Navy team had been defeated by Texas in the Cotton Bowl. Senator Everett Dirksen of Illinois gave me my award.

After the presentation of the trophies, a solemn moment was given over to the memory of our fallen President. All heads hung and most eyes closed during the silence. Then many of us retired upstairs to a large hospitality suite. In one bedroom was a gambling setup, including a blackjack table and poker table, and there were a bevy of hookers showing their wares.

Maybe I shouldn't have been shocked. I'd just spent a year among sixty football players who divided their time between talking football and sex—with sex claiming more minutes. But I believed that men who'd just paid their respects to such a great man should not be soiling sheets with professional hookers.

So I had a few drinks and called it a night.

My innocence received another jolt a few months later when *Sports Illustrated* sent Dan Jenkins to interview me. Helen and I were delighted at the prospect of being featured in a national sports magazine. Back then we were filled with optimism, goodwill, and trust.

Dan Jenkins taught us just how naive we were and how much we had to learn. Jenkins stayed on the Illinois campus for two days. While his photographer snapped away, Jenkins threw more questions at Helen and me than we had answers for. But we tried our best to accommodate the slick writer from the big city, partly because *Sports Illustrated* was the sports publication of record and partly because Jenkins seemed like a nice guy. He was funny, bright, and, yeah, I guess he was charming, too. He was pure Texas by way of New York: quick with a quip, a cocky walk, and his suits, shirts, and ties were straight off Savile Row.

The first day went fine. I showed Jenkins around the campus, introduced him to lots of folks, and took him to the field house. We went over my family history, my youth in Roseland, high school ball. But on the second day, his questions began to touch a few sensitive areas. Jenkins asked me about my grades, why had I picked Illinois, and whether I took school all that seriously. "Why," he asked, "are you majoring in something as silly as physical education?" That should have told me something, but since he'd been so nice the day before, I gave him the benefit of the doubt. However, I did ask the photographer if Jenkins could be trusted. He told me that Jenkins was one of the best sportswriters in the country. "He'll write it exactly the way you say it," the photographer said. "Don't worry, he's straight."

So I leveled with Jenkins. I said that I took phys. ed. because I thought it could help me in football. I told him that I planned to play in the pros and spend the rest of my life in the game, and I thought phys. ed. would help me toward that end a lot more than, say, history or English. I was trying to explain to him—and I am certain he understood—that if I didn't make the pros, I wanted to coach. I remember that he nodded sympathetically, as if to say, "Yes, I see. That makes sense." Then I said something I had thought many times: "If I wanted to be a doctor, I would major in premed."

Well, if Jenkins wrote the story straight, something disastrous must have happened to it somewhere between his typewriter and the newsstand. In a November 23, 1964, cover story entitled "A Special Kind of Brute with a Love of Violence," I was portrayed as a mindless, cold-eyed, and possibly sadistic primate. The word "brute" was applied to me six times. Helen was made out to be a dizzy blonde with enough space in her head to park a car. "She just giggles," said the article, "and turns on *The Red Skelton Show.*" And

maybe worst of all—at least it was most hurtful to me—
Jenkins took what I said about majoring in phys. ed., twisted
it, and screwed it into my back. "If I was smart enough to be
a doctor, I'd be a doctor. I ain't, so I'm a football player. They
got me in PE."

Clearly, Jenkins saw Helen and me as a couple of children
who were out of our depth. On a typical weekday, according
to Jenkins's article, "Dick struggles to classes, including one
that sounds terribly intellectual, kinesiology, the study of
muscle movements. After that he naps. Then he makes tackles, and when Helen comes home they watch television. 'It's
been fun,' she says." He also had me saying "ain't" throughout the 3,000-word piece. Yeah, I said "ain't" once in a while,
but not nearly as often as Jenkins had me saying it.

What got me in immediate trouble was Jenkins's descrip-
tion of the University of Illinois as a "football factory." That
remark—and others aimed at the campus architecture—
landed like a bomb in the dean's office. Pete Elliott and I were
called on the carpet. When I explained what had happened,
things calmed down. But the damage had been done. The
Sports Illustrated story was to haunt me for the rest of my
career. It had labeled me as big, dumb, and vicious, setting a
tone for future writers who would draw on the story as reliable resource material down through the years.

Jenkins had blindsided me. I had trusted him, let him inside my head, and he had misrepresented me—intentionally
or otherwise. It has been written—the first time I think by
columnist Red Smith—that sports are played by little boys.
Well, maybe so. But when one of us little boys makes a mistake, the loss is measured in yards or runs or baskets or goals.
And we pay for it on the spot. When a writer makes a mistake
of the kind Jenkins made, the bill is often picked up over and
over by the player. If sports *are* played by little boys, then I'm

wondering just how young you have to be to write about them.

Anyway, that was my first truly unpleasant encounter with the media. Little did I know then how many more times it would sting me. Nor did I have any idea just how perverse and seductive it would get in the decades ahead.

But I did learn a very important lesson from the Jenkins experience: I would never place my trust in a writer again until I got to know him.

———

The Illini played well enough in 1964, but we had lost the element of surprise that we'd enjoyed in 1963. Every other team in the Big Ten was psyched to play us, and few teams in history have been able to stand up under that kind of pressure. We were the gunslingers—conference champs, Rose Bowl winners—and they came at us with everything they had in every game we played that year. Even the lowliest opponents were out for blood, just to say they had beaten last year's champs.

Meanwhile, the NFL and AFL drafts were approaching. It was a good time to be a college player with professional ambitions. The two leagues would not merge until 1970, even though they secretly would agree to a merger in 1966. Fortunately for me, they were still battling for the best college players and the bidding wars for top prospects were intense. I must have known I would be drafted, but in order to stay focused on playing my best, I didn't allow myself the luxury of such a thought. Then Bill Taylor came to me in midseason and said I would be taken high, meaning I was one of the prime college players, and asked me if I would be interested in having someone represent me.

That's how Arthur Morse came into my life. Primarily

an entertainment lawyer who dabbled in sports, Morse had negotiated a few deals for the Illini basketball team, primarily with Chicago Stadium, where they played a few games every year. Morse was a true North Sider: wealthy, influential, and downtown all the way. He was not my type of guy. But what did I know about lawyers? I didn't even know I needed one until Bill Taylor told me I did. I was so green that you could have sliced and diced me and put me in a salad.

I knew there were NFL and AFL drafts. But I didn't know much more. I never read any stories in the sports pages that described how the drafts were conducted, how the pro teams picked the players. And there was no ESPN in those days to televise the proceedings. About all I knew was they took place in New York in December. If anything, I thought the teams drew lots out of a hat, then took turns picking players.

With Arthur Morse at my side, I was to learn that things were not as simple as they seemed. His connection was with a man who would permanently influence my life: George Halas, the founder and owner of the Chicago Bears, a father to every man who ever wore a Bears uniform. Halas joined the pros when he became player-coach of the Decatur Staleys of the American Professional Football Association in 1920. He took over as the owner and moved the team to Chicago in 1921. In 1922 George Halas changed the name of his team to the Chicago Bears and, at Halas's suggestion, the league was rechristened the National Football League.

The stories of those early hardscrabble days, when baseball was America's second religion, are filled with boom-or-bust drama. Halas—along with owners Wellington Mara of the New York Giants and Art Rooney of the Pittsburgh Steelers—is a mainstay of NFL legend. Was he tough? You tell me. In his early days, the former Annapolis midshipman was a pro in four sports: football, baseball, basketball, and boxing.

When he started the Bears, he was player-coach-owner. If the tradition of toughness ascribed to the Bears is legitimate—and I think it is—then George Halas alone engendered that toughness. Not the city, not the players. But I'm getting ahead of myself.

As my last season at Illinois began, I was rated by many experts as the top pro prospect in the country. How do I know this? The question ought to be: How could I not know it? I read it every day. I saw my name in so many newspaper and magazine stories that even *I* got tired of reading about myself. Pete Elliott was still beating the Heisman drum, and some pundits even said I had a reasonable shot, largely because the preseason favorite, quarterback Roger Staubach of Navy, was injured. I had placed sixth in the balloting the year before, and Pete, who had predicted we'd win the Rose Bowl in 1963 and that I'd win the Heisman in 1964, was hell-bent on making good on his word. As it turned out, I ended up at number three in the final tally—not bad for a middle linebacker.

Meanwhile, I was getting the Sunday sports section of the *Dallas Times* sent to me every week by Gil Brandt, the Cowboys' famous scouting guru. Apparently he knew Bill Taylor pretty well, and I guess the strategy was to get me interested in his team. But Brandt could have saved himself the cost of the postage. Not because I wouldn't have liked to play for the Cowboys, but because the whole thing had been figured out like a Hollywood script.

In the newspapers, the drama of the upcoming draft played out in a variety of story lines. One said the Green Bay Packers and the Chicago Bears were in a fierce battle over me. Each organization was supposed to be gathering first-round picks in order to be in a better position to draft me. The Bears had collected three top picks, while the Packers had two. Although some writers were buying into the idea that the battle was really over Northwestern's star quarterback Tommy Myers, the insiders were convinced that I was stamped "prime meat" by both front offices.

Green Bay definitely held some allure for me because my friend Ray Nitschke was such a force for them. Green Bay had always seemed like the ultimate pro football town to me. I was also attracted to its smallness (less than 50,000), like Champaign, full of spirit and good fun. Of course, there was that great Packer team led by the venerable Vince Lombardi, and I didn't think it could get any better than that.

But the Bears were also a powerful draw. Playing for them would be the fulfillment of a young boy's dream, a dream that began on summer porches in the rain, in my bunk at night, and out in the front yard with a football and an old Skippy jar. By then my old buddy Ed O'Bradovich was playing for the Bears, and I thought it would be neat if we were on the same team.

There were also more practical reasons for wanting the Bears instead of Green Bay. Both teams had future Hall of Famers at the middle linebacker position. The Packers had Ray Nitschke, while Bill George filled the middle for the Bears. Ray was still young, but Bill George was coming to the end of a brilliant career. This situation did not escape me as I watched the predraft drama unfold in the newspapers. The Giants were also in the early running. Wellington Mara was supposed to be interested in me, but the word was that coach Allie Sherman was lobbying hard for Auburn star runner Tucker Frederickson—and the New Yorkers only had one high pick.

The AFL was also showing a strong interest in me. This was a little surprising because the new league was not known for its great defensive teams. Balls in the air and points on the board were the AFL's primary technique for attracting fans

to the games and higher ratings on TV. To that end the owners zeroed in on the best passers, runners, and receivers.
Among the passers was one of the best ever: Alabama quarterback Joe Namath. Joe's personal flare, strong arm, and
fearless demeanor caught the eye of Broadway impresario
and Jets owner Sonny Werblin. Starmaker Werblin was convinced that Joe Willie could lead his struggling New York
team into the black, if not into the playoffs.

The talent wars between the leagues were being fueled by
big television contracts. NBC had lured the AFL away from
ABC in 1965, offering the league a walloping $35 million over
five years; CBS countered with a $24 million two-year rights
package for the NFL. Everyone knew that money was not a
major factor for either league in the signing of new talent.
Since I figured to be one of the first to go in the draft, Helen
and I were a little overwhelmed at the numbers being tossed
around in the newspapers and on TV.

Meanwhile, as the pundits in the press box alternately
ruminated on the upcoming draft and my prospects regarding the Heisman Trophy, I was pretty busy having a good
season, even if the Illini were not quite living up to expectations generated by our success the previous year. We lost
three games—a big comedown from our 8–1–1 mark.

The last game of my senior year was at home against
Michigan State, the team we beat a year earlier for the Big
Ten championship. This time only pride and the conference
running title were on the line. Jim Grabowski was having a
great year for us, but the Spartans' Dick Gordon was a few
yards ahead of him. By game's end, Gordon had netted just
30 yards, while Grabowski had gained 185, cracking the
1,000-yard season mark for only the second time in Illini history.

We won, 16–0. I made eighteen tackles, including nine

solos, and closed out my career with a goal line stand in which I stopped the runner four straight times. My line coach Burt Ingwerson said it was the best goal line performance by a single player he had ever seen.

After the game, a scout named Red Miller, who later became a coach for Denver, told me that the Broncos were interested in my services. He said the ownership—the Phipps brothers—was intent on bringing defense with a capital D to the AFL and would be willing to go a long way toward making me financially secure.

Somehow word of the Broncos' intentions leaked out to the press, and suddenly, along with being billed as the most sought-after player in the country, I was being hailed as a rich man before I'd even been drafted. They had been talking "mere buckets" money. Now it was "wheelbarrows."

It's strange having your financial picture painted in the newspapers when you hadn't even been offered a job. So far I hadn't heard a word from Chicago, Green Bay, or any other team, officially or unofficially—and for all I knew, I could be playing for the Massillon Tigers in 1965.

Late in November, a whisper from Chicago reached Champaign. It came in the form of a telegram from the Bears' front office. It was addressed to Burt Ingwerson. In the expert opinion of several scouts, it said, I had slowed down on pass defense, and it asked if there was anything physically wrong with me. It was pure, unadulterated bullshit.

Looking back from today, I think the telegram was sent for two reasons. One, the Bears' brass must have known I had an injury or two, and they wanted to find out if I was healthy. They must have figured that if there was a problem, then Burt, who had once played for Halas, would tell them for old times' sake. And two, if there wasn't a problem, then the odds were that Burt would show me the wire. In that case, they hoped it would take some of the air out of me, soften me up when it came time to negotiate. As far as I know, Burt never answered the wire.

The fact was: I hadn't slowed down a bit. But now I wondered just who in the hell the Bears had sent to scout me.

The only thing that I knew for certain was that Burt Ingwerson would not lie to me. He was a straight guy, a gentleman, like all the coaches under Pete Elliott. Anyway, if the Bears had seen my play diminish over the past year, the real experts, the coaches, hadn't. They picked me to be a First-Team All-American. I was one of three who repeated in 1964. Then, as if to nail the lid on the Chicago lie, the coaches picked me as the College Player of the Year.

A couple of days before I was to go to New York to accept the All-American award from *Look* magazine and to appear on *The Ed Sullivan Show*, Arthur Morse called to say we had a meeting with the Phipps brothers of the Denver Broncos. At this point in the story, my memory must have sharpened because I can recall everything as though it just happened.

We met in Arthur Morse's offices on LaSalle Street, just a short walk from the Bears' corporate headquarters. The Phippses seemed like nice guys, tanned and jovial and rich, and I listened carefully as they started throwing numbers around. When the figure of $400,000 was mentioned, I was suddenly all ears. But I soon got lost as words like "deferment" and "signing bonus" and "shelter" entered the discussion.

As I was trying to make sense out of what was being said, a question started to nag me. I thought to myself, *How can these guys be so sure they are going to be able to draft me? I understand that sometimes you have to discuss details of a future deal as though it is going to happen. But not once have I heard the word "if" sneak into the discussion. You'd think some-*

*body, if not the Phippses then Arthur, would have used the word
or a similar qualifier at some point along the way. Do they know
something I don't?*

As one of the brothers was discussing bonuses, shelters,
and deferments, Morse started looking at his watch. "Look,
gentlemen," he said, "we are going to have to wrap this up.
Dick and I have a meeting with the Bears in ten minutes."

This was news to me. Then one of the Phipps boys asked
us what we thought of the offer. Morse said, "Well, it's fine.
But I think we'll spend Dick's money the way we think it
should be spent."

Both Phippses blinked at that, and so did I—but for a different reason. They, no doubt, were taken aback by Arthur's
abruptness, while I was surprised at his liberal use of the collective pronoun "we" in connection with *my* money.

Ushering the Phipps brothers to the door, Morse said,
"Good day, gentlemen. We'll be in touch." Pointedly ignoring
Morse, one of the brothers turned to me and said, "Nice to
meet you, Dick, and we hope you come out to Denver and
play for us."

I said, "I would like that."

Then I stood there and watched $400,000 walk away.

Arthur dismissed the Phippses' offer, saying that playing
in Denver would be like playing in Gary, Indiana. I thought,
Well, maybe he's right. Denver had a lousy team at the time.
But I thought I could be happy anywhere with $400,000.

As we hit the street, Arthur told me he knew Sonny
Werblin, the owner of the Jets, and if I was going to play in
the AFL, it was going to be in New York—and for a lot more
money than the Phippses were offering. Anyway, I was feeling pretty valuable as we hurried down LaSalle Street, turned
right on Madison, and finally entered the building at 173 for
my first meeting with the man who would hold sway over

my life for the next decade. In the elevator, I reminded Arthur of the telegram to Burt Ingwerson. Arthur looked a little vague, as though he'd forgotten what I had told him. Then, remembering, he assured me, "We're going to get that matter cleared up right away."

Up three floors in the old elevator, and into Papa Bear's cave we walked.

George Halas, Papa Bear himself, sat behind a large desk. With him was Muggsy Bear, his son, and his defensive coach George Allen, a man I would grow to love—but not right away, not at first. The Bears' offices were not very fancy, certainly not like most front offices are today. But then again George Halas wasn't very fancy either. He didn't need a stage: He *was* the stage *and* the play. On this December afternoon, with Chicago sliding into the deep freeze outside his window, he was warm and friendly. Mugs Halas sat quietly off to his father's right and watched me. Arthur and I were seated across the big desk. George Allen had pulled up a chair and sat just to my left.

Compliments on my college career flowed concurrently with condolences on the Bears' poor season, an understandably sore subject that quickly turned into bright views of the future, of greener fields and more championships.

At which point, my memory gets even sharper. Arthur says, "Well, Mr. Halas, is it fair to say you are interested in acquiring the services of my client?" Halas nods in the affirmative.

"Absolutely," he says.

Mugs nods and Allen says, "Yes indeed."

Meanwhile, I'm looking at Arthur with a large question mark on my face, eyebrows raised, eyes wide.

Arthur says, "Well, if that's true, if you're really interested in Dick, then there is a little matter we have to clear up before going any further."

"Oh?" asks Papa Bear.

Arthur responds, "Not long ago, your office sent a telegram to one of Dick's coaches." Arthur turns to me. "Who was that, Dick?

"Burt Ingwerson," I answer.

"Oh, yes," says Papa Bear. "I know Burt from way back. How is he doing?"

I say, "Burt's doing just fine."

Then Arthur describes the content of the wire as I had told it to him, verbatim.

Confusion reigns as Halas looks at Mugs, and Mugs looks questioningly at George Allen, who just can't understand this, can't comprehend that such a wire would have been sent. Then he asks me, "Did you actually *see* this alleged telegram?" I say, "No, but I believe Burt told me the truth."

Halas says, "So do I, Dick. George, shouldn't we have that wire on file?"

Allen shrugs and says, "I should *think* so, Coach."

Halas then sends Allen on an errand. "Go find that wire, George. So we can get this matter cleared up right now." Halas turns to me and adds, "I can't believe we would ever send a telegram like that."

Allen hurries out—and we wait. Mugs sits there bobbing his head. He had a nervous condition. He was always turning his head, like someone was tapping him on the shoulder. Poor Mugs, living in the dark shadow of the Old Man. Like a guy crouched under the rim of a volcano, waiting for the eruption he knew would come.

Meanwhile, Halas starts clicking his teeth and insisting that he can't imagine anyone in his organization sending such a wire. "Must be a mistake," he says. "Never heard of such a thing. Outrageous!"

A few minutes later, Allen returns empty-handed. Halas

looks at Allen. Allen looks back at Halas and says, "Sorry, Coach. I can't believe it, but the secretary must have misplaced the wire to Dick. If there *was* such a wire."

Arthur looks at me as if to say, "Are you satisfied?" Well, I wasn't, but what could I do? No one says anything for about a minute. Then Arthur breaks the silence. "Okay, here's the deal then. Dick would love to play in Chicago. It's his hometown. His friends and family are here. All that. But he is prepared to go where he is most wanted. Denver has made a very substantial offer. If you can match it, Dick will sign with the Bears."

"How much?" Mugs wants to know.

Arthur describes the Phippses' complicated offer.

The Old Man's eyes get heavy. "Well," he says, "we'll have to talk about that."

Arthur says, "Fine, we can talk. But Dick has to get on a plane to New York in about an hour to attend *Look* magazine's All-American ceremonies, then he has to appear on *The Ed Sullivan Show*."

So we all shake hands and off we go, Arthur and I. Before I enter the cab to the airport, Arthur tells me that I should call his office when I get to New York and leave a number where I will be that night.

"Why?" I ask.

"Because," says Arthur, "Halas will be calling me to iron all this out."

So I get on the plane, wondering how in the hell Arthur knows that Halas will be calling so soon. But again, there was a bigger question. I thought to myself, *Why are they all so confident that Chicago will get me in the draft? Sure, they have three of the first six choices, but New York has first pick, and didn't Mara say he just might tap me? Don't any other teams have something to say about that? How about Dallas, for exam-*

ple? *Have they been sending me the Sunday sports pages all sea-son just to be nice guys?*

Hell, I was green, but I wasn't *that* green.

Anyway, while questions and doubts persisted, the overwhelming feeling was something close to pure happiness. Here I was, little more than a dozen years after kicking that football over our white picket fence at 10324 South Lowe, flying to New York in a first-class seat knowing that I had reached my goal. How many kids grow up to live their lifelong dream?

It was a clear day in New York. Manhattan looked like a postcard. The roofs and spires of the stacked buildings glittered. The stewardess was pretty. The drink tasted good as I finished it, strapped myself in, and settled back, deciding that wherever I landed would be just fine.

———

An hour later, I arrive at the Waldorf-Astoria, check into my room, and the phone rings. *Arthur Morse already? Wow! Things sure happen fast in the big time.* But it's not Arthur. It's some guy in the hotel. Name of Vern Buol. Says he's from Chicago, a friend of Halas's, and he wants to have a drink. So I go to his room and he tells me he is in New York to see that I get whatever I need. I tell him, "I don't need anything. The room and all my expenses are being paid for by *Look* magazine."

Vern seems like a nice guy. I have a drink or two with him. Then things start happening fast. Next thing I know Bill Taylor has joined us—and we are off to Madison Avenue. After a meeting where we are prepped for our appearance on *The Ed Sullivan Show*, I do a bunch of quickie TV news interviews in the lobby. Then it's back to the Waldorf to shower and change before an early dinner with Bill Taylor. Buol spots us in the lobby and joins us. Later, when Taylor and I go out on the town with a bunch of players, Buol is *still* with us.

At some point, I whisper to Bill, "Who *is* this guy?"

Bill says, "He's Vern Buol. He owns a meat company in Chicago and is a friend of George Allen's."

"He told me that much," I say. "But what is he *doing* here?"

Taylor explains, "Each pro team has *friends* like Buol. Guys who want to *help out*. Kind of like recruiters, only they aren't called recruiters, you know?"

I shrug, say, "Yeah, I guess so. Whatever." But I still didn't understand why a player would need a recruiter if he had already agreed to sign with a team and if the deal was right.

Anyway, we all have a great time, bouncing from one spot to another. Some of us wind up at the Latin Quarter, a nightclub owned by Lou Walters, Barbara Walters's daddy, and as I look around I notice that practically every player has a guy like Buol hanging with him. The loudest is some guy from Dallas. He's attached to Craig Morton like a third arm, ordering champagne, steak sandwiches for everyone, slipping cash to the waiters, the maitre d'. Meanwhile, I don't see Vern dip for a thing. I didn't know it then, but Vern's slow reflexes were a harbinger of things to come. Like most of the old NFL order—the Maras, the Rooneys—the Halases gave away nothing.

But Vern turned out to be a really good guy. Sometimes when I visited Chicago, I would head over to Haymarket Square, where sides of beef still hang out on the street like discarded football players, and have lunch with Vern. We usually ate in one of the gin mills, sharing the loud, smoky space with butchers in bloodied white coats, which always made me feel like I was home again. Chicago is a place where most things are still out in the open. Good and bad.

Anyway, back at the Latin Quarter in New York, the booze is flowing, the band is playing, the girls are dancing, and Milton Berle is shouting at the people at the next table. Suddenly I notice Mike Taliaferro, our quarterback in the Rose Bowl, waving at me from another table. Mike was drafted by the Jets last year, and he's sitting with Walt Michaels. After a bit, Taliaferro comes over and invites me out to the Shea Stadium the next morning, which is Saturday—draft day. He says Weeb Ewbank would like to meet me. Before I can answer, I feel a little pressure at my elbow. I look over and it's Vern; he's practically in my lap, trying to hear Mike through the noise. So I wink at Mike and we shake hands and he leaves.

So Craig's candyman orders another round and maybe an hour goes by. Then the maitre d' shows up again to tell me that I have another call. So I grab Bill Taylor and head for the lobby. I pick up the phone. It's Arthur. He says, "See, Dick? Just like I told ya—the Old Man came back to me. Just got off the phone. Now, here's the deal. The Bears are gonna match the Phippses' offer." He pauses, then says, "So what do I tell them?"

I put my hand over the mouthpiece and relay Arthur's words to Bill Taylor. Bill's mouth drops. I start to giggle. I say to Bill, "Say something, for crissakes! What do we do?" Bill doesn't think anyone will go higher. "Take it," he says. So I uncover the mouthpiece, take a deep breath, and tell Arthur, "Okay, it's fine." Arthur responds enthusiastically, says I made the right decision, and tells me he is going to meet Halas right away and shake hands on it. Then he says, "Remember, Dick. A deal's a deal, right?" I say, "Of course. I know that." "Okay," he says.

I no sooner hang up and there's Vern standing next to Bill. "Who was that?" he asks. I tell him who it was but not what went down. Although he seemed like a good enough guy, I certainly wasn't about to share such a confidence with him. Or with anyone else except Taylor. Hell, the draft wasn't until the next day, and I was wondering how everything could be sewed up with the Bears the night before. I wasn't even sure that what had just gone down between Halas and Morse was legitimate. Then Vern pulls a cigar out of his pocket and gives it to me as though it's a bar of gold. It was the only thing I got from Vern Buol on that trip to New York.

On the way back to our table, Taliaferro buttonholes me and gets me to promise I will go out to Shea in the morning. But I nod toward Vern, who is hovering close by. I ask Mike, "How am I gonna get rid of this guy?" Taliaferro tells me to be down in the lobby at 8 A.M.

As I get back to the table, the main attraction walks onto the stage. Then Milton Berle turns and tells *us* to keep it down. Berle would become a friend down the line. As the lights go down, I sit there quietly, smoking my cigar. I'm a player, watching the show. Then one thought occurs. *Wait a minute! Since I forgot to call Arthur and tell him where I would be, how did he know where to call me?*

When I got back to my room that night, I lay awake for a long time. Thoughts ran like runaway trains through my mind. First, I was a professional football player. Second, all that remained was to stay in shape and make the team in the summer. And third came the big G—guilt. I'd agreed to visit the Jets tomorrow, the day of the draft. I thought to myself, *What if somebody finds out? What if Halas finds out and nixes the deal? Then what will happen?* It sounds crazy now, but I was very concerned about doing things right.

I don't think I slept for a minute. At 8 A.M. I was downstairs and there was Mike waiting by the revolving doors that led onto Park Avenue. We went over the Triborough Bridge to

Shea Stadium, met Weeb, and looked at their locker room. Meanwhile, back in the city, the two leagues were drafting players, each league pretending the other didn't exist.

When Mike dropped me off at the Waldorf later that morning, my head was spinning. *Why did Weeb want to meet me? We didn't discuss anything about my playing for the Jets.*

Up the elevator to my floor and the first person I see is Tom Nowatzke. He's in the hallway talking to someone, probably a reporter. He tells me he's been drafted by Detroit. I congratulate him. Then he says, "Everybody's been looking for you. You were picked by Chicago. Gale Sayers and Steve DeLong, too," he says as he walks away down the hall. So I shout back, "Oh, *really?*"

Now I was playing the game, too.

The drafts took place in separate hotels, the NFL in the Waldorf and the AFL just a few blocks north on Lexington Avenue in the Summit. Yet when I walked into the hospitality suite, there was Lamar Hunt, owner of the AFL's Kansas City Chiefs. As the night wore on, other AFL owners showed up and began talking to the players and drinking NFL booze. It just seemed strange to me. Wrong somehow.

But it seemed even stranger when Hunt tried to get me to talk up Kansas City to Gale Sayers. I guess Hunt thought I was going to sign with the Denver Broncos, since they had drafted me in the AFL. It all seemed like one big club. More like a theatrical group. And, in a way, I guess it was, for I learned years later that the two leagues had secretly agreed to merge in 1966, four years before it actually happened.

I understand now that if the owners had gotten really competitive, played on the open market in the way they seem to do today, the real winners would have been the players, the guys whose knees and futures were on the line. But things were different back then. More under wraps. Each draft was a relatively quiet affair, attended by a dozen New York area sportswriters, the wire services, and a few television crews. I am sure that the thought of putting one on national television would have been greeted with a monumental yawn.

That's why I couldn't believe it when ESPN covered the draft live back in the eighties. Now, of course, it's a big TV event, watched by millions. Like the Oscar or Emmy awards. What, I wonder, is so interesting about some kid getting picked by a pro team? I guess it's the money. Frankly, it turns me off to see several pounds of gold dripping from the necks, fingers, and ears of some of those kids. Where did they get that stuff? I'm betting those trinkets aren't family heirlooms. Wasn't it Charles Barkley who joked that he took a pay cut when he went from college to the NBA? Maybe Barkley wasn't exaggerating by all that much.

It all seems like a circus now.

Where once the fans cared only how a player did on the field, now the emphasis has broadened to dollars, endorsements, and lifestyles. Everyone knows about Deion Sanders's deal with Dallas and Nike, or about Warren Moon's marital difficulties a couple of years ago, or, before that, the Fridge's eating habits. The change started about the time that Joe Namath emerged as Manhattan's most eligible bachelor. Joe Willie—who, one former girlfriend jokingly told the press, had weak knees and a quick release—reached a new pinnacle during the let-it-all-hang-out era by doing panty hose commercials, much to the tittering delight of viewers.

The race from in-the-mud football to the ridiculous is not over—and where it will stop, nobody knows. No longer is it how the game was played, or even whether it was won or lost. Winning is no longer the only thing. It may not even be the main thing.

I went back to Champaign feeling pretty good.

Although I didn't understand very much about how it all had worked, I knew that I had been drafted by the Bears and that Halas had agreed to match the Phippses' offer. All that remained was for Arthur to negotiate the finer points of the deal with Mugs. When that was done to everyone's satisfaction, a contract would be drawn up and I would be called up to Chicago for the grand signing—and my lifelong dream would be a done deal.

My life was expanding like some beautiful cloud with colors I never knew existed. One of those colors was U.S. mint green. Yeah, I know, in this day and age, it's hard to believe, but the money factor had never really entered my mind. For me, the rewards of football had always been in the doing, the playing. That's why I could never understand why some guys tried to get out of practice. Sure, there were times when I hated some of the drills that Bill Taylor, a former Marine, dreamed up. But I did them anyway, feeling my lungs burn and my legs turn to water. I did them because I believed they would help me play better, keep me strong late in the game.

One of the many things I learned at Illinois was that there wasn't a whole lot of difference between the top teams in the Big Ten. We were all talented—or we wouldn't be there. Some of us may have been a little faster, or quicker, or stronger than the other guy. But that was not the main reason we won or lost. The difference could always be attributed to desire. The need to win, the will to practice hard, the determination to play through pain, the sacrifice of ego to teamwork. These were the tenets of my faith.

Excessive praise in the press and on campus never sat comfortably with me. And even the money took some time to get used to. It was pure, high-confection icing to a cake that was ten years in the making. Too sweet to taste. Yet, as the weeks rolled by and Christmas came and went, Helen and I slowly worked up an appetite for that icing.

Then one day in January a call came from Arthur Morse. "Come on up to Chicago. The contract's ready to sign." So off I go to the Bears' offices, my head tingling with thoughts of what all that money could buy—for Helen and me, and for our parents. It was like a new world was opening. I had a big-time lawyer, an accountant. I was a player now, not only for the Bears. But with it all, there was some trepidation, maybe even a little fear.

First there was a press conference, me signing a phony contract with the bulbs flashing like the lights you see when you get hit hard, and all the while Mugs smiling over my shoulder, looking for all the world as though he had landed the big fish. Then I stood up before the press and carefully avoided any mention of the size of the contract, because that is the way the front office wanted it. "Uh, Dick, when they ask you about the money, don't get specific, okay? The Old Man doesn't want the other players to get all bent out of shape. You understand?"

Yeah, I understood. They had their deals and I had mine. It was nobody's business anyway—how much I was getting. So the cameras clicked and the questions popped and the hands slapped my back and Mugs got all puffed up and full of himself, predicting a shining future for Chicago, maybe even a championship. And soon it was all over, the reporters and photographers were gone, and Arthur and I headed over to his office, where the real contract awaited my signature.

In the quiet boardroom, the pages of legalese lay on the shining mahogany table. A gold-trimmed fountain pen rested nearby.

I sat down, picked up the sheaf of papers, and began to read what Arthur and Halas had concocted. Most of it was like a foreign language to me and my eyes moved across the words and down the lines until they hit a set of six numbers.

There they stopped, fixed on the amount: $204,000. I don't know how long I looked at the total. It seemed an eternity. Finally, with a loud buzz in my head, I looked across the table at Arthur.

"Is this all?"

Arthur blinked.

"Yeah, that's it, Dick."

"But this is only about half of what I expected. You told me on the phone when I was in New York that Halas had agreed to match the Phippses' offer."

"Oh, no way," says Arthur. "Dick, you must understand, this is a helluva deal. Remember, the Phippses' offer was inflated with all kinds of phony perks. Trust me. This is an outstanding contract."

"Yeah, maybe so. But . . ."

"Look," says Arthur, "you were celebrating pretty good that night in the Latin Quarter, and why not? You deserved it. Listen to me. This is the best deal you could ever get. No team in either league could beat it. I promise you."

Then Arthur showed me what he had done. There was a $6,000 signing bonus, which I told him to send directly to my ma. The rest would be paid out over the five-year life of the contract, mounting from $18,000 the first year to $60,000 the final year. "This," Arthur explained, "puts us in the best possible bargaining position for the second contract."

I had to admit it seemed like a pretty good move on Arthur's part. Of course, now I realize that it also benefited Halas. He got to keep the bulk of the money longer. So I took a deep breath and signed the damn thing. At only half of what I expected it would be, the contract called for more money than I had ever imagined I would get for doing the thing I loved.

Yet I have often wondered what really went down between Halas and Morse.

======

A week or so later, my mother received the bonus check in the mail and called to say thanks, her voice quavering. Then, instead of buying a new television or a bunch of fancy stuff for the kitchen, what is the first thing she does? She goes out and buys burial plots for herself and my father in St. Casimir's Cemetery, where Rita and Le Roy were buried. That's the way my parents were.

If anything, the money made me a little nervous. I was raised on the theory that you earn what you get, and so far I hadn't done a thing for the Bears. The way I figured it, I owed them now. And since I had been trying my hardest all these years for the sheer love of it, I would have been in a lot of trouble if I suddenly considered money to be an accurate measure of my effort, my output.

I remember when Pete Rose got a huge raise, doubling his salary—and the very next season his batting average dropped like a stone. He explained that the raise had played with his mind, made him think that he had to do twice as well, try twice as hard. Well, like Pete, I was incapable of trying any harder. I'd always played with the pedal to the metal.

======

During that last winter at Illinois, I played in a bunch of postseason contests: the Shrine Game in San Francisco, the Hula Bowl in Honolulu. Abe Gibron, who the year before had predicted we would be together someday, came up to me in the locker room before one of these games and said he had just been hired as a coach for the Bears. "See, big guy?" he said. "Honest Abe is always right. I said we'd be together again." Well, the news made me feel good. Now, in addition to Ed O'Bradovich, I'd have another guy I knew when I arrived at the preseason camp in Rensselaer, Indiana.

Then, in June, with classes over, I said good-bye to every-one, to Pete and Bill, to the trainers and equipment people, and to a few other people who helped me through a four-year rite of passage, helped shape the shy, callow, sometimes angry player from the other side of the tracks. I headed home to Chicago, up along the cornrows and into a new life in the city where I grew up.

Well, maybe it wasn't such a new life right away. We went back to Roseland and moved into 10324 South Lowe with my mother and father, because we still hadn't received that first check from the Bears.

Helen and I had seen an apartment at 222 East Pearson, which my sister Babe showed to us. It had one bedroom and it overlooked Lake Michigan and part of the Gold Coast. We loved it. The price was right, too: $240 a month. When we showed it to my mother, she said nothing. But on the way home afterward, she cried. I was never sure whether she wept out of happiness for Helen and me or out of sadness at losing me to a world she didn't know. Probably a little of both. She and Helen were very close by this time, often standing as one against me in a dispute, and no doubt my mother wept for Helen as well.

C H A P T E R

5

My first professional football experience came in mid-
August when the College All-Stars played the Cleveland
Browns, the 1964 NFL champions. The game was the unofficial start of fall for pro fans. But you wouldn't have known
it that night. The air was as thick as warm soup as we took
the field to the cheers of a packed Soldier Field in Chicago. It
was alive that night, filled mostly with Bears fans, some
70,000 in all.

Banks of brilliant light hit us as we came out of the tun-
nel, and the smells of hot prairie air and summer grass
flooded our senses. The PA announcers solemnly called for silence and we stood, our helmets on our hips, as the national
anthem welled up into the night. My eyes were moist, my
stomach was flipping, and my heart was racing. Underneath
it all, I was praying that I wouldn't screw it up.

I was in the best of company. Roger Staubach and I had
been voted cocaptains of one of the greatest all-star squads
ever assembled: Lance Rentzel, Craig Morton, Ralph Neely,
Bill Curry, John Huarte, Tucker Frederickson, Steve DeLong,
Bob Hayes, Jack Snow, Marty Schottenheimer, Fred Biletni-

koff, Ken Willard, Roy Jefferson, Jerry Rush, Harry Schuh, Archie Sutton, and my future teammate, fresh from the cornfields of Kansas, the one and only Gale Sayers. These were players I would face again and again in the long seasons ahead.

Gale and I held our own in that game, toiling under that warm, wet blanket of a night. Of my fourteen tackles, a few were applied to Jim Brown, and yes, he *was* tough to bring down, his body harder and stronger than most. He was the most agile runner I would ever face, capable of reducing the angle of almost any tackle. During the first half, the heat was almost overwhelming, but Jim just kept coming. Then, in the third quarter, a cool, silvery rain fell on us through the lights. Afterward the air smelled of the coming fall as Gale and I finished out our debut.

There is one thing about that game that I will never forget. It happened late in the fourth quarter after the night had cooled down. We had put on a blitz. I shot the gap between the left guard and tackle and there, standing between me and the quarterback, was Jim Brown, the man who, according to the sportswriters, never bothered to block. Well, he was waiting for me *that* night. When we made contact, we seemed to freeze for an instant before I started to make a move to get by him. Suddenly he had my left arm clamped under his left arm, and when he began to roll to his left, I realized that if I didn't get my arm out of that vise Jim had it in, he'd either hyperextend my elbow or break the arm altogether.

I slipped free just in time.

Why did he do it? I don't know. Maybe he didn't like the way I hit him earlier in the game. But deep down I think it was because he was Jim Brown. He was not going to let me get by him, even though it was just an all-star game. Like all great athletes, Jim had a hidden reserve that he called up on special moments.

So much for those who said Jim Brown didn't block. Although I would only play against this man one more time—in a Pro Bowl—my impression at the time was that he might be the best back I would ever play against. That turned out to be true, despite the likes of Jim Taylor, Leroy Kelly, and all the other notable backs of the era.

That night registers sweet and sad and a little vague in my memory. But I remember clearly how I felt, and for that I'm grateful. Chances are I will never know it again, never know a similar honor. Maybe for a surgeon, it's that first operation when his hands do exactly what they'd been trained for years to do. For me, it was that all-star game, my first trial against the best players in the land.

Although I've heard it said that in one's last days the glories of a life are played out on a canvas so bold and brilliant that the memory lives in startling detail. I hope that's true, for I'd like to see the high moments of my playing life once more before I go. Certainly that all-star game of 1965 would be high on the list of my special requests.

But if Chicago was friendly to Gale and me, the players didn't exactly lay down the welcome mat. A week before the game at Soldier Field, the College All-Stars scrimmaged the Bears at their training camp down in Rensselaer. On one pass play, I saw Mike Ditka pull up lame after he was pushed out of bounds. He sprained the metatarsal in his right arch. Ditka got over it, of course, and played another seven years, ending his career in Dallas. But I believe the injury altered the way he ran. Even now he walks slew-footed, rolling on his foot instead of flexing it. Of course, I'll probably never know if I'm right. Ditka wouldn't even tell his priest something like that, much less me.

Anyway, during that scrimmage I heard lots of pointed remarks across the line about the money I was making, like

"Hey, rookie, who's your banker?" I couldn't blame them, really. Gale and I were the beneficiaries of the two-league competition and the big television contract the NFL had signed with CBS. But there was another reason why I received special heat.

For fourteen years, Bill George—a legend in Chicago— had played the middle linebacker position with unmatched brilliance, reading rival offenses in ways that had never been done before. Then along came this kid with the press clippings and the big contract to take his place. Later, long after he retired, Bill George recalled, "I've never seen anyone who was such a cinch. The day Dick showed up in camp I knew I was out of a job."

Well, I certainly didn't think I was a cinch or that Bill George was history, but after I reported to the Bears' camp, remarks seemed to fly my way every time I turned my head. Little zingers about the money I was supposed to be making or about the press I was getting because I was the Bears' first draft pick, the third pick overall. It would begin at breakfast in the cafeteria. Some veteran would spot something about me in the sports pages and make a crack intended for my ears. "Hey, look at this," he'd say to one of his buddies. "They're writing about Richie Rich again." Then maybe someone would look over at me and shout, "Hey, Dick, got change of a hundred?"

The needling continued through the two-a-days. Everybody had a nickname and mine was "Paddles"—because of my size 12EEE feet. All day I would hear that name. "Hey, Paddles, you okay?" Or, if I read something wrong, "Wrong way, Paddles, wrong way."

None of it was particularly vicious or even mean-spirited. But it bothered me because it didn't let up for a long time and I was beginning to wonder what the hell I had to do to please these guys. Of course, the money thing is what ate at them. And, in a way, I guess I couldn't blame them. But having lived under the tyranny of four older brothers—hell, I *still* have to put up with their bullshit—and getting similar treatment at Illinois because I was the top recruit, I knew how to handle the ribbing. I worked hard, kept pretty much to myself, and, whenever I got the chance to knock one of them on his ass, I did it with *feeling*. I don't know if any of them respected me for the hits I put on them, but I know none of them liked it.

My biggest and toughest adversary was the Bears' defensive system—one of the most complicated in the league. I knew that once I mastered the schemes, I would begin to gain the respect of everybody. George Allen was invaluable. I don't know if anyone else could have prepared me better for the pro game. No coach ever loved the game more or knew it better than Allen, and although I didn't trust him at first—because he couldn't find that telegram the Bears sent to Burt Ingwerson—I soon realized that he was on my side. And as those sweltering late-summer days passed, Allen and I grew closer and closer. I'd always put my trust in my coaches and soon Allen had joined my growing line of mentors, taking over where Bill Taylor left off, just as Taylor had taken over for Bernie O'Brien.

Through the five-game exhibition season, Allen was unrelenting. He took detailed notes, marking down every mistake on a clipboard he must have slept with, and went over them with me until he was satisfied that I understood. He told me, "You can no longer rely on your instincts. This is the pro level. Up here the play is faster, more precise. Every mistaken 'read' is punished by a loss of yards and sometimes by embarrassment. Bill George," he reminded me, "has set a new standard for linebackers. His ability to dissect the offense is respected throughout the game." It quickly became clear to me that George Allen was going to make sure that I carried on the tradition.

It felt as though I was back in school, learning a system more complicated than anything I had ever known. The basic game of football doesn't change all that much whether you're in the sandlots or the pros. There are only four or five defensive systems, each devised to counter a particular offensive setup. But within those schemes there are dozens of variations that change every year, each dictating that you make a slight adjustment.

From my very first day in camp, Allen quizzed me on the various Chicago defenses. Most of it was a new language to me. Allen had a whole glossary of terms. "Mac" meant the middle linebacker. "Stub" was the strongside linebacker and "buck" was the weakside LB. "Pow" and "post" were zone coverages. "Colors" signified offense alignments. There were pages of these terms, most of them Allen's brainchildren. Then there were the numbers for various defenses: 56, 54, 46, and on and on. Each scheme had several subschemes. I think Allen was a kind of football genius. He approached every game like a military tactician approached a battle.

He invaded my brain and emotions with his passion for the game. "You are the detective," he would say. "It's your job to spot the clues, determine the enemy's intentions, and make the right calls to your teammates." This mental approach fascinated me. It was what I always believed, what I always loved most about the game, even more than the hitting, and I soon realized that George Allen could help me get better—a lot better. Some of the other players didn't particularly like Allen because he didn't drink or smoke or curse or chase women. These were serious drawbacks to some guys. But the players respected him.

Although Halas and Allen shared an intense passion for

the game, the two Georges could not have been more dissimi-
lar in other ways. For one thing, they spoke a different language. If Allen spoke inspiringly from the pulpit, Halas
commanded his inland ship like an Ahab, tongue-lashing his
players on to greater efforts and heaping obscene derision on
any official who didn't see it his way. Halas regarded officials
as his personal property. He'd hired many of them when the
league pretty much belonged to him, and he could blow sky-
high when one didn't give him the proper respect by calling a
close play the other way. Halas's favorite phrase for such an
ingrate was ''Hey, you fucking asshole.'' Sometimes I'd hear
Halas scream ''asshole'' so often at some poor official during
a game that I'd start thinking maybe it was the guy's middle
name.

I got my first hint that just maybe I was beginning to be
accepted by some of the older players. One day, O'Bradovich
came over to me on the practice field and said that if I was a
good boy I might be invited to Bob Wetoska's birthday
party—an annual semisecret affair held at a local saloon in
Rensselaer. The party was not so much to mark another year
in Wetoska's life as to celebrate the end of our stay in two-a-
day practice hell. Bob was a veteran offensive tackle and a
cocaptain. I respected him a great deal.

When I joined the veterans at the party later on, I found
out that everybody was invited. So much for OB's private in-
vitation—and my thinking that I was becoming accepted.
Strong safety Richie Petitbon was there, along with reserve
quarterback Frank Budka, tight end Mike Ditka, defensive
end Doug Atkins, and all the other rookies, including running
back Brian Piccolo, who never had to go through the ragging
I did.

The beer begins to flow immediately, and pretty soon
someone suggests a drinking contest among the rookies, and

OB nominates me to represent the defense because he remembers my high guzzling aptitude from that first semester at Illinois. Somebody picks Piccolo to swig for the offense. This pleases me. It means payback time for all the snipes and insults I received from the veterans while Brian usually got off unscathed.

Ditka wraps his head with a bandanna and declares himself the referee. A table is cleared and two large glasses of beer are set down. Brian and I face off on either side of the table. Ditka slaps his big mitts, signaling the start, and I drain my glass before Brian barely has his to his lips. Applause and hoots and hollers from the defense rock the saloon, and the gambling begins. Petitbon and OB bankroll the effort, and pretty soon I am beating everyone the offense throws against me.

After about an hour of this, I am getting pretty shit-faced. But I'm still functioning. Then someone yells, "Hey! We gotta get to our meeting! It's almost seven!" Chairs scrape back as everyone gets up to leave. Everyone except Doug Atkins. He is standing at the door with a bottle of Wild Turkey, informing us that nobody is going anywhere. As big as some of us were, Doug Atkins was in a league by himself. I never saw anybody like Atkins. *Nobody* ever saw anybody like Atkins. Six-foot-eight, 275 pounds, and not enough fat on him to cook an egg. On top of that, he was not your typical gentle giant. Dougie's exploits were legend in pro football camps from Baltimore to Oakland.

There we were, all gathered around the door, pleading, "C'mon, Doug, don't be like that . . ." and . . . "Gee, Dougie, we don't wanna get in trouble on our last day in camp." But Doug's resolute. "We ain't gonna go to no damned meeting. I'm tired of this bullshit." Then he takes another jolt of Wild Turkey and stares at all of us. Finally someone promises him that we will come right back after the meeting, so Doug says, "Well, okay then. But first everyone has to take a swig of this Wild Turkey."

So we all line up and take our medicine, which does not sit all that well on top of a couple of gallons of beer. I jump in my Buick Riviera and fly to the local hall where we held our team meetings. As I arrive at the building, I neglect to hit the brakes in a timely manner and the car stops halfway up the stairs leading to the front door. I'm lucky I don't kill anyone. Inside, Frank Budka produces one of those plastic horns the fans use to make noise at games and he starts blowing into it, which gets everybody's attention. Happy as hell with himself, he belts out a song:

> Hooray for Halas, hooray at last!
> Hooray for Halas, he's a horse's ass!

Just as Budka is finishing his solo, in walks the Old Man—with rockets going off in his eyes. He rips the horn out of Rudy's hand and raps him over the head with it a couple of times. Then he says in that grating voice, "You son of a bitch! You're drunk! Now quiet down, all of you—you crazy bastards! Break into your groups. NOW!"

Everybody gets real quiet and I notice that Atkins is sitting there in the back, shaking his head in dismay at such juvenile behavior, while up front Papa Bear, his big hands on his hips, starts in again, cursing everybody's mother. Over to one side, George Allen is waiting for the thunder to subside, and I'm thinking, *Wow, so this is the NFL!*

When Halas finally calms down, our defensive unit gathers around Allen. Seeing—and no doubt smelling—our advanced state of intoxication, Allen quickly reduces his syllabus to a few simple points and lets us out of school early. We promptly return to the saloon, but Atkins gets there first and takes his position at the doorway. Our ticket inside was another swallow of that Wild Turkey.

That was the first of many team parties.

―――――

George Allen was a very special guy. He was one of the greatest tacticians in the history of the game, and he was deeply appreciated by many veterans. Allen seemed to breathe new life into them. He was every bit the coach Halas was, and he proved it years later when his "Over-the-Hill Gang" of Washington Redskins made it to the Super Bowl.

The older players respected and feared Halas. Two years earlier, they had won the NFL championship with him at the helm. At first I was in awe of him, knowing he could just as easily break me as make me, and I wanted to stay on his good side, which I found to be fairly easy. Years later, only Gale and I would negotiate our contracts with him face-to-face.

George Halas was the iron fist in the iron glove. Nothing got by him at Rensselaer or at Wrigley Field, our home field through the 1970 season. Our practice field was a prison yard; we were the lifers and Halas was the warden. No one ever dared to talk back to him—at least not while he could hear them. No one except Atkins, that is. There were numerous stories about Atkins telling the Old Man off. Usually this was done by telephone when Atkins was tanked. Yet Halas put up with Atkins's bullshit. I have no idea why. Maybe it was because Doug was a great player. Or maybe because he was a favorite of Allen's, and the last thing Halas wanted to do was annoy the best defensive coach in the NFL. What I think is most likely, however, is that Halas loved Atkins for the same reason I suspect he grew to love me. Doug and I were throwbacks, balls-out players who reminded Papa Bear of what the league—his beloved NFL—used to be like back in the days when the Bears played the Canton Bulldogs.

For whatever reasons, Atkins was usually allowed to do his thing. During weekday practices at Wrigley, for example, when the defensive unit would be running drills in preparation for Sunday's game, Atkins would hang out with the groundskeepers, trading jokes and helping them sweep up. Halas and Allen would be working the offense and defense at their respective ends of the field, and there would be Dougie in the stands with a broom in his hands. When his services were absolutely necessary to a particular play or defensive scheme, one of the coaches would request his presence and he'd disengage from the groundskeepers and shamble onto the field. I don't remember hearing anyone complain about Doug's special treatment.

Doug owned a pit bull named Rebel. Some Saturdays, when the defensive team would meet to go over plays for the last time before home games, Doug would show up with this dead-eyed dog of his, one of the nastiest-looking creatures I've ever seen. We would meet in the locker room at Wrigley, which must have been originally designed for a two-man bowling team, and Doug would sit in the back, his legs reaching practically to the first row of desks, and next to him would be his vicious mutt.

After the meetings, Doug would take Rebel out onto the field and start snapping a towel at him. Naturally, Rebel would grab the towel in his teeth, and they would play tug-of-war, each time finishing with Doug swinging the towel over his head with that idiot of a dog hanging onto the other end. After about six rotations, Doug would let go of the towel and Rebel would fly 30 or 40 yards and land with a bounce on the right field grass. It was one of the craziest things I've ever seen.

Then one Saturday OB decided to bring his dog to the meeting. It was a Great Dane, as big as a Shetland pony, and probably required more food than the Fridge. OB started bringing the beast on a regular basis. So every Saturday, while Allen and the other coaches tried to keep our attention on the blackboard, Rebel and the Great Dane would glare at each other and do their heavy-breathing act.

Occasionally—and it always seemed to happen when Allen was about to explain something important—Rebel and the Great Dane would begin mouthing off at each other, their snarls and growls and barks raising a din in the small meeting room. We'd all shift nervously in our seats while Allen would close his eyes and seek divine intervention. As for OB and Doug, they'd each blame the other's mutt for initiating the outburst. After they'd get their mutts to quiet down, we'd go on with the meeting as though nothing had happened. *Wow!* I'd think. *So this is the big time!*

———

The differences between the pros and college were enormous. The level of play and the money were improvements, but everything else seemed to go downhill. Take the equipment, for example. At Illinois our uniforms were first-rate. Not only was each player carefully measured for his helmet and shoulder pads, but every other pad, especially knee pads, were also highly functional. Even the jerseys and pants were made out of the latest materials, light and strong.

When we arrived at the Bears' camp, however, our attention was directed to a large hamper that sat in the middle of the locker room, and we were told to find a pair of shoulder pads that would fit us. Luckily, I had kept my college pads. I wore them for the next five seasons, throwing them away only when they couldn't take any more patching up.

I could write a whole chapter about the crappy Bears' equipment. Even those celebrated "black" jerseys were a disgrace. First of all, they were actually a dark blue. Second, when it rained, their weight doubled and they hung on us like hair shirts. Everything from the shoes to the jocks had been used before. These days in the NFL it's different, of course, but back then the Old Man was not about to spring for such sissy stuff as first-class gear. He probably told himself that playing in used gear helped make us tough, and no doubt he applied the same logic to the field we played on for the first six years of my tenure in the pros. Many players thought the field at Wrigley was a joke. But not me. I loved that little bandbox and I still do.

Wrigley was originally a baseball field—a small baseball field at that—so small that wooden extensions had to be built over one of the dugouts to make room for the end zone. Then there was the locker room, barely big enough for a baseball team, only half what it should have been for a football team. Narrow wire-mesh lockers were jammed together and rusting metal folding chairs competed for space. Hell, we even had it better back at CVS. Cleanliness was a distant concept for the Chicago Bears. One time I smelled something awful and accused my teammate Doug Buffone of having rotten shoes, only to discover a dead rat behind my locker. But hey, that didn't matter to me because I was in the pros. And if this was how it was supposed to be, then it was just fine with me.

I loved the craziness of our big, dysfunctional family: Papa Bear and Muggsy Bear and Uncle George Allen, big brothers OB and Doug Atkins, and little brothers Gale Sayers and Brian Piccolo. I guess it made me feel at home. Better than home, really—because these guys were not really my brothers, so there was no emotional baggage to carry. Yet my teammates were brothers in many ways, and even today I miss that family more than I like to say or even think about.

Maybe that's why I waited so long to write this book. I

knew that sweeping the dust off some of the memories would be difficult. I guess football has really been a family thing with me. I'm beginning to think that what I was really looking for was a sense of belonging—first at CVS, then at Illinois—and that's what the Bears were that first year.

But one memory, in particular, is funny. Our second exhibition game was against the Redskins in Memorial Stadium. In the middle of the second quarter, I was kneed in the head while tackling the running back. The next thing I know I'm sitting on the sideline, looking up and down the bench. There's Rosey Taylor, OB, Atkins, and all the rest. Then Allen comes down, his clipboard under his arm, and he leans over and looks into my eyes and says something like:

"You okay, Dick? You ready to go?"

So I say, "Am I okay? Yeah, I'm okay. Let's go."

Then Allen says, "What's the score?"

I look at him like maybe he's drunk, which would have been a first, and I say, "You're asking me what the score is? We haven't even started yet."

Then I see that some of the guys are smiling, and I look back at George and ask, "Have we?"

George says, "Just sit there and take it easy."

Then it occurs to me that I'm all dirty and sweaty, so I look on the field and of course the game is going on. Then I look at the scoreboard. It's the beginning of the fourth quarter. I'd been out to lunch for more than half the game. Well, my eyes must have looked okay, because Allen sent me in soon after that.

I played reasonably well in that exhibition season. I split my time at middle linebacker with another player, Mike Reilly. I played the second and fourth quarters, Reilly the first and third. He was pretty good, and I wasn't at all sure I would get the nod to start in the season opener against the 49ers.

Our last exhibition game was against the St. Louis Cardinals. By this time, I was feeling fairly confident about my play, thanks to a lot of hard work and George Allen's brilliant coaching. In the locker room before the game, you could almost feel the start of the season approaching. The veterans seemed more animated, especially Ditka, who stood at the doorway as we filed out on our way to the field, urging each of us to suck it up and play hard.

In the second quarter, Jackie Smith, the Cardinals' great Hall of Fame receiver, cut across the middle and I tried to clothesline him. When he got up, he looked at me and said, "Hey, rookie! Don't start that bullshit or you'll never make it into your second year in this league." I suggested a place where he could put his comment. Smith just walked away, shaking his head and no doubt thinking I was way out of line, which I probably was.

After the game, the Old Man announced I would start against the 49ers. As I rode in the plane to San Francisco, nursing a sprained ankle I'd picked up against the Cardinals, I thought back to my first college game against the Washington Huskies and how even then I was limping from an ankle injury sustained in practice. I also remembered the knee injuries; one that kept me out of several games in my sophomore year, and the one that cost us the city championship back at CVS. I was reaching that age when you begin to notice cycles in your life, the relentless repetitions from which you learn or don't learn.

But nothing had prepared me for Dr. Theodore Fox, the Bears' physician of record. I had managed to hide the fact that my left ankle was not 100 percent for most of the week. But one of the coaches spotted me limping on Thursday, and sent me off to get it looked at. There I was, lying on a table, undergoing the first of many examinations by Dr. Fox.

He probed and poked, and his eyes seemed to glow when he hit a tender spot. He reminded me of Laurence Olivier in the role of the sadistic dentist in *Marathon Man*. He marked the spot with a fountain pen. He didn't use X rays, just his fingers. Then Fox turned to veteran defensive tackle Johnny Johnson, who was also there to be "fixed up," and said, "Does Dick know my nickname?" Johnson shrugged, and Fox looked at me and smiled. "They call me 'Needles.' "

Then he took an economy-size hypodermic needle and stuck it into the center of the little circle he had drawn on my ankle. That was novocaine to anesthetize the area. But before it got a chance to work—I mean seconds later—Fox stuck another needle in there, pushing it deep into my ankle joint.

"Hydrocortisone," he said, savoring the word like it was the name of his favorite wine.

He pulled the needle out a fraction of an inch, rotated it, and injected more juice at a slightly different angle. Meanwhile, I tried not to scream, it hurt so much. No way had that novocaine begun to take hold. Needles repeated his pincushion technique maybe half a dozen times, laying down a field of fire all around the contours of my ankle. The whole time I was wincing in pain, a hair's breath of jumping off the table. Fox knew he was hurting me and he just laughed. He thought it was hysterical that he could make Mr. Tough Guy jump. But it wasn't just the pain. I hated the sight of needles. I would hear that weird laugh hundreds of times in the years ahead.

People say that I had a great tolerance for pain. Since I have never lived inside another player's body, I have no idea if that is true. But I do know that I wanted to play football better than anyone else, and perhaps that explains why I was able to push the pain down, lock it in until the game was over. I didn't know it then, but pain would be with me for the rest of my life. Toward the end of my career, my joints would hurt so much on Monday mornings after a game that I would sometimes have to crawl from my bed to the bathroom.

I mention pain now because I might not later. When I start this trip back into my pro years, the physical pain most likely will be forgotten as it was on the field. Of course I have tried to remember all the injuries, because they reappeared throughout my career. But I won't dwell on them now. The only thing that mattered in those days was playing ball. I just couldn't get enough of it. Between the seasons I waited for August and training camp at Rensselaer, between games I waited for the practices, and on Sundays after the first kickoff I waited for the opposition to take the field. Then, with my heart pounding, my mind clear and focused, I waited for the snap of the ball.

CHAPTER

6

"*O*kay, listen up! Especially you rookies."

This was our last team meeting before traveling to California, where we would play two games in six days. First to San Francisco for the season opener at Kezar Stadium against the 49ers, and then, after practicing at the Oakland Raiders' camp in Santa Rosa, we'd head for Los Angeles to play the Rams in the Coliseum.

The voice was Papa Bear's, of course. He was preparing us for our flight into Babel.

"As many of you know, tomorrow we are going to that cesspool of sex: Godless California. All you two-suiters, listen up. If you have any ideas about dipping your wicks in the human trash out there, forget it. We are going there to play football. That's what you are getting paid for—so leave your fucking suits at home, you understand?"

It was one of his better speeches. But the term "two-suiter" escaped me until O'Bradovich explained it to me on the plane. In those days, the team traveled in blue blazers and slacks, white shirts, and ties. Each blazer bore the Bears' logo on the breast pocket. So to escape detection, some players would pack a suit and make a quick change the minute they hit their hotel rooms. Then out they would go in search of nocturnal playmates—female variety.

Halas was a mass of contradictions. He was the most profane man I ever knew, a man who could outcurse a platoon of drill instructors or make even Lenny Bruce sound angelic. Yet Halas was so pure when it came to sex that he could have lectured Cotton Mather. But there may have been a practical side to Halas's puritanism. He truly believed that sexual activity drained an athlete of his ability. As Papa Bear put it: "I don't want any of you guys leaving your games on some damn whore's bed!"

Halas might have saved his breath as far as I was concerned. Virtually all my free time was spent going over the playbook with George Allen. In his patient way, Allen drilled me on the 49ers' offensive setups, their audibles, and their fancy stuff. He outlined the tendencies of quarterback John Brodie: what Brodie usually did under certain circumstances and who his favorite receivers were. And Allen clued me in on the running backs, especially that old master John David Crow.

That Sunday I got my shot. I played in my first NFL regular season game.

Before 33,000 in little Kezar Stadium, the 49ers pounded us into the ground, 52–24. It was the worst opening day in the Bears' history. We held our own in the first period, but then it all fell apart. From the second quarter until well into the second half, the 49ers scored on six consecutive possessions, making our defense look about as bad as it could get.

Our offense was not much better. Neither of our quarterbacks, Rudy Bukich or Bill Wade, could get things going. Gale Sayers did not start. When Gale finally got his chance, he couldn't keep his footing on the soft turf. Twice he slipped just when it appeared he was going to break loose for a long gain. He also had trouble holding on to the ball and fumbled twice.

I was amazed by the 49ers' level of play. Brodie was a maestro, mixing his plays with intuitive genius, but I was especially impressed by the 49ers' offensive line. Those guys were really good, working off each other and executing their plays with efficiency. The exhibition season had not prepared me for such a tight, quick offense. But I caught on and made fourteen tackles before the gun sounded.

I also made a few rookie mistakes. We kept trying to red dog them and I guess I was too anxious to get in there and some of their runners got by me. I admitted as much to the press after the game in the locker room. "I'll get better," I promised. But apparently that was not good enough for Cooper Rollow of the *Chicago Tribune*. Rollow walked into the trainer's room just as Dr. Fox was giving me a postgame shot, which would become another ritual. "Hey, rookie!" he said. "What happened on that big run by Crow? Was that your fault? Looked that way to me."

Maybe it did look that way if you didn't know the game very well. The defense on that play was a 46 wide blow, which called for me to shoot the gap on the left side of the center and the weakside linebacker, Jimmy Purnell, to shoot through on the right side. Well, for some reason, Jimmy didn't get there on time and John David Crow busted through the hole for about 50 yards on those ancient legs of his. I wasn't about to explain myself to a newspaperman I didn't know, so I kept my mouth shut. Rollow stood there for a while, looking down at me on the training table, then he walked away. The next day I was not surprised to read how I had blown a number of draw plays. Nailed again. With Dan Jenkins I had talked too much. Now I was damned by my silence. George Allen was quoted as saying, "Butkus did a fine job," but the damage had been done by Rollow's words.

Over the next nine years, Rollow and I would achieve a friendly relationship, a kind of agreement to disagree. I came to respect him, and years later, in 1979, at the final vote on that year's Hall of Fame nominees, Rollow stood up and officially entered my name for the vote with the words "From the Chicago Bears, Dick Butkus. Enough said."

But it wasn't only the curiosity of the press that I had to worry about. The next day I was allowed to rest at practice because I had gotten another shot in the ankle. While I was watching from the sideline, I fell into a conversation with Atkins. I noticed Halas looking over at us as we were shooting the shit, and I wondered what was bothering him. That evening at dinner Halas announced in front of the players that he wanted to see me in his suite.

When I finished eating, I went in to see him. He was sitting in a chair, all smiles and friendly. "How's the ankle? You played pretty good on Sunday. Don't think too much about the loss. We'll get better." Meanwhile, I was nodding and saying, "Yes, sir," "No, sir," "Thank you, sir." Then Halas asked me what Atkins and I had been talking about at practice.

I told him we were discussing defenses. He leaned forward, elbows on his knees, and came out with it: "Was Atkins grilling you about your contract?"

"No, sir," I said.

Halas paused for a long moment, his eyes searching my face. He was no longer smiling. "Listen to me, kid," he said. "If Atkins or anyone else does ask you about the money, you tell him it's none of his goddamn business! You understand me?"

"Yes, sir," I said.

He didn't have to worry about me. I would have done

anything he asked. I was so damned proud just to be playing for my hometown in Wrigley Field. Hell, this was the pros! We could adapt because we were tough, because we were pros. It wasn't like college with fresh socks and clean jocks. This was South Side football, blue-collar, rag-tag, ass-busting football—just how I liked it. Cheap uniforms and cramped quarters. Tough, down-and-dirty football. George Halas breathing fire at us all the time. Man, it was great! I was in football heaven.

The distrust Halas showed that night intensified over the years. He formed a tight circle of house rats, informers who reported privately to him, and he hired gumshoes to shadow players whose nightlife was more active than he would have liked or whose friends and associates may not have been of the Halas stripe. He even had players investigated, including Ditka, Bill George, and Atkins. He may have had me tailed for all I know. If he did, the guy must have been bored stiff.

I'm sure Halas considered such tactics vital to the health of the league and the Bears. But there was more to it than that. His advancing age began to lay claim to the thing that had mattered most to him. His love of the game was dying. The money was all-important now and I watched it drain him of the exuberance that made the Bears such a powerful force in the NFL.

It's a shame what age and wealth do to some men, warping their judgment so they don't know who their real friends are, and then they start listening only to those who will tell them what they want to hear. Often enough these are family members, maybe the heirs to their power and wealth, often undeserving, inept, and hungry. Near the end of my playing days, I was to feel the sudden chill of George Halas's disaffection, and it was almost as if my own father had deserted me.

But this was my rookie year. Now that I had one league

game under my belt, I was convinced that I could play in the NFL, maybe even excel. I could also sense that a few of the veterans were beginning to soften their attitude toward me. O'Bradovich had stuck by me and the older players respected him. Also, I had been given the starting middle linebacker job at the end of the exhibition season. By now it was clear to everyone that Bill George would not be playing much. He had not come back from a knee injury and after the season he would be traded to the Rams, where he would finish a great career.

On that evening when Halas requested my presence in his suite, I was feeling a sense of belonging for the first time since I reported to the Bears. But Halas had put me in a compromising light.

Ditka and Wetoska called a meeting later that night and urged the younger players to forget about the loss to the 49ers and focus on the upcoming game against the Rams. When the rah-rah was over, I raised my hand. I knew everyone had seen me go into Halas's room, and I wanted to say something for the record. I didn't expect some of the veterans to believe me. But I didn't say it just for them. I told everyone, "I want you all to know that I am not a teacher's pet. Never was, never will be. I am here for one reason only. To win football games."

We went down to Los Angeles and lost a squeaker to the Rams, 30–28. Like us, the Rams had been beaten badly in their season opener by the Lions, 20–0. One of the sparser crowds in recent memory showed up for our game with them.

Both teams therefore were motivated to play their very best. The Rams scored first when defensive back Aaron Martin intercepted a Bukich pass and raced 36 yards for a touchdown. But we struck back on their next possession. Bob Kilcullen broke through the line to block Bruce Gossett's field goal attempt and Rosey Taylor picked up the ball and raced 60 yards to paydirt.

We struck again on their next possession. As Ram quarterback Bill Munson dropped back to pass, Atkins blew in from the right side and hit him so hard that the ball popped free. I scooped it up for the first of my twenty-five career total fumble recoveries and took it upfield 22 yards to the Rams' eighteen. Then Gale, who again did not start this day, was inserted by Halas and we watched him take a handoff from quarterback Bill Wade, fake a pass, then behind a neat block of linebacker Cliff Livingston by flanker Johnny Morris, the "Kansas Comet" zipped 22 yards into the end zone for the first of his 56 professional touchdowns.

By the end of the third quarter, we were ahead, 28–9.

Then we fell apart or "ran out of gas," as Papa said afterward. Our defense was melting in the California heat and Bill Munson began to hit Terry Baker and Tommy McDonald with passes while fullback Dick Bass moved the ball on the ground. With less than a minute to go in the game, Munson found Baker in the end zone and the Rams nailed the victory with their third touchdown in twelve minutes.

At some point in that miserable fourth quarter when our offense was on the field for a brief appearance, a drunken fan ran onto the grass and started dancing in little circles and waving his arms. While the crowd applauded his rude idiocy, I sat on the bench praying he'd come within range so that I could demonstrate my appreciation. Ditka did it for me. As the fan approached the huddle, Mike straightened up, took a couple of steps, and leveled him with a forearm. That's when I realized just how much he hated to lose.

We returned to Chicago in time to read our notices in the local press. A few stories wistfully harkened back to that championship season two years earlier when the Bears had finished at 11–1–2 and then beat the Giants, 14–10, for the NFL crown, which at that time was the top of the pro game. (The Super Bowl would not take place until January 1967 when Green Bay would defeat Lamar Hunt's Kansas City Chiefs, 35–10.)

With two straight losses to our discredit, a few home-town writers began to wonder just how good I was and whether Gale was too small for the pros. But most writers chose to measure our improvement rather than fit us for coffins. While Gale had not broken a long gainer yet, they noted that he was showing signs of getting his pro legs. And they gave me some pretty good grades, too.

The next week we went north to Green Bay. We landed at Austin Straubel Field, a small group of Quonset huts with a single runway in those days, on Saturday in the early afternoon. We then went by bus to the old Northland Hotel in the heart of the downtown district. I liked the place immediately. Big old lobby, all dark wood and overstuffed couches and chairs, potted palms, high ceilings, tall windows, and a mezzanine from which you looked down on it all.

When we arrived, a wedding reception was in full swing. There were people everywhere and a band was playing stuff like *Lady of Spain* and *The Girl That I Marry*. Some of the wedding party spotted us at the check-in desk and the hoots and boos began. But it was done in such good fun that you had to laugh. There's something about Green Bay fans—the way they are about their football team—that made me think of my college days. Sure, they wanted their Packers to win and they let us know it, but they didn't hate us in the process. And if the Packers didn't win, the fans didn't tear them apart afterward.

You had to ask yourself how an NFL team survived in Green Bay. That in itself was a miracle to me. With a population around 50,000 and Lambeau Field holding 35,000 when filled to the gills, which it always was, win or lose, Green Bay was a beacon of sportsmanship in a sports world that was already changing for the worse.

Anyway, with the wedding reception getting louder and crazier by the minute, we checked into our rooms and gathered immediately for a meeting with Papa Bear. He was smart about meetings. He knew that once we hit the bar downstairs, he might as well have been in Duluth for all we would have cared. The only available spot was on the mezzanine, so that's where we met. While the band played on just below, Halas launched into a pep talk straight off a page by Knute Rockne.

The tale spun by Papa concerned a certain Lord Baltimore, who inspired his battle-weary troops to charge the encampment of an army many times its size, thereby catching the enemy unaware and achieving an upset. Halas was a trip. You could see the excitement on his face, so you had to listen. When he finished the tale, Halas told us to be sure to get a good night's sleep. Then he left the mezzanine. Atkins, who had experienced many a blowout with the Old Man, leaned over the railing and addressed everyone below in a booming voice:

"Paging Lord Baltimore! Will Lord Baltimore please report to the Chicago Bears!"

The wedding reception carried on into the wee hours. At least twice that night, zealous Packer fans (or maybe it was one of the Packers) set off the hotel's fire alarm system. The next morning a few other players and I went to Mass at St. Willebrord's with the Old Man, his son Mugs, his daughter Virginia, and her husband Ed McCaskey. As we settled into one of the pews, we saw Vince Lombardi with his family and a few players. This was no surprise. I knew that Vince was a devout Catholic. But after the Mass was over, I saw someone outside the church who almost put my system into shock: Paul Hornung, football's consummate playboy. In the years ahead, Paul and I would become good friends. But that morning I learned that you should never judge someone you don't know solely on the basis of their reputation.

It's doubtful that things would have been any different even if Lord Baltimore had showed up that afternoon. We lost our third straight, 23–14. I don't remember much about the game, except that I played pretty well, and so did the rest of the Bears, especially in the second half when all the parts seemed to start working together. It was also Gale's first start—and he made the most of it, gaining 80 yards on 17 carries and picking up his second and third NFL touchdowns. The second score was one for the books. Gale took a little flair pass from Bukich, spun free of his coverage, and broke into the Packers' secondary, streaking 65 yards into the end zone. But Gale's heroics were not enough that day. Only perfection would have beaten the Packers.

They were the best team in football. In 1961 and 1962 they had beaten the New York Giants for the NFL championship, and they were on their way to the top again in 1965. Some say they were the best team on any field in any season. It would be hard to argue with that assertion. What a backfield! Bart Starr at quarterback, cool and precise; Paul Hornung, the triple-threat "Golden Boy"; and Jim Taylor, as tough a runner as ever lived. Receivers Boyd Dowler, Max McGee, and Carroll Dale—all battle-hardened, no-frills guys who could get it done. Up front were four of the best ever. Fuzzy Thurston and Jerry Kramer were Bart Starr's "guardian angels." They were flanked by Forrest Gregg and Bob

Skoronski—and all four were anchored by center Ken Bow-man—unsung today, but a great one.

In his book, Kramer remembered one play against us when Bowman forgot the release signal in the count. So Bart yelled, "Hut!" and started pulling back. Kramer and Fuzzy stood up in pass-blocking position as the defensive tackles charged across the line. There was only one problem: Bow-man still had the ball. "About that time," wrote Kramer, "Butkus and Bowman looked at each other." Bowman sup-posedly said, "Oh shit"—just before I ran about three yards and smacked him ass-over-tea-kettle back into Starr, who was standing there without the ball.

I honestly don't remember the play. I was involved in so many situations like that, I can't remember them all. For ex-ample, they tell me that in one game I tackled Jim Taylor so hard that he coughed up the ball twice—only to be saved each time by a quick whistle, but I don't remember that either. What I do remember about Taylor was that you had to tackle him hard and hang on or he would slip away somehow. An-other thing about him was that Taylor loved contact. He would just as soon run into you as around you. In fact, I think he preferred it.

On the downfield side of the ball, the Packers were just as deep in Hall of Fame talent. Ray Nitschke at middle linebacker and Henry Jordan at tackle led a whole raft of tough guys who were afraid of no one, except perhaps the man on the sidelines, Mr. Vince Lombardi.

Despite the loss against the Packers, there was a positive feeling among our players and coaches as we headed back to Chicago. We knew we were getting better. In the two weeks since the 49ers blew us out, Halas's "kiddie corps" had aged dramatically, and the older players seemed to be getting younger. Gale was looking better and better, and I was beginning to feel more comfortable out there. Now we would play several games on our own turf. If we were going to have a decent season, we would have to start winning.

I loved playing before my hometown at Wrigley. Traveling was exciting, but I liked being home. I guess the familiarity made me feel more secure. Each week we followed a program. If we played on Sunday, we were given Monday off. On Tuesday, we reported to Wrigley and watched films of the upcoming team in their most recent game. In this case, it was the Rams, who had beaten us by two points two weeks earlier. Then we went outside and ran a light workout. No equipment to speak of. That night the coaches would put in the game plans.

On Wednesdays, we started practicing in full gear. First thing in the morning, we had a general meeting. We'd start practice by lining up in one of the end zones and running a couple of laps. Then we broke up into our separate units after doing a standard set of exercises. Often the three linebackers and four defensive backs would play against three receivers and four backs, including the quarterback. The drill, known as seven on seven, required us to employ the defensive schemes of our upcoming opponent against our own passing plays. On Thursdays, we would reverse the process and focus on defense, using the seven on seven drills with the defense adjusting to the offensive plays of Sunday's opponent. We'd practice new stunts and red dogs and work on our zone setups.

In those days, the defensive unit was treated like a poor cousin. This was true throughout the league. The offense would get the best practice fields and meeting rooms. At Wrigley we had to squeeze into the visitors' locker room. In hotels on the road, the defense would have to meet in the cramped meeting rooms, while the offense relaxed amid the quiet comfort of real meeting suites.

But this just made me more motivated. While some play-ers let it bother them, I would take the inequity and throw it into my own personal mix of mind dynamics. As the days went by, my anger would brew like strong coffee until game day arrived. Then I would be so focused that even my own teammates tiptoed around me. Ditka once told a writer: "He stokes his anger all week and by game time he doesn't even talk to you. You're lucky to get a grunt out of him."

But that doesn't mean I walked around all week like a caged animal. Each afternoon after practice, I would visit Helen at her new job with Blue Cross, Blue Shield, which was conveniently located on the same block as our apartment. Then I would go home and take a nap. In the evenings, we kept pretty much to ourselves, eating at home or maybe visit-ing our parents back in Roseland.

On Thursday nights, I would sit in my apartment and study the films, running them over and over on the projector until every pattern and individual movement was burned into my memory. Then I would study the various calls, so I would be prepared on Sunday: the red dogs, the special zones, the overs and the unders, the full complement of devices de-signed by Allen to thwart a particularly hot receiver or run-ner. Allen's plans required a lot of work because he would revise them from week to week.

Fridays were usually a light workout that included some laps around the field and some calisthenics. Back then almost no one in the NFL lifted weights. Hell, the Bears didn't even have a weight room. Most of us had been told that weights were not good for football players, that they hampered movement. One player disagreed. Dick Evey worked out all the time and had a great build, leading me to suspect that maybe the popular view about weights might be wrong. In Evey's case, lifting helped him make the pros, providing him with additional weight and strength.

On Friday afternoons, George Allen and I would have a late lunch with Vern Buol at the Golden Ox, a German restaurant located near Haymarket Square. Vern would knock back a few cocktails and I would quaff a couple of liters of beer while consuming a platter of broiled red snapper. Allen would sip some soda pop and eat something terribly healthy, never seeming to care when Vern and I got a little buzz going.

Vern was the official baby-sitter of the Bears, and our friendship extended beyond football. In the off-season, Vern and I did a lot of things together, one of which was fishing. He had a friend named Rollie, a successful attorney who kept a forty-two-foot sportfisherman down in South Florida. Sometimes we would go to the Biminis, a pair of tiny islands eighty miles off Miami in the northwest section of the Bahamas. One time in the early spring, Rollie invited Vern and me down to fish for swordfish at night. We had a great time out on the water, knocking back brews and hauling in those bruisers by moonlight. Rollie insisted that we tag each fish and release it. Back then all I could think of was all those swordfish dinners swimming away, but now I realize that we did the right thing.

Anyway, after the Friday lunch at Haymarket Square, I would go home to 222 East Pearson and take a nap. After dinner, I might watch a little TV or read over Allen's game plan before going back to bed. I knew by now that sleep might not come easily the night before a game, so I made sure that I got as much rest as I could on Friday.

Saturday occasionally began with one of those infamous defensive meetings where Atkins's pit bull and OB's Great Dane would steal the show. Then we would go out on the field and run through our punt and kickoff returns. After that we'd break up into offense and defense. The offense would run their plays against the defensive subs while the offensive subs would run the opposing team's offense against the defense at the other end of the field. Since there weren't enough offensive and defensive subs, we would "show them a picture" of the play we were going to run.

During slow periods, we'd play different games with the ball. If you hold a football a certain way and throw it underhand like a softball pitcher, you can make it dip and dive like a knuckleball. We'd play catch this way, each guy trying to make the other miss the ball. Another game involved hand strength. Each guy would grip half the ball and the idea was to twist the ball free of the other guy's grip. Besides having big hands, I had another advantage. Due to a bad sprain that had never healed correctly, I could take my right thumb and bend it back all the way to touch my arm. This allowed me extra purchase on the ball because I could curl the thumb around the ball like a meat hook while holding it on top with the other four fingers. It was almost impossible to get the ball from me. This grip of mine turned out to be one of the main reasons why I was able to rip the ball away from opponents so many times.

I was always playing with the football: bouncing it off the grass, or spinning it on my fingertips, or just holding it. Now receivers do it all the time. I used to imitate Johnny Unitas of the Baltimore Colts, the NFL's premier quarterback. Unitas had that quick-step shuffle, his body swinging back and forth as he dropped back to pass.

Another drill was to stand with your back to the guy with the ball and not turn around until he yelled. By then the ball would be at least halfway to you. It was either catch it or get whacked in the face. The drill was a great sharpener of reflexes. As the seasons went by, we would develop some of these games even further. A few are still played today.

Then it was home again for more study and a good

night's sleep if possible. But sleep came late the night before our second Rams game of 1965. I don't remember exactly what ran through my head as I watched the first light of dawn materialize behind the curtains. We were down 0–3 and needed a win if we were going to have a good season. Then there was the excitement of playing my first official NFL home game in Chicago, in the stadium where I once hit a baseball off the outfield wall. I hoped I could perform half as well this time.

I got up very early and walked over to Mass at the Holy Name Cathedral. After receiving Communion, I knelt in the back pew and prayed for a win, then offered up a few words on behalf of my knee and finished by asking for some guidance on the field. I returned to the apartment, where Helen cooked me a steak and eggs breakfast.

By then I wasn't talking much. It must have been difficult for Helen to understand why I pulled so far into myself before playing a game. Now she just rolls her eyes at the memory. But it was the only way I knew how to gather myself. I am not mean by nature. In fact, I am really quite the opposite. My friends are always telling me to get tougher in business because I tend to trust the wrong people. Maybe that's one reason why football appealed to me. You never ran into very many lawyers or agents or writers out there on the field. Reading the players was always very simple. The bad guys wore the other uniform, and it was my job to make their lives miserable. In order to do that at the highest possible level, I employed every mind trick I knew. By the time I got to Wrigley Field on game day, I had psyched myself into a state of pure hatred of the enemy.

When I'd pull into the parking lot, I would see the kids. They didn't know me too well in my rookie year, so there wasn't much bullshit about autographs. They'd watch me turn off the engine and get out of the car. Standing off at a respectful distance, they'd say, "Have a good game." Sometimes they'd say, "Hey, Dick, do you think you could get us in?" I'd take a close look at them. If they seemed okay, I'd usually say, "Yeah, follow me in." I figured that if these kids were there that early, then, by God, they deserved a shot at sneaking into the game. The guys at the gate usually looked the other way.

The locker room would be mostly empty and quiet except for the sound of an occasional footstep on the hard floor or the closing of a door. The silence reminded me of a church an hour before Mass. The trainers would be preparing the various tape jobs for some of the players. Dr. Fox would be lurking somewhere and maybe a few of the Early Birds would be suiting up.

The Early Birds group was formed by Halas as a bulwark against one of his greatest fears: the formation of a players' union. According to a story I heard, Bill George, my esteemed predecessor at middle linebacker and an early agitator for a union, was called in to the big office on LaSalle Street by the Old Man one day.

"So what's all this crap I've been hearing?" asks Halas.

"Well," says Bill, "some of the boys think they should have a union and they elected me as player representative."

Halas's teeth start to click. "You guys don't need no fucking union."

"Well, I don't know," Bill says. "I think we do."

At this point, the Old Man looks off toward the window as if in deep thought. Then, with pain in his eyes, he addresses the bearer of this nightmare.

"I'll tell you what I'm willing to do, Bill," he says. "I'll give you $25 to shag balls. But you gotta promise me to keep the other players from talking union horseshit."

Bill George accepted the offer, successfully ending the first player-owner negotiation in the long history of the Chicago Bears, and the Early Birds were born. Since Bill George was a linebacker, who do you think got first crack at being an Early Bird? I had to be there anyway to snap balls to the punters, so I picked up an extra $25 for nothing. By today's standards, it doesn't seem like very much. But back then, $400 a year, which included exhibition games, could buy a lot of groceries.

The Early Birds had fun out there. One Sunday morning, the extra-point kickers kept lofting the balls into a small crowd that had gathered in the stands behind the uprights. The fans would scramble to catch the balls and throw them back to us. Then one joker decided to keep the ball, so we started yelling, "Hey, motherfucker! Throw the ball back, you asshole!" Stuff like that. Well, what made it funny was that one of our coaches was a member of the Christian Fellowship Athletes Association. "Gosh darnit," "Gee whiz," and "My heavens" were his saltiest expressions, while we were yelling the rottenest things we could think of at this fan. "Guys, guys!" he yelled. "He's a paying customer." "Fuck him," we said. So he would get all upset. That coach was the only guy I ever knew who showered and shaved before every game.

That first home game against the Rams set us on a winning course that would draw raves from around the country. It also gained Gale Sayers and me our first notes of genuine respect—which, in Gale's case, would develop into universal awe by the middle of the season.

It was quite a turnaround for Gale. He had already displayed flashes of the future in the first three games, especially against Green Bay. But he still hadn't gotten completely untracked. All of us, except a few newspapermen, knew he was going to be great. One writer remarked that he "couldn't block a dummy.'' Still another, who claimed to have seen him play at Kansas, made one of the worst accusations: ''Sayers never did like the rough going.''

Let me tell you a few things about Gale Sayers. Since I had played against Gale in a couple of college all-star games, I already knew that he had better moves than anyone I'd seen so far in the pros. I was convinced it was only a matter of time before he broke out. Ditka and the other veterans had seen enough of Gale to know it, too. In a preseason game against the Rams, Gale returned a punt 77 yards into the end zone and ran a kickoff back 93 yards for another score. Then he threw a 25-yard completion for a touchdown. Gale was in a league all his own. Nobody could change directions as fast or as often—and no one could accelerate quicker, then gear down on a dime and accelerate again.

In our home game against the Rams, Gale put on a show that made believers out of the doubters. On one play early in the game, Gale took a screen pass and broke free for 80 yards and a score. As Hall of Fame tackle Rosey Grier later recalled the play: ''I hit him so hard near the line of scrimmage I thought my shoulder must have busted him in two. I heard a roar from the crowd and figured he must have fumbled. I was on the ground and when I looked up he was 15 yards down the field and going for the score.'' Gale ran for two more touchdowns that afternoon, putting up some big numbers for the first time, and before the week was out the writers had dubbed him the ''Chicago Comet.''

Again they were calling Sayers and Butkus the greatest tandem of first-round draft choices in NFL history. Some pundits predicted that we would win dual Rookie of the Year honors. Meanwhile, Bukich was having a great season, completing a high percentage of his passes. Ditka was doing what he always did at tight end: opening holes for Gale and Jon

Arnett and catching little passes on third and long and taking the ball beyond the first-down markers, often with a couple of defensive backs hanging on him.

On defense we allowed only 6 points by the same Rams team that had scored 30 two weeks earlier. I was beginning to feel confident on every series now, correctly reading my keys time and again. Doug Atkins was in his next to last year at defensive end, and he wasn't going quietly. He was awesome, especially on the pass rush. His six-foot-eight frame flying in from the right side would rattle the coolest quarterback. The other linebackers were veteran Joe Fortunato on my left and Larry Morris on my right. Not much got by us.

In the third quarter, I nearly lost it. I intercepted a Munson pass over the middle and began running it back when Ram halfback Tommy McDonald blindsided me, then grabbed my face mask and tore it off my head. When the refs made no call, I went nuts. There's a picture of me on my knees, holding the ball, looking at the official who is holding his arms out as if to say, "Easy does it, kid."

In general, I had pretty good relationships with the referees and umpires. They got a kick out of my antics. I was always excited and consumed by the game, and sometimes they seemed to actually appreciate my vocal abilities. I fooled around so much with the officials and the other team that I don't remember a lot of the things I said and did. Someone once told me that during a game I kept bitching so much to an official about a missed call that he turned to me and said: "Dick, if you don't shut up, I am going to bite your head off." To which I am supposed to have replied: "If you did that, you'd have more brains in your stomach than you do in your head."

That story may have originated in some writer's head (and if it did, it's pretty funny) like many of the malapropisms attributed to Yogi Berra. But recently I read it again in *Sports Illustrated*. Who knows? Maybe it was the work of my old pal Dan Jenkins.

———

The next week we beat the Vikings in Minneapolis, 45–37. With less than two minutes to go in the game, Gale took a kickoff at the Bears' four yard line, headed up the middle into the point of the wedge, cut left, then ducked back to the right and scampered for the sideline. Once he reached the sideline, it was clear sailing to the end zone and Gale left the would-be Viking tacklers in his wake. Nobody even touched him. We went ahead, 38–37. A few plays later, quarterback Fran Tarkenton passed on the run out of one of his patented scrambles. I snatched the floater at about midfield and ran it back to the ten. On the next play from scrimmage, Gale scored his fourth touchdown of the day.

The next week we bagged the Detroit Lions, 38–10, improving our record to 3–3. Our season slate had been wiped clean. Our next game was against the Green Bay Packers at Wrigley Field. The buildup in the media—the newspapers, TV, and radio—was at playoff volume. And why not? Although we had lost to Green Bay at Lambeau Field a few weeks earlier, we had played them tough enough for the local scribes to predict a victory at Wrigley.

Green Bay was the class of the league, and nobody wanted to beat them more than I did. Years later, Helen heard a story from Fuzzy Thurston. It seems that before our first game against the Packers, Vince Lombardi openly discredited me to his troops, saying that I was slow and that I usually overcommitted. After we played against them, Lombardi apparently revised his opinion because he warned his players about me: "Watch that Butkus character. He's really something."

We were all something that day. George Allen had tweaked our defense, and with better execution, we were able to put some pressure on Starr. We accomplished that by constantly shifting and stunting, making him try to catch us out of position with a quick snap. This messed up their timing on offense, resulting in a number of offsides calls, and after two quarters we were in charge of the game. Throughout the second half, we increased the frequency of our shifts and stunts. Starr eventually settled down, but it was too late. We won handily, 31–10.

Halas started veteran quarterback Bill Wade against the Packers, but replaced him with Rudy Bukich early in the game. It was the right move. Bukich called a great game and we gave him the game ball. I led the team in tackles with fourteen and broke up one of Starr's passes. After the game, Lombardi praised Halas's kiddie corps to the press, saying that we had given the old-timers "a shot in the arm." Then the wily Lombardi said something that may have cost us a victory down the road. "This Bear team is better than the 1963 bunch that won the championship."

Blessings from the Pope couldn't have had greater powers than Father Lombardi's remark. They played the quote on the radio and TV all week like it was the number-one hit on the charts. And we of the kiddie corps listened, each time feeling a little more hot air enter our systems. Then the Baltimore Colts blew into town with a chill wind at their backs and turned us colder than those sides of beef down on Haymarket Square. Leading the charge was Johnny Unitas, the best quarterback of my time—and maybe of all time.

I had spent years reading quarterbacks, but I couldn't read Unitas. He was the consummate poker player, using his eyes as diversions instead of windows into his thoughts. He'd hunch behind the center, his eyes moving but never resting on any particular spot. Then he'd take the ball and start stepping back with that patented shoulder swing copied by every teenage quarterback in America, his head steady on its base, the eyes seeming to see all and nothing at the same time. Then, as if in response to some inner rhythm, he would launch the ball toward its target. If it wasn't caught, it usually wasn't his fault. Number 19 was very good.

The game with Baltimore was the most consistently bruising affair I had yet encountered on any football field. It seemed as though all the blocks and tackles were just a little harder, a little nastier. Players were limping to the sidelines with regularity. In my eighth NFL game, my reputation was beginning to precede me and double teams became a regular tactic intended to slow me down. My number 51 was becoming a target. This was fine with me because it meant someone else—usually Doug Atkins or tackle Earl Leggett—was free to make mischief in the backfield.

But for all the mischief we made that day in Wrigley Field, the Colts survived and limped home winners, 26–21. Gale and I had played well, however—and the Bears' Rookie of the Year boosters continued to beat the drums for a dual award. We paid as little attention as possible to the publicity. But it seemed the newspapermen were always throwing the possibility in our faces. While I just didn't answer, Gale fielded the writers' queries with the same deftness he used to elude tacklers, slipping by them with a remark about how well Ditka or Bukich or Atkins was playing or how important Ron Bull's blocking had been to his running that day.

Meanwhile, Papa Bear dodged nothing thrown at him by the press. Since his team was suddenly back in the national limelight, writers around the country were seeking a Halas interview. George had his favorites. Usually they were writers who had been there when he started the Bears: guys like Ring

Lardner, Grantland Rice, Frank Graham, and Red Smith, gentlemen writers with a sense of history and regard for what football players did out there. Some of them even remembered Halas as a player and sometimes would recall in their stories the day in 1923 when Halas snatched a fumble by Jim Thorpe of the Oorang Indians and outran the greatest Native American athlete of all time some 98 yards for a touchdown and an NFL record, a record that would hold up for forty-nine years.

After beating the St. Louis Cardinals by a score of 34–13 the next week, we went on the road for three games—against Detroit, New York, and a rematch with the Colts in Baltimore. I loved playing against the Lions. At one point, Detroit general manager Russ Thomas called me an "annihilating S.O.B." Veteran Lion tight end Charlie Sanders went Thomas one better, describing me as "a maladjusted kid" after I had cracked a couple of his ribs. I accepted such remarks as tribute to my talent.

I was finding in my rookie year that intimidation worked up in the pros just as it had in college and high school. Guys didn't get any tougher because they made the pros. No matter what you say about the game, football at its base is pure violence and mayhem, bound loosely by rules and tightly by the clock. Every player—including me—who ever worked on an NFL field has thought about getting hurt. If I could tap into a player's physical fears, I knew that he was mine—not only for that play or even that game but from one season to the next.

You might wonder how I handled my own fear. At six-foot-three and 245 pounds, I wasn't the only big guy out there. Fear can be a debilitating force if left unchecked, but I pushed it back through sheer willpower and with a lot of humor. I learned early in my rookie year that the officials in the NFL allowed a lot more self-expression on the field than we had enjoyed in college, and I adjusted accordingly. I never stopping running my mouth. All week I would slowly withdraw into myself, each day growing quieter and quieter, which allowed me to focus on Allen's defense game plan. Then I would find my voice right after the opening kickoff— and I usually didn't stop using it for the rest of the game: badgering the opposition, complaining to the referee, and boosting my teammates.

I remember yelling a lot in Yankee Stadium the next Sunday, especially at Tucker Frederickson, who I had met on my visit to Florida as a high school senior. As the Giants' leading ground-gainer, Tucker was the Eastern writers' favorite to win the Rookie of the Year award. But if Gale had a good game in New York and I could contain Tucker's excellent running game, then the focus would shift to the Chicago Comet. As for my chances, I never seriously considered that a linebacker would get the award over a runner or quarterback. And anyway, I really didn't care any more about Rookie of the Year award than I did about the Heisman Trophy back in college. As far as a dual award for Gale and me went, that was just bullshit to sell newspapers.

Yankee Stadium was packed. There hadn't been an empty seat in it for a decade or more, and although the Giants' glory days were clearly waning, there was still a lot of punch and pride in the Big Blue. You can say whatever you want about New York, but I love the vitality that runs through that city. I can't say I always liked the sports fans there, but I've always respected their knowledge of the game. In New York, you usually get booed or cheered for the right reasons.

There was little cheering that day for the Giants. While Gale ran through New York's vaunted defense, I took care of Tucker, leveling him as often as possible. I did it so often that he was looking for me every time he carried the ball. Whenever I got close, I'd yell at him, "Over here, Tuck!" Then I'd knock him down. Gale had another 100-yard game, his fourth in the last five games, and we won, 35–14.

On to Baltimore with a chance at redemption for our earlier loss at Wrigley. We arrived on Saturday, December 5, with a 7–4 record. The Baltimore fans showed us absolutely no respect. They abused us every chance they had—at the airport, in the hotel, and on Sunday morning when we arrived by bus at Memorial Stadium. Halas, who always rode with the team, brought a friend who was a priest to the game. When the fans saw him get off the bus, one of them sneered, "You're going to *need* a priest today, Papa Bear." I was impressed by the Colt fans. They never failed to fill Memorial Stadium whenever their beloved wizard and sleight-of-hand expert Johnny Unitas was dealing the cards.

In the second quarter, Unitas got knocked out for the rest of the season. We put on a blitz and Doug Atkins and tackle Earl Leggett blew into the backfield. Leggett got there first. While Atkins jumped clear of the turmoil, the two tackles leveled Unitas before he could set up, tearing a ligament in his right knee.

We went on to win, 13–10.

Then came the return match with the 49ers at Wrigley. In the season opener, the team led by John Brodie and John David Crow had dismantled us, especially the rookies. They had scored 52 points in that game, and I took the loss personally. Since that humiliation, we had improved enough to win eight of our last nine games, but now we would have a chance to find out how much better we really were.

It rained heavily in the early morning hours of Sunday, December 12, 1965, and I remember getting up and going out to Mass in the dark with the wind sweeping torrents off Lake

Michigan. And later, after one of Helen's great breakfasts, I drove to my Sunday job at Wrigley Field. On the way, I thought about the 49ers' front line—Bruce Bosley, Walt Rock, Len Rohde, Howard Mudd, and John Thomas—and about John Brodie and John David Crow, the running legend who had made that 50-yard run against me. I thought about how disorganized we had been in that first meeting and how far we had come, now 8–4 on the season after losing our first three games. And I thought how Ditka and the other veterans—Bukich and Morris and the rest of the offense and Atkins and OB and Petitbon on the defense—seemed to have become younger and more energetic as we rookies matured.

It was as though we had breathed some of our youth into what remained of the Monsters of the Midway. It's no use being coy here. There were two primary players in the Bears' resurgence, a two-man shock troop that invigorated a team that had been going downhill. I did it on one side of the ball, raising hell with the officials and disturbing the opponents with every tactic I knew, and Gale did it on offense with the football in his hands.

Gale would take a kickoff or a deep punt and start downfield, eluding the first tackler and the second, and with the crowd noise swelling, he'd cut to the sideline or across the middle and turn on the afterburners. Then we would all be on our feet, ready to kick ass by the time he was tackled or driven out of bounds or had scored. He was instant adrenaline to all of us. Every time Gale touched the ball, you knew in the back of your mind that you might be witnessing something that might never happen again. Gale's running was pure creativity, and I have never seen his like since.

From day one back at training camp, Abe Gibron had me on the kickoff return team. At first he put me at the point, but sometimes when I peeled back I tended to knock my own men down as the wedge—four of us, shoulder to shoulder to protect the ball carrier—turned back on itself to pursue the ball carrier as he sought a sideline lane. Later he put me far-ther back in the wedge. This allowed me to see the field better and make strategic blocks to free up Gale. As I watched the ball spiraling over my head, I would tell my team, "Wait . . . wait . . ." When Gale had gathered the ball in his arms and was five yards behind us, I'd yell, "Go, go, go!"

It was everyone's job to hit at least one man as the wave of defenders converged on Gale. The trick was to time our blocks just as Gale arrived. When it worked—as it so often did—it was beautiful to experience. I don't know how many times I found myself on my ass after a block, watching Gale burn one player after another, leaving them strung behind like so many disabled vehicles.

It had stopped raining by the time I pulled into the park-ing lot. The morning's downpour had been working on me in a negative way. But I loved it when it rained because it slowed down the game. I wasn't sure how well we would play in the quagmire that was waiting on the other side of the green-and-white stands. A knot of die-hard kids was there and I let them follow me in, the guards looking the other way as usual. *What the hell*, I thought. *There will be lots of no-shows in this weather.*

After we Early Birds had each earned our $25 by shag-ging booted balls, we came into the locker room and let every-one know that the field was a mess. Gale just shook his head. He worried about performing in such conditions. He needed a firm field to make his cuts, and there was also the distinct possibility that he could tear a muscle or pull a hamstring. If that happened, our season would be over.

We had an outside shot at a playoff spot. But we had to beat San Francisco and Minnesota first, then hope that Baltimore and Green Bay each lost one. Not a likely scenario, but stranger things had happened at the tail end of an NFL season. We suited up and went to find out just how good we were. In the process, we walked into history.

Gale struck in the first quarter by taking a screen pass from Bukich and running 80 yards through the slop into the end zone. On the next possession, he broke through left tackle and took it in from the twenty-one. With his number 40 obliterated by mud, he scored from 7 yards out, and again on a 50-yard whirling dervish performance. His fifth touchdown was a 1-yard plunge over the right side and his sixth was an 80-yard punt return that will live vividly in the minds of the 46,278 who actually saw it—and the half million or so who claim they were there.

Gale tied the record for most TDs in a game, equaling the feats of fullback Ernie Nevers of the Chicago Cardinals in 1929 and halfback Dub Jones, who did it for the Browns in 1951. Sayers's sixth touchdown was his twenty-first of the season, breaking an NFL record held by Lenny Moore and Jim Brown. In that game, Gale ran for 118 yards, caught two passes for another 80, and picked up 134 returning punts and kickoffs for a total of 332 yards.

The final score was 61–20—the most points ever scored by the Bears in a regular season game. We had exacted our revenge, using a rookie who just weeks before had been described by some writers as a loser and even a coward. With his fragile knees, the greatest halfback I ever saw danced in the mud that day, not caring one bit about himself. To lift yourself above your own concerns and perform at the highest level is greatness.

Halas hailed Gale's feat as "unbelievable" and called it the "greatest performance ever by one man on a football field." Who would argue the point? No one I know ever did. But something other than moisture must have been in the air that day. In Baltimore's fog-bound Memorial Stadium, Paul Hornung had been almost as good, scoring five TDs as the Packers ripped the Colts, 42–27.

With nothing to gain by a win, we finished the season by losing to the Vikings, 24–17, the next week at Wrigley. Gale scored another touchdown, raising his total to 22. Meanwhile, the Packers and Colts ended the season with identical records, 10–3–1, forcing a playoff game to decide who would face the Cleveland Browns in the championship game. The game was a classic, going to the wire. Tied at 10, the two teams played into overtime and the Packers' Don Chandler ended the sudden-death match by kicking a 25-yard field goal that Colt fans still claim went wide of the uprights.

Then in early January, the Packers beat the Browns in the mud at Lambeau Field, 23–12.

Gale Sayers won the Rookie of the Year award hands down. As for my season? Even in my dreams it could not have been better. In those days, no official sack records were kept in the NFL offices in Manhattan. But it didn't matter because I knew I had a great season, and so did everyone else in pro football. Gale and I were the only two rookies to make All-Pro that year, and I went to my first of seven Pro Bowls.

After our first three losses, we had played well—going 9–2 the rest of the way. I had weathered my rookie year, and now I looked forward to the seasons ahead when I could only get better and better. Little did I know there was only one more winning season in my future.

7

*T*he roots of the Bears' future were rudely pulled from the earth by George Halas before the next season even got started. He let one of the best coaching minds in the history of the game escape to the West Coast. How Halas, presumably sound of mind and body, managed such a stroke of supreme arrogance I will never know. We needed George Allen like the South needed Robert E. Lee.

George Allen was everything on the Bears' staff. He was their main scout, defensive coordinator, trade negotiator, head of player personnel, and teacher of the game. If Halas was Papa Bear—and indeed he was—then Allen was our uncle. He was the go-to man when a defensive player needed advice. His knowledge of football and life was huge. But his salary was only $18,000 a year.

So along came the Rams with an offer that Allen couldn't refuse. The story goes that Allen actually solicited the offer from Rams owner Dan Reeves and then asked Halas for permission to talk with Reeves. Halas replied that Allen could indeed talk with Reeves but only to inform him that Allen still had two years remaining on his contract with the Bears.

Reeves then announced publicly that he and Allen had reached an agreement. Papa Bear raged and stormed for weeks. He considered Allen's backdoor communication with the Rams "a betrayal" and Reeves's offer a "flagrant case of tampering with a coach under contract." Meanwhile, NFL commissioner Pete Rozelle stayed clear of the fuss, except to say, "It has been traditional with the NFL and throughout sports that assistant coaches are permitted to take advantage of opportunities for advancement."

Halas then decided that the matter was too big for the league and he brought suit against Allen and the Rams. Early in 1966, in a Chicago courtroom, the contract was ruled to be valid. Having made his point, Halas then withdrew the suit and let his best football mind go West to become the head coach of the Rams.

This was one situation where Papa definitely did *not* know best. Halas should have appreciated Allen for what he was and might have been—the Bears' future savior. Papa was approaching his seventy-first birthday and it was time for him to consider stepping down from a brilliant coaching career that included a record six NFL championships. The bells had to be tolling his head, telling him to let some fresh coaching blood rush into the Bears' system. Instead, he held on for two more seasons, finally handing the reins to Jim Dooley in May 1968.

By then our downward journey into the ultimate embarrassment had gathered too much momentum for any coach to stop. If Halas lost his right arm, he didn't seem to know it. I lost a confidant, a friend, and a teacher, and the city of Chicago lost its pro football future for more than a decade.

As for Allen, he went on to bigger and better things, of course, eventually as the coach of the Redskins driving a bunch of overhauled retreads called the "Over-the-Hill Gang" to the Super Bowl in 1973 when they lost to the Miami Dolphins, 14–7. As to his unpleasant departure from Chicago, Allen never displayed any rancor toward Halas or the Bears' management. If anything, he remained gung-ho for the Bears all through those years afterward. He almost seemed like a fan.

In 1990, I interviewed Allen for CBS Sports. He was coaching at Long Beach State and I thought it would be interesting to show him as excited about his college team as he ever was about the pros. When the cameras weren't running, we talked about the days we had been together, about my rookie season, among other things—and for just a moment it seemed like the only item that was missing was his clipboard.

Later he died on Christmas Eve.

Not long after the Allen–Halas schism came more bad news. Pete Elliott, Bill Taylor, and the entire Illinois football coaching staff had been fired. Elliott had just been named athletic director and Bill Taylor had just been named head coach when some so-called NCAA violations had mysteriously come to light. Rumors circulated about foul play. Someone at Illinois who felt he should have gotten the athletic director's position had concocted a slush fund and reported it to the dean's office.

That someone was Mel Brewer, who was assistant athletic director at the time. When it was decided that Pete Elliott would get the head job, Brewer couldn't accept being passed over and that very day in December 1966, he pulled a folder out of the football file cabinet and presented it to the dean. In the folder was proof that Illinois had violated a couple of Big Ten rules.

The "evidence" showed that the athletic department had paid bills in two local restaurants for Sunday meals served to football players on scholarship. In those days, a scholarship player received all meals except on Sundays, when the cafeteria was closed. Since another Big Ten rule did not allow scholarship players to work during the school year, eating on Sunday could be a problem, since most of them came from working-class families who couldn't afford to send meal money to their kids.

The meal money fund had been in operation for many years. The total outlay during the seven years that Pete and Bill had been there was $17,000. Bill recently told me that when he and Elliott arrived to take over the reins of the football team, they reviewed the rules and expressed their concern about the cafeteria being closed on Sundays, and that it was none other than Mel Brewer who told them about the fund, which had been set up many seasons earlier.

Bill Taylor went on to the Dallas Cowboys and later worked at Levi Strauss and Company in California. Pete Elliott went to Indiana to run a private business for three years before moving onto the University of Miami, where he was athletic director and head coach of the football team for a few seasons. Recently he retired as executive director at the NFL Hall of Fame in Canton, Ohio.

Mel Brewer went into seclusion after he blew the whistle and died several years later.

The effects of that scandal are still being felt by the Illinois football program. The school was well on its way to establishing itself as a major Big Ten power under Elliott and Taylor. But the program is still struggling to attain respectability.

It took me many years to feel comfortable about what happened at my alma mater. In fact, I didn't return to the campus until my number 50 was retired next to Red Grange's jersey.

The Bears were among the most highly regarded teams going into the 1966 season. Bill George had left to join George Allen in L.A., but we drafted Doug Buffone from the University of Louisville to spell the aging Joe Fortunato at left linebacker. We also signed Frank Cornish, a big defensive tackle from Grambling, to help bolster the defensive line. Brian Piccolo was healthy for the first time since joining the Bears, and as the nation's leading collegiate scorer in 1964, he promised to add another dimension to Gale's running attack.

But for all the seeming improvements, our performance did not approach the level of the previous year. We began well enough during the preseason, losing to the Philadelphia Eagles, but then beating Green Bay and the Washington Redskins, who were now coached by Otto Graham, the former star quarterback of the Cleveland Browns. On September 2, we took the field against the St. Louis Cardinals at the annual Armed Forces benefit games at Soldier Field. St. Louis always gave us a good physical match, probably because they used to be our crosstown rivals in Chicago before they relocated in St. Louis in 1960. In fact, the Cardinals had won the last three Armed Forces games, trouncing us, 25–3, in 1965. The Cardinals were considered contenders in the NFL's Eastern Division, but they had been having their troubles during exhibition play. They had already given up a total of 65 points in losses to Baltimore and Los Angeles.

Our offense started out slowly. Roger Leclerc booted three field goals in the first half, but it wasn't until the third period that quarterback Rudy Bukich finally got the attack going, driving 80 yards and scoring on a touchdown pass to end Jimmy Jones. With twelve minutes remaining, I dropped back into the secondary to pick off a Charley Johnson pass meant for Jackie Smith to eliminate the Cardinals threat. We eked out a win, 22–20.

The next week we opened our season at Tiger Stadium against a Detroit team that we heard was riddled by dissension and disorganization. I remember how confident we felt before that game. We were almost cocky coming off a 3–1 preseason. Leclerc put us on the board with a field goal in the first quarter, but that was it for our offense. Meanwhile, the Lions' fullback Tom Nowatzke broke through for a TD, and Pat Studstill caught a Milt Plum pass for another to bring the score to 14–3. That's all the Lions would need that day. After the game, Ditka said what was on all our minds: "Lack of offense, that's what killed us. We haven't put a good touchdown over the line in a long time. It finally caught up with us today."

The following week we flew to Los Angeles to play the Rams. The Rams had ended the 1965 season in the toilet, but now they were coached by George Allen, who knew our defensive schemes almost as well as we did—maybe better. Although we led at halftime, 17–14, the Rams marched 65 yards to a touchdown from the second half kickoff, and they never looked back. O'Bradovich and I each recovered a fumble from the small but very speedy Dick Bass, but both times our offense gave the ball right back to the Rams. We lost, 31–17, and after the game Halas announced, "We are off to another one of our patented slow starts."

Against the Minnesota Vikings on October 2, we rallied from 10 points down in the fourth quarter. Rudy Bukich passed 19 yards to Ditka for a TD, and Leclerc kicked two field goals to put us ahead, 13–10. Then with twenty seconds left, Dick Evey lined up in the wrong place on the field but was still able to block a Minnesota field goal attempt that would have tied the game.

Defensive coach Jim Dooley had given me a little freedom to concentrate on the ball carrier in rushing situations, and we remained cautious on our pass defense against Fran Tarkenton's scrambles. I managed to get into the backfield and harass Fran much of the time. It was our first victory of the season, but it really didn't feel that way. In the locker room, we cut the ball into eleven pieces and each defender took one piece. We were 1–2 and already playing catch-up to the 4–0 Packers and the 3–1 Rams. But we were at least moving in the right direction.

On October 9, we came home to Wrigley for the first time that year and played tough against the great Johnny Unitas and the Baltimore Colts. We won, 27–17. I set the tone for the game on the first play by hitting Colt fullback Tony Lorick so hard that after the game he complained over the extreme viciousness of my tackle. Unitas could only put together one touchdown pass to John Mackey. I remember after the game Atkins and Evey recalled the hits they gave to Unitas. "I could see his eyes glaze over," Atkins said. Our slow start was officially over, and we were in third place in the Western Division. In seven days, we would face the first-place Green Bay Packers, who had just lost a squeaker to the 0–2 San Francisco 49ers. Things were beginning to look up.

But the Packers charged back from the previous week's upset, shutting us down, 17–0. They held Gale to 29 yards and our entire offense to 60 more. The Packers could be devastating in those years. They were all good players, but it was their execution that made them great. Most of the time we knew exactly what play they were going to run. But it didn't matter because they always executed their plays with precision. Lombardi was a great coach because he was able to get his players to perform selflessly—which in the case of Green Bay was easier said than done. Everybody knew he was a great motivator. He could handle talents like Hornung, Nitschke, and Taylor, and he could inspire excellence from everyone. Some players you can be on top of, some you can't, and Lombardi knew the difference. In that game, Green Bay intercepted three Chicago passes and never let us get beyond their twenty-six yard line until the fourth quarter when quarterback Bart Starr fumbled and I recovered on the Packers' ten. At the time they were ahead by only 10 points, so we still had a chance to make it close. But Jon Arnett fumbled the ball and the Packers recovered, effectively ending the threat.

Our defense played well that day, allowing Green Bay only one sustained drive. On one play, one of our guys broke through and chased Starr to the sideline. We thought we had him boxed in, but he made a desperation pass to Jim Taylor and came up with a 12-yard gain. That hurt. At times Green Bay just seemed lucky. But you make your own luck in football. Without any offense, our efforts seemed futile. In 95 games against Green Bay, this was the eleventh time they had held the Bears scoreless. The loss pushed us down to fifth place.

The next week we redeemed our earlier loss to the Rams by beating them by a touchdown, 17–10, at Wrigley. The game was almost all Gale. He gained 241 yards, returning two kickoffs for 129 yards, 87 yards on rushing, and 25 yards on passing. When the Rams had an opportunity to take the lead in the final minutes, we came alive and preserved the victory. I had to leave the game with a pulled muscle, but Jim Purnell came in and twice read the pass correctly, knocking the receivers for losses.

The next Sunday we traveled to St. Louis to take on the Cardinals at their plush new Busch Memorial Stadium before the *Monday Night Football* audience on ABC. Doug Atkins and I didn't play in the Halloween game due to leg injuries we sustained against L.A., but our defense played well without us. Bukich threw two interceptions that led to touchdowns, and a penalty prevented us from scoring a critical tie-break-ing TD. We went down, 24–17. It was our fourth loss, most likely eliminating us from contention in the Western Division. It was the only time an injury kept me out of a game in my first eight years with the Bears.

In the next two games, against Detroit and San Francisco, we settled for ties. This was before the sudden-death rule had been instituted in nonplayoff games. In the first game against Detroit, Roger Leclerc missed a 25-yard field goal attempt in the last sixteen seconds to give Detroit a 10–10 tie. The next week against San Francisco, Joe Fortunato was ejected from the game, resulting in a 15-yard penalty and a game-tying field goal for the 49ers. Joe was ejected for retaliating after San Francisco end Monty Stickles whacked him on the back of the neck following a fourth-down play. Everyone in the league knew that Stickles was a cheap-shot artist. He'd do something to you and then laugh if he wasn't caught. A very tough guy, Joe was always in control on the field. Stickles must've hit him hard for Joe to react the way he did. Of course, since the refs were looking the other way when the real infraction occurred, Joe was booted and Stickles re-mained in the game.

Earlier in the quarter, we were down, 17–10, when Bukich threw two touchdown passes, one to Gale Sayers and one to Jimmy Jones. Minutes later, OB scooped up a Brodie fumble that had been forced by Dick Evey and ran into the end zone. A miss on the extra point, and the score was sud-denly 30–17.

Then the 49ers fought back, scoring a quick TD and a field goal, narrowing the edge to 30–27. With thirty seconds remaining, the 49ers tied the game, 30–30, with a little help from Stickles.

These games were very frustrating for me. We should've

won them hands down, but instead they put us behind both San Francisco and Los Angeles in the standings. It seemed as though we always found a way to beat ourselves.

On November 20, we visited Green Bay to take on the Packers for the second time. Although we lost, 13–6, we showed them once again that we had one of the best defensive lines in the league. We held Jim Taylor to 49 yards and the entire Packer offense to 69 yards on the ground. When Bart Starr went out on the second play of the game with a pulled hamstring, Zeke Bratkowski came in and after a slow start didn't miss a beat. He connected on 14 passes for 187 yards. In the fourth quarter, when the score was still 7–0, we closed the gap to a point, but Roger Leclerc's extra-point kick was blocked. Green Bay put up another 6 for insurance.

The Atlanta Falcons were the new kids on the block, and their 1–9 record proved it. It almost seemed easy, especially after the Packers. Our offense racked up 466 yards on the way to a 23–6 trouncing in a downpour that kept most fans away from Wrigley. We were able to prevent the Falcons from entering Bear territory until midway through the last period. But even when they were on the Bear six yard line, the Falcons couldn't bring it home. It was a good game for morale. I'll be the first one to admit it: It's fun to so completely dominate a game. Through the rain and the mud, we gave our fans a good show that day.

Then it was off to Baltimore to take on the Colts and the damaged Johnny Unitas. Baltimore needed to win in order to salvage their title chance, and we were going to try to keep them from it. And we had them, 16–14, until the last five minutes of the game when Unitas marched his troops up the field in five plays and capped the drive with a touchdown pass with only thirty-nine seconds remaining on the clock.

In our last game of the season, the Minnesota Vikings

saw Gale Sayers gain 197 yards to capture the National Football League rushing title with a total of 1,231 yards for the season. Gale also set a new NFL record with 2,440 combined yards gained for the season.

———

Looking back on the 1966 season, I can't help but wonder what went wrong, why we didn't do better than we did. It's true that quarterback Rudy Bukich had lost his prime target, Johnny Morris. The fleet receiver who led the Bears in receptions in 1964 and 1965 was hurt early in the season and spent most of the time on the bench. But does the loss of one receiver adequately explain the drop in Bukich's completion percentage from 56 percent to under 50 percent? Our total points scored dropped from a Bears' single season record of 409 to 234. We finished the season in fifth place with a 5–7–2 record.

To explain our poor season, maybe we should look at a thing called chemistry. Take Bill George, for example. Although he hadn't played in 1965, his presence mattered in the locker room, on the sidelines, in the meetings, and in the practices. Bill was a force and his winning personality and his desire were like a drug for some of the players—especially those on defense. I learned a lot from him, but he also was such a good motivator, even when he wasn't playing. Bill would never again put on a Bears' uniform, but his reputation as the man who changed the focus of his defense from a middle guard to a true standup linebacker would live on in the history of professional football.

Halas was getting older. By now he was no longer an important part of practices, preferring to work through his assistants and ride around the field in his golf cart. And George Allen—who can adequately measure his contributions? Cer-

tainly his loss was felt in a major way by the defense, but
what did Allen's enthusiasm and work ethic bring to the offensive players and the coaches, maybe even including the Old
Man?

Up in Green Bay, major changes were also in the air. No
one was sure just how many games were left in the legs of
Hornung, thirty-six, and Taylor, thirty-five, and to bank
against the future, two running backs were added to Lombardi's roster. Donny Anderson out of Texas Tech and my old
college teammate Jim Grabowski were financial beneficiaries
of the two-league scramble for college talent. The cost for
both was estimated at $1 million. This kind of high-stakes
poker was soon brought under control during the off-season
by the owners when they announced that the AFL and NFL
would officially merge for the 1970 season and that a single
draft would be instituted immediately.

The Packers won all but two games in 1966. After beating the Dallas Cowboys for the NFL championship, 34–27,
they went on to win the first Super Bowl—the game was not
officially named the Super Bowl until 1969—by running over
the Kansas City Chiefs, 35–10.

Gale and I were named to the All-Pro team for the second
time.

The Falcons were followed by the New Orleans Saints in
1967, raising the total of NFL teams to sixteen. Pete Rozelle
and the owners decided to reconfigure the two conferences
into four four-team divisions called the Central, Coastal, Capitol, and Century divisions. We landed in the Central Division
of the Western Conference with Minnesota, Detroit, and
Green Bay. We would compete for the conference title with
the Coastal Conference: Los Angeles, Baltimore, San Francisco, and Atlanta.

If our roster changes between my rookie year and 1966 had been few, such was not the case in 1967. Doug Atkins, now thirty-seven, was traded to the Saints for offensive guard Don Croftcheck. Quarterback Bill Wade, who had sat for most of the past two seasons, retired at thirty-six. Rudy Bukich, also thirty-six, stayed on as a backup to our new maestro, Jack Concannon, who came to us from Philadelphia in a trade for Mike Ditka.

We started out the 1967 season on shaky ground. Our second exhibition game was in Kansas City against the Chiefs, who had been humiliated by the Packers in Super Bowl I. The Chiefs wanted to prove that the American Football League was for real and they were better than they showed against the Packers the previous January. They hit us with everything they had. We surrendered a total of 66 points. But Halas remained upbeat, telling reporters after the game that we would learn from our mistakes.

In our next exhibition game, we once again met the St. Louis Cardinals in the annual Armed Forces benefit game at Soldier Field. Backup quarterback Larry Rakestraw would be given his first start. Going into this game, Brian Piccolo was beginning to get his sea legs and had already racked up more yards in preseason play than Gale Sayers. Every team we faced knew what Gale was capable of doing, and they always sent a few guys to mark him.

The night before the game, Halas put us up in a local hotel because a lot of guys still had to find apartments for the season. That always seemed to build our camaraderie and the next day we showed that we were contenders. Devastated by the Chiefs the week before, we trounced the Cards, 42–14. Rakestraw had a great game, scoring two touchdowns himself, but more importantly, he brought drive and purpose to a Bears' offense that had been lacking in leadership. With help from Andy Livingston, Gale Sayers, and Brian Piccolo, who made a great catch in the end zone, Rakestraw was able to chalk up 35 points in the first half. The defense also came alive, holding down young Jim Hart's impressive passing game. Richie Petitbon, Bennie McRae, and Joe Fortunato made interceptions, while O'Bradovich and I helped shut down the Cards' running game. Through our constant stunting and shifting tactics, we were able to hold them to a total of 3 yards in the first half.

Our next preseason game would be against the Philadelphia Eagles, but before that game we lost one of our greatest linebackers, a true mentor to everyone on the team. Hobbled by chronic knee problems, Joe Fortunato was placed on injured reserve. Joe was a thirteen-year veteran, and his loss meant the signal calling for the defense would fall on my shoulders. Signal calling in those days was much different than what NFL players do today. A week before the game, we would start preparing by watching game films of our upcoming opponent, trying to figure out their tendencies in certain situations. What might a team do on second and short yardage or on third and long? From these films we would determine the different ways to defend against the offense. I would try to pick up a few clues or tendencies by watching how the different players broke the huddle and came to the line, then I would call the play I thought they were about to run. These days the coaches will determine an opponent's tendencies and then relay the calls out to the players for them to execute. It probably cuts down on mistakes, but it makes defense much less of a mind game.

At one film session later on in my career, we were watching footage from the previous game, trying to pick up some clues as to how a particular offense blocked for their quarterback. On the screen, O'Bradovich is trying to get to the ball carrier, but he has to go through about five guys to get there. The first guy, a tackle, hits him, but OB is able to spin away. Then the tight end tries to cut-block him. OB stumbles but stays on his feet. Several more blocks are thrown until the fullback hits OB so hard that his helmet turns sideways on his head and he can barely see. But OB still doesn't stop. He's on his knees with bodies all around him and he's getting closer to the ball carrier. Then I slide past the destruction and make the tackle, Coach Gibron says, "Good job, Butkus. Let's see that again. Watch yourself, OB." We had a good chuckle over the fact that Gibron had congratulated me on the tackle while basically OB did all the heavy lifting.

The Eagles would be an interesting match for us because Halas had traded Mike Ditka for Jack Concannon in an attempt to bring a fresh arm to the quarterback position. We all knew Ditka had played well with the Eagles so far, having caught 9 of Norm Snead's 42 completions. They were 4–1 in preseason play, and Snead had thrown for 652 yards and eight touchdowns in three games.

Jack Concannon started the game, but he couldn't put any points on the board and neither could Rudy Bukich. We were able to hold the Eagles' offense scoreless for the entire game, and in the second half Larry Rakestraw tossed two touchdown passes, one to Dick Gordon and one to Gale Sayers, to bring home the victory, 14–0. I remember one play when Ditka was coming across the middle, looking for the quick pass from Snead. If anyone knew our defense, it was Mike. In the middle of his run, I yelled, "Hey, Mike, look out!" Our impending collision must've flashed through his mind because he stopped cold, and Snead's pass flew over his head. The game ended our preseason on a positive note.

Three days before our match against Pittsburgh, Larry Rakestraw was again given the starting quarterback position.

During the early part of the season, we practiced on the golf course at the Tam O'Shanter Country Club, where it was rumored that gangsters like Al Capone brought their molls in the 1920s and 1930s.

Although we started out well enough in our first game of the 1967 season, going up 13–3 on Gale's 103-yard kickoff return and Rosey Taylor's interception leading to a touchdown, the Pittsburgh Steelers were able to stall our offense by holding Gale to only 2 yards from scrimmage. On defense we just played badly, allowing a young Pittsburgh offense five touchdowns. Larry Rakestraw was equally ineffective, completing on 7 of 13 passes, and only being able to put together one sustained drive the entire game. It was an opening game that we would just as soon forget, which was easy because the following week we were to face the world champion Green Bay Packers.

This would be Green Bay's first game of the season, but by the end of regulation, they hardly resembled the Packers from the year before. After going scoreless in the first quarter, fullback Jim Grabowski punched into the end zone, and Don Chandler's 20-yard field goal put them up 10–0. I always enjoyed seeing Jim when he was with Green Bay. He had gone to Taft High in Chicago, a CVS rival, before we played together at the University of Illinois. When we got on the field, it was a different story. A former track star at Illinois, Jim was gone if he was able to get by you.

We came back when Mac Percival, another teacher-turned-football-player, kicked a field goal and Gale's 13-yard sweep in the fourth quarter gave us the tie. The Packers turned the ball over eight times—five interceptions and three fumbles. Richie Petitbon got three in the air and I picked up two fumbles. Frank Cornish, Doug Buffone, Bennie McRae, and Rosey Taylor all played great. We reversed our dismal performance of the week before in Pittsburgh. We made the plays and were able to get good field position. In the final two minutes of the game, Dick Evey and Ed O'Bradovich appeared to have cornered Bart Starr for a loss what would've eliminated a field goal attempt, but Starr somehow escaped and gained 4 yards on the play. Now within kicking distance, Chandler came in and gave the Packers the 13–10 win. We lost again and our record dropped to 0–2, but we felt good about how we had played and were looking forward to the Vikings.

When two winless teams get together, it's not always a pretty sight. On October 1, we played the Minnesota Vikings, and although we brought home our first victory of the season, it was nothing to be proud of. Both the offense and defense produced touchdowns against the Vikings, but it was during one set of downs that the Bears' offense moved the ball 46 yards to the Vikings nine yard line, only to *retreat* 44 yards due to successive penalties of clipping, holding, offsides, and a run by Jack Concannon that lost 3 yards. By the end of the series, it was fourth down and 63 yards. Everyone on the defense made sure to thank the offense for the wonderful field position we got after the punt.

The next week took on the 3–0 Baltimore Colts at Wrigley. It was our home opener, and we wanted to win for the hometown fans and even our record. As a team, we played well—in fact, we outgained the Colts on the ground and in the air—but as often happens against good football teams, our fate hinged on three plays. In the first half, we held the score to 3–3. But in the second half, Richie Petitbon, who had been covering John Mackey well all game, was called for holding on the same play that Rosey Taylor intercepted a Unitas pass, returning it 33 yards to the Colts' eleven. The play was called back and Unitas took his team into the end zone.

Rudy Bukich then threw an interception to Rick Volk, who sprinted in for the touchdown. A little later, Bukich fumbled and the Colts' defensive unit produced another score. We lost, 24–3, and now, despite playing well against Green Bay and the Colts, we were 1–3. Our 1967 season was not looking up.

On October 15, the Detroit Lions—the only team to have dented Green Bay's armor with a tie—came to a wet and rainy Wrigley Field to try to secure their second-place standing in the division. It was the first game in which our offense would escape without making a lot of costly mistakes. Staying on the ground with Gale Sayers, Ronnie Bull, Ralph Kurek, and Brian Piccolo, our rushing game ate up the yards. The defense also played well, preventing the elusive Mel Farr and the Lions from getting into the end zone. Bennie McRae made two interceptions, one of which he returned for the second touchdown of the game. The 14–3 win gave us second place and that same week last-place Minnesota upset the decaying Packers, which meant we were all of a sudden very much in control of our own destiny.

The next week we traveled to Cleveland to take on the Browns, but right before the pregame warmup, our hopes were dashed when Dr. Fox announced that Gale would not be playing due to a mysterious leg injury. Without Gale's running to worry about, all that stood in Cleveland's way was our defense, and I suspected that we wouldn't be able to contain the Browns' offense for the entire game, especially if we were on the field all day. As it turned out, all of Cleveland's 24 points came in the last seventeen minutes. Our offense only managed to put together one threat, advancing to the Cleveland seven yard line. But Concannon fumbled and the Browns recovered. That was it for the offense. We didn't have a chance without Gale. The loss pushed us back down into third place, behind Detroit, who demolished San Francisco that week.

Gale was ready to go the next week against the Rams in Wrigley. We had beaten Los Angeles seven straight at home, and we figured the 3–1 Rams would follow the same pattern. It didn't work out that way. The Rams outscored us 14–7 in the first half and 14–10 in the second. The game was rough and wet, and George Allen's team committed a couple of mistakes that we should've capitalized on. On one, Mac Percival's kickoff was high enough to cause receiver Wendell Tucker to fumble. Charley Brown recovered on the seven yard line, but Concannon and Company failed to cash in. On the first play, Gale fumbled and the Rams recovered. The Rams had a good offensive line, and we all had a difficult time with our coverages. Although Doug never got as much recognition as me, he was a terrific player. He fit the role of what a Bear linebacker should be: never a guy to lie down on the job and tougher than nails.

Los Angeles mostly concentrated on shutting down Gale and the Rams did a good job of it. He gained only 13 yards in 13 attempts. As a result, Concannon became our leading ground-gainer with 77 yards—not bad for a quarterback. He threw plenty of passes but only completed 8. At one point in the first quarter, our offense moved down to the ten yard line, but through a series of mishaps, they were pushed back to the Bears' 49 and the count was third and 51. Thanks again, offense!

On November 5, we found ourselves at Tiger Stadium, home of the Detroit Lions. Back in October, we had beaten the Lions, 14–3, at Wrigley, but in the intervening weeks they had won one game and we had lost two. We needed to prove that our first win against them wasn't a fluke.

The stars of the show were Gale on offense and everyone on defense. Gale terrorized the Lions, first running 63 yards to set up a Concannon 1-yard sneak, then going 97 yards on a kickoff return. Playing both offense and defense to compensate for the injured Bob Wetoska and Dick Evey, Ed O'Bradovich forced the Lions into a fumble, which Doug Buffone picked up and carried in for another score. Frank Cornish and Rosey Taylor played an extraordinary game, shutting the Lions down with our nickel defense. In those early years, the Bears' defense was a real close-knit group. We socialized together and we brought that same closeness to the field because we knew it was up to us to win games.

The New York Giants paid us a visit at Wrigley the next week and we sent them packing, 34–7. The Giants were known as one of the most efficient scoring machines in the league, and for a brief flash in the first quarter they lived up to that reputation, going 65 yards in ten plays for a 7–0 lead. In the second quarter, Jack Concannon was knocked out of the game by the Giants' defensive ends, and Larry Rakestraw came in at quarterback. Then we got down to the business at hand, and on five plays handed the offense great position to produce real numbers. Frank Cornish intercepted Tarkenton twice and recovered a fumble, keeping the Giants deep in their own territory. The key to shutting down Tarkenton was not going straight after him in the middle but going to the outside to contain the scramble. It was the Giants' poorest offensive showing of the season.

With our momentum up, we won again the next week, this time against the St. Louis Cardinals, knocking them out of first place in the Century Division. We held the Cards to 3 points, while Jack Concannon ran 6 yards for a touchdown in the first quarter and threw three terrific passes to put the game away in the second quarter. In three games, we had scored 91 points while holding our opponents to 23—and two of those teams had been highly ranked. Were the new Bears for real? The answer to that question would follow our game against the 7–2 Packers the next week. The offense was finally hitting on all cylinders and the defense was working better than ever. With only four games to go in the season, this would be our last chance to get close enough to challenge the Packers. It had all come down to one game, and we were ready.

The game was thrilling, but it all came down to two mistakes. Their first touchdown came after Jack Concannon hit Packer linebacker Dave Robinson with a perfect pass. The interception gave them perfect field position at the Bears' nineteen and they scored a few plays later. Gale provided the day's highlight when he wove his way through the Packers' line to go 44 yards for our only touchdown of the day. Later in the game, Gale fumbled a punt after we had pushed the Packers back to their five yard line. They recovered and Don Chandler kicked the field goal. We lost, 17–13.

That was it. With three games remaining on the schedule, the Packers had cinched the Central Division's only playoff berth, and we were out of the running. We went on to beat the 49ers and Falcons, but tied the Minnesota Vikings for a final record of 7–6–1.

Jack Concannon was not the Bears' savior in 1967. For one thing, his completion percentage was—like Bukich's the year before—below 50 percent. I suppose part of the reason for Jack's disappointing performance was due to the fact that he didn't have a healthy Gale Sayers in there to draw the attention of opposing defenses. Gale had injured an ankle early in the season and never fully recovered, dropping from the league's top rusher the year before to third place.

But for all our problems in the first half of the season, winning only two of our first seven games, we played well the rest of the way, losing only once, 17–13, to the Packers. We finished in second place in the Central Division, while the

Packers went on to win the NFL championship against the Dallas Cowboys. In one of the most famous plays in NFL history, Jerry Kramer blew Jethro Pugh out of Bart Starr's way for the winning score as the clock in Lambeau Field ticked down to zero. The Packers went on to defeat the AFL champs, a tough Oakland Raiders team, 33–14, for their second straight Super Bowl win.

For me, 1967 was another good year. My right knee held up reasonably well and I was reading the offenses accurately and moving with confidence on every play. Two years in the league without serious injury had given me time on the job to refine what Bill George had taught me. From here on, I could only get better. But would the Bears get better? I hoped so. I always hoped so.

But there would soon be reason to think otherwise.

CHAPTER

8

*E*arly in 1968, I watched two generals give up their field commands. Vince Lombardi announced his retirement as coach of the Green Bay Packers right after Super Bowl II, and George Halas announced that he was stepping down as head coach of the Bears in May. His arthritic hip had deteriorated to a point where he could no longer coach from the sidelines. "I realized this when I started rushing after a referee who was pacing off a penalty and it suddenly dawned on me that I wasn't gaining on him."

Although the Old Man's retirement came as no surprise, I felt it deep in my heart. Besides being one of the founders of the NFL and the creator of the Bears, his was a name that had been a fixture in the Chicago papers since before my high school days. Playing under him was a dream come true. Sure, he scolded, bullied, punished, and cajoled us. But he also taught us. He was very funny, always joking around with his players, but he was from an era in the NFL that produced names like Red Grange, Curly Lambeau, Bronko Nagurski, and Sammy Baugh. He was loud, profane, tougher than you would ever believe, and there were times when we all hated him. He had coached the Bears for forty years; won eight divisional titles, six championships, and 324 games, with 31 ties.

Without Halas and Lombardi on the sidelines, the greatest rivalry in NFL history would never be quite the same. Less than twenty-four hours after announcing his retirement as head coach, Halas held an elaborate press conference and named assistant coach Jim Dooley as his replacement. No one was surprised by his decision. The hint had come in February when Dooley was named coach of the offense, but some observers felt Halas would wait a year or two before handing the team over to him.

On the surface, it seemed as though Dooley was the right guy for the job. He was bright, young at thirty-eight, and hardworking. He impressed Halas with his desire to please, but his deep knowledge of football and his talent for innovation put him above the rest. I believe it was that first "quality"—his loyalty to the boss—that convinced the Old Man to give him the job.

Actually, I read someplace where former quarterback Bill Wade may have been offered the job first. There was only one problem: He didn't know it at the time. At a coaches' meeting in February, Halas said that he was purchasing a new overcoat and wondered who he should give his old one to. Abe Gibron suggested that Wade get the coat. So the Old Man put his long black coat—the one he wore on the sidelines—on Bill's shoulders. Then he told Wade to call him on May 1 and said that there might be a nice surprise waiting for him if he decided to come back to the Bears.

Wade called Halas on the appointed date and told him he wasn't coming back to the Bears. The Old Man seemed disappointed, repeating that if he did return there might be a nice surprise. Wade did not change his mind. A couple of years later, a friend explained to Wade that it was an old custom among his people that a businessman give his coat to the individual he'd chosen to take his place.

Dooley looked down a difficult road. Not only would he have to coach under the unsparing eye of Halas, he would have to do it with men who owed their livelihoods to someone else, even though Halas said he would give Dooley total control. He retained every staff member: Abe Gibron, Ed Cody, Luke Johnson, Chuck Cherundolo, Babe Dimancheff, Phil Handler, Sid Luckman, and Joe Fortunato as coach of the defense. A few of these men had been Dooley's rivals for the top job after it had become apparent that the Old Man was thinking of stepping down.

"There has been talk in the past that the coaches were jealous of each other, and that certain coaches would try to make themselves look good to Mr. Halas," said Dooley. "I've probably done that a little myself. Everybody wants their boss to feel they've done something well."

In an attempt to end the dissension that had developed over the previous couple of years, Dooley created two coaching councils: one for offense and the other for defense. "From now on," he said. "When we do something well, it is the group that has done it; and if we should lose, then it's the group that has to take the blame."

There would be more blame to share than credit.

Since the "miracle draft" of 1965 that brought Gale and me to the Bears, the choices had been disappointing. Without George Allen to evaluate the talent, the Bears turned up a few fair players but no exceptional ones. In 1966, defensive back Charley Brown and tackle Bob Pickens never really panned out, and the next year defensive end Loyd Phillips, end Bob Jones, and defensive back Gary Lyle didn't live up to expectations. Big Mike Hull was the number-one choice in 1968. He couldn't make the grade as a runner or a tight end. In addition to new talent not shining, some of the old stars were dimming. Flanker Johnny Morris hanged it up after the 1967 season, leaving an already ragtag receiving corps in terrible shape.

If there weren't enough capable hands to catch the ball, we had plenty of quarterbacks who wanted to throw it. In fact, there were four: Jack Concannon led the group in the early going; then there was the aging Rudy Bukich, who at thirty-seven could still get it done; he was followed by journeyman Larry Rakestraw, who in turn was followed by the highly touted rookie Virgil Carter. Carter had been drafted out of Brigham Young and was ready to come off the taxi squad on a moment's notice. This was like having four leading men signed up for the same part in a movie.

The Old Man was still a presence during our preseason sessions, although he stayed out of the way and let the coaches do their jobs. But we were beginning to notice little things about Dooley, things we had never seen before. For one thing, he treated the players differently. OB, for example, could never do anything right around Dooley. If Ed was a pound overweight, Dooley would fine him.

I have asked Ed why he thinks Dooley didn't like him. Ed doesn't really know, but he makes two guesses. One, that Dooley, like most coaches, doesn't usually appreciate a player questioning his decisions. Ed would do that occasionally, but it was always for the good of the team. Ed just wanted to win. The other possibility for Dooley's apparent dislike for Ed goes back to the last year Dooley played and Ed had joined the Bears after his stint in the Canadian Football League. The Bears' defense was awesome then, and whenever they would stop the opposing team, Ed would come off the field and say to the offense, of which Dooley was a ranking member, "Okay, fellas, hold 'em now, and we'll get another score for you."

Meanwhile, 300-pound lineman Frank Cornish could never do anything wrong. One day during rope drill—that's where the players high-kick it through a grid of ropes—Frank was skipping whole sections, and Dooley didn't seem to notice. Seeing this favoritism, I decided to test Dooley's even-handedness by enlisting a number of players to run through the drill the same lame way as Cornish had. To a man we were criticized by our coach and made to do it again.

Despite these limitations, we respected Dooley and we won all but one of our exhibition games. The most convincing victory was against Washington, 45–13, the team we would face in our season opener. Our performance led Dooley to believe that we were in better shape than was previously thought. This ebullience made him do things that seemed a little strange to me. One occurred during the week before our opening game against Washington when Dooley and the staff held a barbecue for the players and their families at the Tam O'Shanter Country Club in the suburb of Niles, Illinois.

Everything was going along fine when an armored car pulled into the club and parked near us. Two guards got out, opened the back door, and withdrew a large canvas sack. Dooley gave the nod and they emptied the sack: 25,000 freshly minted one-dollar bills. With all of us standing around staring at this pile of paper, Dooley said, "Take a good look, gentlemen. That's what each of you will win if we go all the way this year."

Dooley had two distinct advantages in the coaching department. One was his age. At thirty-eight, he could communicate with some of the players more effectively than the seventy-one-year-old Halas ever could. The other advantage was that he didn't negotiate the players' salaries as Halas had done for forty-eight years in his role as the owner of the team.

Somehow, in all the preseason publicity generated by a new coach and a successful preseason, the fact that quarterback Sonny Jurgensen had not played in our preseason Redskins game seemed not to matter. Dooley was dying to get another shot at Washington, and he told us that we had a great opportunity to show the league what our pass defense could do. In 1967, Dooley had developed a new defense in passing situations, which called for a fifth back to come in for one of the linebackers. It had sort of worked in one game.

"That Jurgensen will probably throw fifty passes against us," he told the reporters with wide-eyed enthusiasm. "Think of it! Why, there's a heck of a chance to snag a few of those fifty. The more they throw, the happier our defense should be. It's a marvelous opportunity for interceptions or for getting to the passer."

Despite Dooley's attempts to fuel our drive with a display of 25,000 one-dollar bills and this latest bit of bravado in the newspapers, it was all for nothing because it was Sonny who was on the money that day. It seemed as if he hit his target every time he threw the ball, and we could do nothing to stop him. The final insult was a 99-yard touchdown pass to Gerry Allen in the fourth quarter. We lost the opener, 38–28. Something had gone wrong with our defense, because while the offense had not gone to pieces as it usually did in those years, our pass coverage was horrendous.

The Bears hadn't won an opening game since 1963, and since I came on board we had always played our first few games on the road. Wrigley was seen as our twelfth player, but in 1968 we embarrassed ourselves in our own home. True to form, we started the season without a win.

The following week we were humiliated by the Lions, 42–0. Four of the six touchdowns were set up by interceptions and a fifth was the result of one of the Bears' three fumbles. But while the offense had reverted to their usual play, the defense fared little better. The Lions' quarterbacks, Bill Munson and Greg Landry, racked up a total of 468 yards. Since we had beaten this team twice the year before, it was our sorriest exhibition.

Jack Concannon was just not doing the job at quarterback, and with three more arms waiting in the wings, Dooley was confronted with his first major decision of the year. Should he bench the man who was supposed to be the leader of our so-called "total offense" and give the ball back to Rudy Bukich or should he hang in with Concannon in the hope that he would start performing at the expected level?

Dooley decided to cling to the status quo. The next week against Minnesota the decision was made for him when Concannon broke his collarbone and Bukich separated his shoulder. The 2–0 Vikings were the most improved team in the league, and some thought they were a developing power in the NFL. Joe Kapp and his offense had already humbled two teams with great linebackers: the Falcons with Tommy Nobis and the Packers with Ray Nitschke. Now they were looking forward to taking on the 0–2 Bears and Dick Butkus. But if statistics tell the whole story, the Bears' defense was clearly the best of their three opponents. We held the Vikings to 158 yards all day, and we won our first of the season, 27–17.

"The game was a matter of survival," said Dooley to the press. "We had to win in order to stay in the race." But it was a costly win, since we lost both Concannon and Bukich.

Larry Rakestraw was given the ball for the next two games and the results were not good. We lost the first to the Colts and the second to the Lions. I hardly played in the first game, pulling myself out after the first series with a strained left knee. All week it had been bothering me, but the coaches didn't want to cut me from the roster against the Colts. After

the game, newspaper stories criticized the Bears' management for not reporting my injury earlier in the week. The
wounded Johnny Unitas sat out of this game, but it hardly
seemed to matter. His replacement, Earl Morrall, threw four
touchdown passes, three of which came in the second quarter. The next week Detroit came to Wrigley in what we figured was payback time. The week before, the Lions had fallen
to the Vikings, the only team we had beaten that season, so
we felt confident on our home turf. Well, the defeats weren't
over yet, as Mel Farr, the 1967 Rookie of the Year, totaled 211
yards to lead the Lions to a 28–10 victory. We had a hard time
stopping Farr, but I could see we were starting to. Twice we
gave the ball to the offense in Detroit territory, but after the
first period Larry Rakestraw couldn't seem to put it into the
end zone. With seven minutes left, Virgil Carter came in and
did some fancy scrambling but couldn't put together a sustained drive. Now we were 1–4 for the season, last place in
the division. It was our worst start in years.

On October 20, we rolled into Philadelphia to play the
0–5 Eagles. It was an error-filled day, but we came away with
a triumph, 29–16, thanks to the sometimes erratic play of
Virgil Carter, who threw a single touchdown, and the steady
toe of Mac Percival, who connected on five field goals, to tie
an all-time Bears' record most field goals in a game. Our defense was finally clicking. Doug Buffone picked up a fumble
and made an interception to set up two field goals, and we
held the Eagles in check for the entire second half. The next
week we returned to Wrigley to take on the Vikings, who had
been slipping in the standings ever since we met them a few
weeks before. Joe Kapp, their quarterback, ruled with a
tough-guy will. Even if his passes were wobbly, you still
couldn't rattle him.

But Kapp had one flaw. He told me the snap count on

every play. He would crouch in the huddle, his back to his own goal posts, and I could see his lips moving through his teammates' legs. This juicy bit of reconnaissance gave me a decided edge, allowing me to break a split second sooner.

Minnesota center Mick Tingelhoff would watch me break right on the snap. After the play was over, he would shake his head. I even started talking to him as he approached the line.

"Hey, Mick. What's the count again—on *two* right?"

Mick would just look at me and shake his head in amazement. Often it meant the difference between failure and success. I made sure to pass this information on to my teammates when I left the game in the third quarter because of bruised ribs.

It was a wildly suspenseful game that flip-flopped a few times in the last quarter, but it really came down to the final minute. Joe Kapp connected with Gene Washington for a touchdown, putting them ahead, 24–23, with less than a minute on the clock. Then Dick Gordon returned the kickoff to the Chicago forty-one, and Virgil Carter scrambled for 10 more yards. With less than thirty seconds left in the game, Carter hit Cecil Turner for 9 yards, then threw the ball out of bounds to stop the clock. Mac Percival came in and kicked a field goal for the victory. Suddenly we were in third place, knocking on Detroit's door.

The next game was against a struggling Green Bay team that had slipped down to last place in the standings, and it was Mac Percival who once again kicked a last-minute field goal to beat our oldest rival. With thirty-eight seconds left, we were tied, 10–10, when someone on the Bears' bench recalled a little-known rule that Paul Hornung and the Packers had used against the Bears four years back. We didn't really understand the rule, but we asked the umpires to check the official rule book and it turned out to be true. After a fair catch from a punt, the receiving team could put the ball in play with a punt or a placekick. In this case, the receiving team must remain 10 yards from the kicker. When the rule had been explained to both teams, Percival connected with the ball squarely and we had ourselves another victory, 13–10.

Two things had given us our last three wins. One was Virgil Carter's ability to get the team within scoring range so that Mac Percival could kick a field goal. That year Percival would kick 25 field goals to set a Bears' record for most field goals in a season. The other reason for our success was Gale Sayers. It took a few games, but he was beginning to have a career season, leading the NFL in rushing. Against Green Bay he ran for 205 yards, breaking his own Bear record of 198 yards set two years earlier. Gale was doing it all: cutting and slashing and burning rubber downfield.

The next week we won, but it was the costliest of victories. We were ahead of the 49ers, 14–0 in the second quarter. Gale was having a tough time because their defense was keying on him on every play. He had only picked up 32 yards on 11 attempts. In an effort to free Gale up, Carter called for a pitchout. Gale cradled the ball and swept wide behind his blockers. Just as he was about to make his cut upfield, defensive back Kermit Alexander slipped through the protection and hit him low, catching Gale's right knee with his left shoulder.

Gale went down for a moment, then leaped to his feet—and went down again. The packed house of 47,000 fans and all the players and maintenance people and concessionaires and ushers—everyone—rose to their feet in shock.

In the silence, Gale was helped off the field.

We went on to win the game, 27–19, and were suddenly locked in a tie with the Vikings for first place in the Central

Division. That night Dr. Fox operated on Gale, trying to repair the ligaments in Gale's right knee. But Gale would not be back in 1968. With five games left in the season, Gale had accumulated 856 yards and was averaging 6.2 yards per carry. He was heading for a 1,400-yard season, which would have led both leagues that year.

The operation by Dr. Fox was described as "a success" in the newspapers the next day. But even though Gale would come back and gain over 1,000 yards in 1969, he was never the same after that operation. No one would ever see his running genius again. I call it "genius" because I never saw anyone else do what he did.

The next week the bad luck followed us to Atlanta. The Falcons still had not put together a solid team. They were 1–8 for the season and were 12-point underdogs going into this game. Despite the loss of Sayers, we felt confident about beating them. When playing against Atlanta, I always felt as though I had to prove myself to the press and the public. They had such a bad team, but Tommy Nobis was a terrific linebacker and people were always comparing us as linebackers. In 1967, Nobis made the All-Pro team ahead of myself and even Ray Nitschke, who had helped get the Packers to the Super Bowl. But the comparisons were never really fair, because it was so difficult to determine who played a better game. In the second quarter, Virgil Carter went down with a broken ankle and we lost the game, 16–13, breaking our four-game winning streak and dropping us out of first place. The next week we lost badly to the Dallas Cowboys, who were playing without quarterback Don Meredith. It was a forgetful match in which there was more fighting than football. I threw a punch, and both teams entered the fray.

But the next week, with a semirepaired Jack Concannon at the helm, we beat the fledgling New Orleans Saints in Tulane Stadium, and we found ourselves 6–6 on the season, back in first place. The defense played well, despite experiencing food poisoning the night before, but the real star of the game was Brian Piccolo, who racked up 112 yards. The Saints had a hard time blocking me out, and I was able to attack on their sweeps and up the middle.

The newspapers devoted plenty of ink to the upcoming games against the Rams and the Packers, for if we won, we would win the Central Division title and go to the playoffs. Dooley told reporters that we would need 17 points to defeat the 10–1 Rams, who were one game behind the league-leading Colts. As 14-point underdogs, this was going to be our toughest game of the season. Without Gale, we would need to pull off a miracle in Los Angeles. But somehow we were able to slip by George Allen's Rams. In the third quarter, I intercepted a pass that led to our final touchdown. Then we prevented the Rams from moving the ball into field goal range in the final minute of the game. Dooley was right: it took 17 points. The final score was 17–16.

The following Sunday we limped back to Wrigley Field to face the Packers in the season finale. If we won, we would go to the playoffs. Behind throughout the game, we were able to mount a comeback in the fourth quarter, scoring 17 points. But it wasn't enough and we lost, 28–27. Our season of broken bodies and bad luck had finally ended.

Gale and I were again named to the All-Pro team.

Considering the adversity we had faced, there was reason to believe in a future. We had battled to a 7–7 season and nearly won our division. With a little less bad luck, we would have improved on that record, and maybe even had a shot at that $25,000 Dooley waved under our noses at the preseason barbecue.

Dooley's assessment of the year was in character. "In the

future, when adversity hits, we'll realize we can come out of it. We'll be able to remember when things were as bad as they can be."

━━━━━━━

Our 1969 season began with injuries, defined misfortune, and ended with tragedy. At 1–13, it was the season I'd most like to forget, but it was also the season I played some of my best football. No one could have predicted what happened in 1969. In only the second season since Halas retired, we sank to a new low in Bears history.

The season began optimistically enough. Dooley had shaken up his coaching staff, bringing in several new aides to replace as many malcontents. The fresh blood included former Packer center Jim Ringo to coach the offensive line and former pro end Bob Shaw to teach the receivers how to catch. From the draft, personnel director Bobby Walston had tabbed Rufus Mayes, a tackle from Ohio State, and still another quarterback, this one from Kansas. A kid named Bobby Douglass.

Rudy Bukich had retired and Larry Rakestraw was traded away, cutting the quarterback count to three: Jack Concannon, Virgil Carter, and the untried Bobby Douglass. A rumor that Dooley was putting Douglass up at his home must not have played well in the minds of Concannon and Carter. We didn't know it then, of course, but that rumor and many others—most of which turned out to be true—would blossom into full-fledged discontent before the season was over.

Dooley's defensive lineup seemed pretty solid. Everyone was back from the previous year, with the significant exception of Richie Petitbon, who'd been dealt to the Rams. The offense seemed intact, except for three significant areas: catching, passing, and running. With the exception of flanker

Dick Gordon, no other receiver was a proven pro player. As for passing, Concannon and Carter both had low completion percentages and Douglass was still an unknown. In the running department there was only Gale, who was coming back after his knee operation. Ron Bull, who was getting old, was mainly used as a blocker.

If Gale went down again, we'd go down with him.

We lost our final preseason game, the annual Armed Forces benefit game, to the St. Louis Cardinals, 37–31. Jack Concannon was back at quarterback, throwing 251 yards for three touchdowns and scrambling five times for 48 yards. But our Bears' defense couldn't contain the Cardinals.

After ending the season with a exhibition 3–3 record, we opened against the Packers at Lambeau Field with Concannon again as our quarterback. I remember seeing THE PACK IS BACK signs all over town. Well, the Green Bay fans were right. The Packers celebrated their fiftieth anniversary by beating us that night, 17–0, for our sixth consecutive opening day defeat. Our offense had even managed to pull together 204 yards—not bad, we reassured ourselves, except most of the yardage came in the middle of the field. Beating the Packers in Green Bay was never easy. We put the game behind us and looked forward to our next game.

But the next game should have told us something. On September 27, we traveled to St. Louis to play the Cardinals. It was the first of our bad-luck games. We lost, 20–17, because of a freak play.

Early in the game, Gale came out of the huddle realizing he wasn't sure what play had been called, and he yelled to Concannon to hold it. Already into a quick count, Concannon called, "Time!" Hearing the word, center Mike Pyle snapped the ball, hitting Concannon in the leg. The ball shot straight up into the air and St. Louis linebacker Larry Stallings snatched it and ran 62 yards for a touchdown. Our guys didn't even chase him, because they thought time had been called. It put the Cardinals up 0–13.

By the end of the third quarter, Concannon had passed for two TDs and with Percival's help we were leading, 17–13. We traded the ball a few times in the fourth quarter until quarterback Jim Hart brought his team down to the two yard line and gave it to Willis Crenshaw for the score. Looking back on that particular St. Louis drive, I should've called more red dogs. I had been using it in the third quarter, but I didn't think the play would be effective this late in the game. Now the score was 20–17, but Concannon brought the Bears' offense back, carefully rationing his timeouts. With a run by Sayers and passes to Austin Denney, Ron Bull, and Brian Piccolo, the offense ended their drive on the Cardinal nineteen with four seconds remaining on the clock. It was a perfect display of offensive football. Percival, our ace kicker, came out to tie the game, but his kick was slightly off to the right. If any game defined the 1969 season, that was it. An early but costly blunder, and then a touch of bad luck to hand us another loss. It would happen another eleven times that year.

The next Sunday in New York, we were ahead of the Giants, 24–21, with a minute to play. Tarkenton had driven the ball deep into our territory. Then, due to a mixup in our secondary, receiver Joe Morrison ran a little cross pattern and was left wide open in the end zone. We lost again, 28–24. The next week we lost to Minnesota, 31–0. Despite our lack of offense in the game, the Vikings lauded our defense afterward. "Their defense has got to be one of the best there is," praised quarterback Jim Kapp, "and Butkus is the best." Another Viking said, "It doesn't show on the scoreboard, but they played one heck of a tough game. It was one of the roughest I can remember, the hardest hitting."

With an 0–4 record, Dooley had to do something. So he did the obvious. He changed quarterbacks, even though Concannon had completed 60 percent of his passes. But instead of tapping Carter, who clearly deserved the chance, Dooley surprised everyone by starting Bobby Douglass. And while the quiet and patient Carter smoldered, the Bears continued to lose. Douglass's arm was strong, but his ability to pick up receivers in the open was weak.

Meanwhile, Gale was having a tough time carrying the ball. He was averaging just 3.5 yards per attempt and didn't have any touchdowns. The sportswriters began to question whether he had fully recovered from the operation. Then Gale spotted something in the game films. He was hesitating a fraction of a second every time he made his cut downfield. When he saw it, he immediately eliminated the hitch and went on to score eight touchdowns and lead the league in rushing with 1,032 yards. His yards per attempt improved to 4.4 by the end of the season, but we would never see that 6.2 brilliance again.

Despite Gale's rebirth and the quarterback change, we continued to lose. In the next two weeks, we held the Detroit Lions to 13 points and the league-leading Los Angeles Rams to 9, but still we couldn't put more than 7 points on the board in either of these games. We were even able to prevent the Rams from getting into the end zone. It was the first time under head coach George Allen that the Rams won without the benefit of a touchdown. You couldn't call it anything but bad luck.

As the writers began to bear down on Dooley, he began to bear down on us, crushing what little morale was left.

Dooley finally snapped when Ed Stone of *Chicago Today* wrote: "Dooley is basically a gentle person. That's not a rap. That's a fact of nature. If Dooley suddenly tried to become a stern commander in the Halas–Lombardi mold, the players would laugh at him." The next day Dooley grabbed Stone by the front of his shirt and raged at him in front of the players. "I'll show you how gentle I am. You're a leech. I don't want you in this locker room anymore, except on game days." Then Dooley turned to us and said, "Don't talk to this man in the locker room during the week."

Dooley then promised a "housesweeping," claiming that certain players were more concerned with their "hairdos" and "clothes" and "outside activities" than football games.

Our game against the Steelers at Wrigley Field on Sunday, November 9, 1969, would be our single victory that season. Dooley had instructed me and Mike Pyle, the offensive captain, to kick anyone out of the game who was not giving it his best effort. We beat them, 38–7. Sometime in the third quarter after a kickoff play had ended, Andy Russell and I walked back to the line of scrimmage, and at some point along the visiting bench, Pittsburgh defensive tackle Mean Joe Greene approached us and started tossing insults at me.

Then he spit in my direction.

I can understand why Greene did what he did. Hell, I did the same sort of thing all the time. He was trying to provoke me, figuring that if I went at him the refs would toss me, which would give the Steelers a better chance of getting on the scoreboard. Another possible motivation for Greene's behavior was that he was a rookie, trying to make his mark. I didn't even mind the spitting that much.

So I stopped, looked at Russell, smiled, and said, "What does this rookie think I'm gonna do? Start a fight and get kicked out?" Then I looked at Greene and said, "You asshole!"

———

Unfortunately, when NFL Films included this scene in a

1995 two-hour history of the league that they were preparing for the NFL's seventy-fifth anniversary, they got it wrong. They spliced an old film of me running off the field with commentary from some Pittsburgh players indicating that I was afraid of Mean Joe Greene. After Greene saw the film, he came up to me and said, "You know, Dick, it didn't happen that way." When I brought this up to the film's editor, he admitted that the shot of me running off the field was taken from another game. Hell, anybody could see it was a splice job.

Let me explain how I feel about fear. For one thing, we all have it. If you don't, you're an idiot. In fact, every player who has ever put on a jersey and pads has experienced fear. The trick is to feel the fear and rise above it.

The only way I know to do that is to get good and mad. The anger defeats the fear every time. This technique is as old as warfare itself. From the Romans to the Native Americans to the U.S. Marine Corps, the battle cry remains the primary method of pushing the fear down so far the whimpering can't be heard. On the football field, there was no one louder than me.

I was never afraid of Joe Greene, or any other individual for that matter. My fears always revolved around getting hurt. My right knee hadn't been sound since my junior year at Illinois, and I knew it would never be sound again. But so far I had been able to shake off the pain and play. So far my knee had survived a number of direct hits and countless aggravations, such as players rolling on it and twisting it in ways it was never meant to go.

Throughout the 1969 season, Dr. Fox was giving me shots of hydrocortisone after each game, then maybe another during the week, on Tuesday or Thursday. After a road game, he would come down the aisle to my window seat on the plane and sink a syringe-full of the stuff into my knee at 30,000 feet. But I managed to play despite the pain.

The win against the Steelers proved to be an aberration. And then things took a turn for the worse. The next week we were in Atlanta, playing the Falcons at County Stadium, when Brian Piccolo took himself out of the game because of a cough. It was hot as hell that Sunday, November 16, and of course we lost, 48–31. For some reason, maybe an interview, I was late coming into the locker room. I was dying for something to drink, and Brian was standing there holding a can of Coke in front of his locker, which was next to mine.

I said, "Give me some of that, Brian."

He started coughing. "No, you might catch this."

"Give me the Coke," I insisted. I took it from him and drank it down.

The following day back in Chicago, Brian was sent to the hospital to have his cough checked out. They must have found something, because the next thing we knew he was in New York for "further tests" at Sloan-Kettering Hospital.

Brian Piccolo had come to the Bears in 1965 out of Wake Forest, where he led the country in total yards rushing. Most scouts had passed on him because he was relatively small and slow for a fullback, the feeling being that he would not be able to perform at the pro level. But Halas and Allen saw something they liked, and they picked him up as a free agent the same year Gale and I were signed.

Bill George was an alumnus of Wake Forest, and he took Brian under his wing. Although George was at the end of a great career, he was still the most influential Bear in 1965, and while I was given the cold shoulder treatment due to my "six-figure" contract and extensive press clippings, Brian seemed to enjoy almost veteran status, and for a while I resented him.

But you had to like Brian. He was a solid player, hardworking, and he could be very funny and very generous. He had a great wife, Joy, and three lovely kids. Helen liked Joy a lot and sometimes we went out with them socially.

I grew to like Brian well enough to play pranks on him, which you might guess by now has been my acid test of friendship since my Roseland days. One time, after picking Brian up at his home in Beverly Hills, the same neighborhood where Bertetto and Richards and I used to confiscate sleds and bikes, I peeled out across his lawn and left a beautiful scar where only green grass had been, wondering as I did so whether the two Ricks and I had ever played "goal line stand" in Piccolo's front yard. Brian just laughed.

The next Sunday, November 23, we were at home against Baltimore. In the locker room before the game, Gale got up and gave a little talk about his roommate. Brian was very sick, he said, and might not make it back to the team. Gale was a stoical guy, but I could see that he was hurting. Then he asked everybody to go out and win one for his friend. Well, we tried, but couldn't get it done, losing 24–21. It disgusted me that we couldn't win even with that kind of motivation.

As we played out that season, Brian was practically commuting to New York for more tests. He was diagnosed with a rare type of cancer. Finally they operated on him and sent him home. Then, in May 1970, Gale went to New York to accept the George Halas Award, given by the sportswriters to the Most Courageous Athlete of the Year.

Gale was courageous in that horrible season. He had come back from the knee operation to lead the league in rushing. But with Brian Piccolo lying in his deathbed back in Chicago, Gale stepped to the podium and told the audience who the award really belonged to. When I read about it the next day in the *Chicago Tribune*, I damn near fell apart.

"You flatter me by giving me this award," said Gale. "But

I tell you here and now that I accept it for Brian Piccolo. It is mine tonight. It is Brian Piccolo's tomorrow. "I love Brian Piccolo and I'd like all of you to love him. When you hit your knees to pray tonight, please ask God to love him, too."

They tell me the big dining room remained silent for quite a while after that.

What I remember most about that time was Joy Piccolo. She was a petite woman and she had already been weakened by the births of three daughters in rapid succession. As the Piccolo watch continued, we all watched her grow ever more frail.

Huge dark circles appeared under her eyes and made her look so damn vulnerable. One day near the end, Helen and I joined a small group at the house to visit with Brian. To see him lying there, all skin and bones, was very hard. Helen had a particularly tough time with it. Still does when she remembers all these years later. Brian lingered for months after that, then in June 1970 we got word that Brian had passed away.

I lost a friend, and Gale lost a brother.

A movie called *Brian's Song* was made from a book that Gale had written. When it aired on ABC on November 30, 1971, much of America wept at the tragic beauty of the close relationship between a black player and white player named Gale and Brian. I was cast as myself, while a couple of young talents, James Caan and Billy Dee Williams, played Piccolo and Sayers. It was my first acting experience, and although I had no clue at the time, it was the beginning of a second career that I would resume after my fall from football.

About the same time that the movie was being made, I was doing quarterback lunches at the Playboy Club in Chicago. Quarterback lunches are usually on Mondays during the season, when a select group of fans pay for the privilege of sitting with some players and discussing the previous day's game. Anyway, Playboy had a resort at Lake Geneva, Wisconsin, not far out of Chicago, and at one of these lunches we decided to hold a golf tournament up there in memory of Brian Piccolo—with the proceeds going to cancer research. That tournament is still held every year, and I have read that the type of cancer that killed Brian is now considered 90 percent curable.

Dooley finally started Virgil Carter in game thirteen against Green Bay. After a dismal first half in which he completed just 2 of 17 passes, Carter was replaced by Douglass, and we lost, 21–3. After the game, Carter blew his stack and called Dooley a liar. "He promised me he wouldn't replace me." Then he demanded to be traded, saying, "The only way I'll come back here is to play out my option, and I hope they won't be so chickenshit as to make me do that."

Halas, of course, backed Dooley. He fined Carter $1,000 and suspended him for the last game of the season. He even went so far as to tell the press, "What a grand young man he was last year. No one can have such a change without someone influencing him or changing him." Carter ended up playing for the Bengals the following year and doing it very well.

On December 21, 1969, we gave our fans a Christmas present by losing to the Lions, 20–3, at Wrigley. With minutes left in the game, the Lions kicked off after a score and the ball squiggled along the ground. I picked it up and headed downfield, knocking a few players over before being brought down 28 yards later. The crowd stood and cheered my effort as the clock mercifully ticked down to end the worst season in the team's history. Then the fans went home to lick their wounds.

I don't remember anyone hanging around the clubhouse that day. We'd gone 1–13 for the year, losing most of our pride in the process. If the fans were wondering what had happened, it was also high time for every member of the team, the coaching staff, and the front office to go home and think long and hard about what he did to contribute to this blackest of years.

The sportswriters began their postseason attack, moving in on the carcass with dull knives. Each story ripped a little more flesh from the Bears' tradition. The cry went up not only for Dooley's blood but for the Old Man's as well. "Halas faces the necessity of making the boldest decision in his fifty years of football," wrote one critic. "He needs a clean sweep that includes himself."

At seventy-four, he was hanging on to the Bears' throat, said the pundits, and the team was choking to death. He ran Dooley from LaSalle Street, they wrote, often using his son Mugs as his envoy.

One writer put it this way: "The season has been continuous chaos, with no one clear mark on the horizon. Dooley has been accused of being indecisive. Maybe it's the nature of the man, but one will never know because Halas has been tapping him on the shoulder all year, and that's certain to make a man nervous."

Halas had always been able to keep the writers on his side. But no more. As the criticism mounted day by day, Halas began firing back. Describing the coverage by the *Chicago Tribune* and *Chicago Today* as a "sackful of lies," Papa Bear added, "I've gone okay for forty-eight years without their assistance and I don't need it now." If the newspapers had lied about anything, it was that we were even worse than they said we were.

As hard as the press had been on the team, I was receiving rave notices in the sports pages and from players around the league. Future Hall of Famer and Lion head coach Joe Schmidt told the writers after our last game: "I have never seen him quit. If he overplays sometimes, it's because he's so aggressive. With less than four minutes to go, he ran down that field trying to score a touchdown with the same desire as if it was the opening kickoff."

"He terrifies you when he comes charging in like a madman," said Lion running back Mel Farr. "He's so quick he's unbelievable." Hall of Fame quarterback Bart Starr chimed in: "Butkus has made the Bear defense what it is. I can't imagine anyone quicker or stronger. He's one of the finest examples of hustle I have ever seen."

I especially liked that bit about "hustle." That's all I really cared about, that I played my best. The fumbles, the interceptions, the hard hits, the sacks. They were all by-products of the effort, the hustle, and maybe the intuition I'd nutured since I was a kid, seeing the play unfold first in my mind.

So ended my fifth year in pro ball. I had made the grade and then some. I had gained the respect I had sought around the league. My first contract had come to an end. It was time to sit down with the Old Man. Time to look back and evaluate, time to add and subtract and to see how far I'd come since that first day at Rennselaer. Then to look into the future.

———

I had gotten rid of my first agent, Arthur Morse. Through my friend Jay McGreevy I was introduced to an associate of superagent and talent manager Mark McCormack, whose offices were in Cleveland. McCormack dispatched Ed Keating to Chicago for a meeting with Jay and me. I liked him immediately and agreed to have him represent me in my contract negotiations with Halas. But George refused to meet with Keating. He wanted me in his office and no one else.

So there I sat in the gloom of that postseason looking

across the desk at the Old Man. I was twenty-six now, which in football terms verges on middle age. Between us was the issue of my right knee. I'd had an assortment of injuries. Several shoulder problems, half a dozen hip pointers, torn rib cartilage, three KO's, broken fingers, and elbow chips that required an operation. But these ailments were sneezes compared to my knee.

Beginning way back in my second year, the right knee had been tender after most games and Dr. Fox had given me shots of hydrocortisone. So I had been able to play at full strength with it, even though I knew the ligaments were getting stretched to the breaking point from the hundreds of hits the joint had absorbed. My knee moved four ways now, the usual frontward and backward motion but also to either side. Dr. Fox knew this—and if he knew it, the Old Man knew it.

"How's the knee holding up?" said the Old Man.

"Fine," I said.

I asked him about his arthritic hips. He'd had an operation in England sometime during the last weeks of 1969.

"Much better, kid. Thanks for asking."

Then we began to haggle, the Old Man sitting back there on his throne, sleepy-eyed and wise, working me over like a three-card monte master.

"You know, kid, the people don't come to see you play."

"Oh no?" I said. "Who do they come to see?"

"Gale," he said, "They come to see Gale. So I can't see paying you that kind of money."

I was stopped cold. I didn't know what to say to that.

"I'd like to make a call," I said.

"What for?"

"I'd like to call Keating and get a response."

"Sure, kid," he said. "Use the office right down the hall. It's empty. Take your time."

Keating had given me a figure to shoot for, and every time I hit a roadblock I went into an adjoining office and called Ed, who was at a public phone nearby. The Old Man must have been laughing his ass off as I went back and forth between his office and the one with the telephone in it. Finally we reached an agreement. A three-year, no-cut contract for a total compensation of $195,000.

Was it fair? Hell, I don't know. It felt fair to me at the time—and I don't know how else you can measure it.

What wasn't fair was the news about Vince Lombardi. In September 1970, as we were finishing an 0–3 preseason by losing to the Broncos, 30–17, at Mile High Stadium, Lombardi had already slipped into a coma from which he would not emerge at Georgetown University Hospital in Washington, D.C., where he was general manager and head coach of the Redskins.

His body was riddled with cancer. He'd had two surgeries over the summer, the last one on July 27, and he had watched the Redskins preseason games on a closed-circuit television installed in his hospital room with his wife Marie beside him. During one game, Vince's eyes seemed closed when Redskin receiver Charley Taylor dropped a touchdown pass. When Marie mentioned what happened, he growled, "I can see."

When I read the story, my first thoughts were about my friend Paul Hornung. When Lombardi took over in Green Bay in 1959, the Packers were at the bottom of the standings. Their one star was quarterback Paul Hornung, who passed, ran, and did all the kicking.

Hornung's nightlife rivaled fiction. When Lombardi arrived, he took Green Bay's Golden Boy aside and told him he was no longer the quarterback and offered to trade him if he wanted. But if he chose to stay, Hornung would have to straighten out his life and become a leader. If he did that,

Lombardi promised that the Packers would soon be champions. Well, the rest is history—and now Vince was dying and Paul was losing the single most positive force in his life. Vince Lombardi built men. Paul Hornung stands today as Vince's best work.

Vince never regained consciousness and died on September 3 at 7:20 A.M. Veteran All-Pro quarterback Bart Starr said Vince's death was like losing a father. Halas said he loved him as a friend. Commissioner Pete Rozelle said the players who will miss Lombardi most "are those who still had yet to play for him, who might have been taught by him, led by him and counseled by him."

When the 1970 season began, Dooley was still there, paraphrasing Norman Vincent Peale's perennial bestseller *The Power of Positive Thinking* so often that we were all sick of hearing it. Dooley was a nice man, but he never understood that cheerleading was not leadership. Why he wasn't fired after that disastrous 1969 season I will never know.

Halas had never fired a coach in fifty years. He tried to keep all his personnel, his players, his front office people, and his field staffs for as long as possible, in some cases for decades. Of course, in those days the price was usually right, and Papa could afford to indulge his benevolent side.

But this owner-friendly climate was changing. The NFL and the AFL had officially merged, and the money was just beginning to flow from the TV networks. *Monday Night Football*, starring the one and only Howard Cosell, was being launched by ABC sports impresario Roone Arledge. It was an overnight sensation. Soon a whole new breed of football fan was emerging as football gained dominance in the Monday night ratings.

────────

We opened our season against the New York Giants at Yankee Stadium on September 19, 1970. It was a Saturday night game. I vaguely remember the beginning of the play, but I'll never forget the end.

Quarterback Fran Tarkenton takes the snap and fakes a draw, but I'm not fooled as I drop back. He swings to his right and I move laterally, staying with him. Then he throws a screen pass back to his left, across his body—and I scramble to recover. Tight end Bob Tucker is waiting for me. He comes in low.

Bam!

A small bomb explodes inside my right knee. I got down, thinking, *Oh, God, please don't do this. Not yet.*

I've never felt anything quite like it. The closest was when the cartilage was torn away from my ribs in 1967. But this is worse because it's the knee. The play is over, and something makes me get up. I stand there as though everything is fine. I don't want the Giants to know that I'm hurt. They'll come after me if they know. The deadness down there in the knee is overwhelming. But I keep playing, but I don't tell anybody about it. I know I'm limping, but nobody seems to notice.

The first half ends with the Giants ahead, 13–10. We have contained the run, holding Tucker Frederickson and Ron Johnson to just a few yards. But Tarkenton is killing us, swinging his backs out into the flat and connecting on 10 of 15 passes. The knee hurts, but I say nothing through halftime and go back out there and play the rest of the game. Coach tells the cornerbacks to play the receivers tighter, to start bumping them at the line of scrimmage. The ploy works as their receivers get thrown off their patterns and Tarkenton starts having problems finding an open man. This gives us more of an opportunity to nail him in the backfield or set up for possible interceptions.

We get two interceptions late in the fourth quarter. One by Buffone that stops Tarkenton deep in his own territory and another by me on the Giants' last possession. We win, 24–16. It is the first time the Bears are 1–0 since 1963, when the Monsters of the Midway went all the way. As Cooper Rollow will write the next day in the *Chicago Tribune*, we "have already equaled last year's highest point."

After the game, the knee starts to hurt really bad. I tell Dr. Fox about the hit and he sinks a double dose of hydrocortisone in there, then pokes around with his fingers for a while and says he'll check it again on Tuesday back in Chicago. He doesn't seem especially concerned. But then again, he wasn't inside my knee when Bob Tucker's shoulder hit it.

Fox gives me another shot on the flight home that night and I stay quiet, my mind focused on the area around my right knee. I know there's something wrong and I'm worried.

By the next morning, the knee had swollen considerably, and I spent the day in bed with my leg mounted on four pillows. I applied a heating pad to the knee—a half hour on and a half hour off. I was restless and it was a beautiful day outside, so I eased myself into some clothes and went out into the backyard of our house in Chicago Heights, a community to the south and east of the old neighborhood. We had lived there for almost three years, and Nikki, who was born in 1966, was almost five. I found Helen and Nikki together out under one of the big old trees. I played with Nikki for a few minutes, picking her up and swinging her and laughing. Helen asked about the knee. I shrugged and said, "It'll be all right. It's a little swollen now, but it'll be fine by tomorrow." I wasn't at all sure of what I was saying, but there was no sense in worrying her. I walked out past the yard into a field that ran behind the house and asked myself, for maybe the first time in my life, what would I do if I suddenly couldn't play anymore. It was midafternoon and the shadows from the trees were creeping across the bright field. I didn't stay long. The thought of not playing depressed me. I limped back into the house and called Jay McGreevy at his office and asked him if he wanted to have dinner. I needed to do something to get my mind off the damn knee.

On Tuesday, the swelling was down and Dr. Fox was encouraged. But he couldn't resist flooding the knee with some more hydrocortisone. The next day I practiced a little, then more on Thursday. By Friday I was going pretty good, maybe three-quarters, and by Sunday the old urge was back and I played a good game against the Eagles at Northwestern's Dyche Stadium. I collected two sacks and fourteen unassisted tackles. The sacks came at the right time. It was late in the fourth quarter, and the Eagles had whittled our early lead—sparked by Cecil Turner's 95-yard opening kickoff return—to 17–16. Quarterback Norm Snead was in a good rhythm and he was advancing the Eagles dangerously close to field goal range. I called a blitz on second down and five and led a charge that included OB, George Seals, and Bill Staley. I got there first and Snead ate the ball for a 9-yard loss. The next play I shot the gap and nailed Snead again. He got so mad that he slammed the ball into the turf and stayed on his knees glaring at me. Percival later kicked his second field goal and we won again, 20–16.

It was our second win in a row, something we hadn't done in two years.

Could it be that the Bears were back? We would find out what we were made of the next Sunday when we played the Lions at Tiger Stadium. The Lions were also at 2–0, but their stats—77 points scored and only 17 allowed—were more impressive. Well, we played a terrific first half, allowing their crew of fine runners just 17 yards, and we opened the third quarter with a 7–0 lead. Then everything changed as Mel Farr and Altie Taylor found their legs. The Lions scored three touchdowns in the third quarter to take a 21–7 lead and then they cruised through the fourth, trading touchdowns with us. Final score: 28–14. We left the Motor City feeling pretty good. Except for that one bad quarter, we had outplayed the hottest team in football. Had Gale been able to play, who knows what might have happened? Anyway, we'd be ready for them three weeks later when they would come into our park—the last of three home games.

We lost all three. First the Minnesota Vikings charged into town and mugged us, 24–0. Next came the San Diego Chargers to roll us at home, 20–7, and then came the Lions to roar their dominance, 16–10. The defense was playing well enough to win; and Buffone, Seals, and I were on our game. But the offense was awful, generating only 17 points over the three-game losing stretch, an average of less than 6 an outing. Although Jack Concannon's recent prominence in Chicago's nightlife had earned him the nickname of "State Street Jack," he made more poor choices than Elizabeth Taylor on three successive Sundays. But it wasn't all Concannon's fault.

On November 1, 1970, we took a 2–4 record into Fulton County Stadium in Atlanta. The Falcons had won five straight games after losing their season opener and were clear favorites to beat us. Our total offense for that game was only 170 yards. But we hung tough when it counted, forcing their running backs to cough up a pair of fumbles, and we led at the half by a score of 13–7. In the third quarter, Falcon quarterback Bob Berry drilled a pass over the middle to tight end Jim Mitchell, who broke three tackles before running into the end zone. Just twenty-six seconds later, Bear returner Cecil

Turner took the kickoff and ran through a huge hole we'd created with our wedge. No one touched him as he loped 94 yards to paydirt. Percival added a field goal in the fourth quarter and we won, 23–14.

The next week we lost to the 49ers, 37–16, as quarterback John Brodie picked our secondary apart with his passes. No one ran very far on us that year, but a good arm with some protection could beat us just about every time. John completed 21 of 28 passes for 317 yards and three touchdowns. His final pass of the day, a 5-yarder to halfback Doug Cunningham, ranked him among Johnny Unitas, Sonny Jurgensen, and Y. A. Tittle as the only players in NFL history to complete 2,000 passes. At 3–5, we headed north to face another great field commander, Bart Starr. At thirty-seven, Starr was pretty banged up. Shoulder and arm injuries had kept him out for parts of the last two seasons, but he was out there that day in Lambeau Field to direct the Packers in their 101st meeting with the Bears.

We were down 10–0 at the half. We got it going in the third period when Mac Percival kicked a field goal and Jack Concannon connected on a beautiful pass to Dick Gordon for a 69-yard touchdown. Percival kicked three more field goals and late in the fourth quarter we were up by a score of 19–13. Then Bart Starr went to work. With 1:33 left and the ball on his twenty-three, Starr calmly completed five straight passes to his receivers. After halfback Larry Krause ran for 11 yards, we got hit with a half-the-distance-to-the-goal penalty and the ball was spotted on our two and a half with three seconds on the clock.

Starr rolled out to his right. Then tight end John Hilton, Starr's intended receiver, collided with Doug Buffone and they both went down. Seeing nothing but grass in front of him, Starr scampered across the goal line before I could get there. Dale Livingston made the extra point and beat us, 20–19. I don't believe there was another quarterback in the league who could have done what Starr did that day in Lambeau Field.

It was a hard loss, but we bounced back the next week and beat the Buffalo Bills, 31–13. Bobby Douglass made his first start—and promptly threw an interception that resulted in a Bills' touchdown in the first period. But Douglass collected himself and went on to throw for four touchdowns, and we won going away. The defense did its job, holding O. J. Simpson to 74 yards—a victory in itself.

As the season went by, the knee loomed as the major factor in my life. The sportwriters were watching me now, describing me in their stories as "gimpy" when I was on the field. But the coaching staff acted as if there was no problem. When Dooley would come into the training room early in the week and ask Dr. Fox how I was, Needles would say, "Don't worry. This guy will be ready."

And week after week I was ready, even when I had no business suiting up. Late in the year, we played the Colts in Baltimore. My knee was raging now, and nothing seemed to help. In the locker room minutes before the game, Dooley asked me how I felt. I swallowed hard and said for the first time in my life, "I don't think I can play, Coach." Dooley then explained that he hadn't reported my condition to the league earlier in the week. He said if I didn't start the Bears would be fined and he would look bad.

"Do me a favor," he said. "Just go out there for the first play. Then we'll pull you."

I said, "Okay."

The Colt cheerleaders lined up and formed a pathway for us to run through when our names were announced to the crowd. Although this is done all the time now, it wasn't a common practice back then. But I liked it—really, you couldn't help but like it. It got the fans all revved up by booing me, which just gave me more incentive to play hard. But not that day. My knee hurt so much that I had to limp off to the side and head for the bench. As team captain, I had to go to midfield for the coin toss. OB remembers me dragging my foot out there, the toe catching the hard turf and making little puffs of powdered dirt, and he thought, *What a sitting duck he is gonna be for all those guys who want to get back at him for all those times he made them pay.*

We won the toss and elected to receive. After our offense went nowhere, I went out on the field and on the first play I grabbed Colt center Bill Curry by the shoulders and began dancing with him, bouncing on my one good leg. I remember him looking at me in shock, probably because I wasn't trying to tear his head off. After the whistle blew, I looked over at the bench and saw that Dooley's back was turned toward me. I ended up staying in for the Colts' entire possession, dancing with a different Colt on every play. Then I went to the bench and watched us lose another squeaker, 21–20.

After losing another close one to the Vikings up in Minneapolis, 16–13, we went home to face the Packers and Bart Starr the following Sunday. Throughout the week, we vowed not to let Starr embarrass us again. We planned to put pressure on him all afternoon, but we didn't have to. Late in the first quarter, Willie Holman and I broke into the backfield and converged on Starr, slamming him down, knocking his helmet off. He got to his feet slowly and started walking toward our bench. When a few teammates turned him around, he left the field. But after we punted, Starr was back. He hit Carroll Dale with a 33-yard pass on the first play of the series. Then he sat down on the field to take a rest. I don't think he knew where he was. This time he was helped off the field.

In contrast to the Starr's quiet mastery, Jack Concannon was wearing a pair of high-topped white shoes for the first time. The shoes seemed to help, at least that day. Concannon threw four touchdown passes and we won, 35–17. Jack explained his new shoes to the writers in the locker room. "I just wanted to jazz up the game. You never know when it will be your last."

Given his coaching record, Dooley should have identified with Concannon's remark. Instead, he was ecstatic. "A little PMA," Dooley gushed in the locker room. "Jack's white shoes, some team defense, and excellent pass receiving were what did it," he said. By PMA, he meant "Positive Mental Attitude." I thought the reason we won was NBS: "No Bart Starr."

This was our last game at Wrigley Field, the funky little park where for five decades the roar of 50,000 voices poured down on the Bears in a wash of human emotion. Although we were gone forever, our spirit seems to remain. Some old-timers say that on autumn Sundays when the wind blows a certain way through the rafters of Wrigley, you can hear cleated feet running on the wooden extension in the southeast corner of one end zone.

They say it is the ghost of a guy named Grange, galloping—which we all know is not true. Right?

―――――

In January, I headed for the Pro Bowl. In all, I played in eight Pro Bowls and enjoyed every one. Each was a true busman's holiday—when a player could finally relax and let his guard down a little. That first one out in Los Angeles was particularly sweet. There were five of us representing the Bears: Ditka, Joe Fortunato, Petitbon, and Sayers. All good guys who liked to have fun. We arrived on Monday, which gave us plenty of time to "play" before the game.

The bar and restaurant of choice was the Bull and Bush. It was a classic sports bar. Great steaks, honest drinks, and lots of attractive women. On Friday when a team would be in town to play the Rams, the Bull and Bush was always jammed to the rafters from lunch until late in the evening.

The Bull and Bush had one of the great bartenders of all time. His name was Harry Hagar. He never did much of anything. While the other two bartenders busted ass keeping up with the orders from the customers and waitresses, Harry would just stand there smoking a cigarette, serene in the eye of the storm. Every so often, someone who didn't understand Harry Hagar would call out, "Hey, Harry. Give me a draft, will ya?"

Harry would look sternly at the guy and say, "Can't you see I'm fucking busy here?" Then he would go back to smoking his cigarette while the place went nuts around him. Harry reminded me of a bartender back in Chicago at a place called Stuka's. One time I brought in Doug Buffone and Ross Brupbacher of the Bears. One of them made the mistake of asking for a little music. The bartender said, "You want to hear some music, go to the fucking theater. There's no *music* here. You're here to drink, so drink for crissakes."

By midnight on Friday, just about every Pro Bowler would be at the Bull and Bush, knocking back a few under Harry Hagar's watchful eye. Everyone would be in a relaxed postseason mood. But that didn't mean we were one big happy family. No way. We still tended to hang out with our own teammates. But it was kind of neat. All these great players in the same place.

As I sat in the Bull and Bush on the night before my fifth Pro Bowl, I wondered if it was my last time in the inner circle. I could feel the knee pulsing. I wondered if it was a countdown.

C H A P T E R

9

Dr. Fox operated on my knee in late January. In the recovery room at Illinois Masonic Hospital, he told me he had tightened all the ligaments and the medial collateral. I asked about the interior cruciate: Had he worked on it at all? He said he had but offered no details. This concerned me. Just a week earlier at the Pro Bowl, Bob Lilly and I had compared the wobble in our knees. His seemed worse than mine, and I asked him why he didn't have an operation. He explained that his problem involved the interior cruciate. He said that few players had ever come back after letting it get tampered with by a surgeon. But Fox termed the operation a "complete success" and said that by the time I reported to Rensselaer in July, the knee would be as good as new. Then he slapped a full plaster cast on my leg and sent me home to convalesce for a month. He gave me a load of Percodans and said to take them when the pain started. He predicted the pain would start to ease off in a week or so.

But about four days later, I began to experience horrendous pain, not in my knee but in my groin. I called Dr. Fox and he told me to come into his office so he could check the cast. I told him I was only getting about three hours of sleep a night. Fox gave me some sleeping pills and more Percodans and sent me home again.

Four or five days later, I had to go back to Dr. Fox's office. A new pain had developed in my knee. Between my groin and my knee, I was now getting no sleep at all. I asked him if this was normal. Fox said everything was fine, then he gave me some more pills and sent me home again. The pain in both places continued to radiate for another month. Without sleep I was getting like a zombie. Helen didn't know what to do, although she tried. She was fully pregnant with Matthew, our third child. I was becoming very irritable, not only from the pain. I was afraid, too, and I spent many long nights trying not to move a muscle and wondering if I would ever play again. Those nights were scary. When I did fall asleep, I often had nightmares. Finally, on perhaps the fifth or sixth visit to the doctor's office, Fox opened the cast and took a look.

I will never forget the look on his face as he cut the cast away. He almost threw up. A huge boil was oozing near the incision and a mean-looking rash covered most of my leg. Fox took a pair of scissors and snipped off the top of the boil. I howled and jumped about three feet off the table. Stuff was squirting all over the office. Fox mumbled something, then quickly slapped a soft cast on the leg, almost as though he didn't want to look at it any longer than he had to. He sent me home again with more pills.

I felt a little better for a few days, but then the pain returned despite the strong medication. I said the hell with it and took off the cast myself. The boil was swelling again, so I squeezed it and it popped. While I was flushing it out with water, I pulled something out of the center, something long and thin like a string. I called Fox and went back to his shop. Needles took one look and put me back in Illinois Masonic

Hospital. Helen was in the room with me when she started to have contractions. She had to leave and drive to Jackson Park Hospital on the other side of the city, a trip she remembers vividly.

Meanwhile, Fox read the new X rays and decided to open the knee up again and take a fresh look at what he'd done. *More surgery?* Bells and whistles went off in my head, but there was nothing I could do about it. So the next morning Fox revisited the interior of my right knee, carving another scar in the process. Before he closed it up, Needles constructed two drainage holes, installed plastic tubes above and below the knee, and hooked the tubes up to a machine that would flush out the joint. Then he put another full cast over the mess. As this was going on, I began to get a sinking feeling about my future. I remembered what Bob Lilly had said about the interior cruciate—and I wondered what Needles had done to it. Meanwhile, in Jackson Park Hospital, Helen gave birth to Matt. When she called me to tell me she was okay and that Matt looked a little like me, it was my single moment of joy in a postseason that had turned into a disaster.

A few days later, Fox walked into my room, checked the chart, looked at the contents of the drainage container, and said, "Well, looks like the knee is flushed clear." Then he grabbed the tubes and yanked them out from under the cast. I remember rising about a yard off the bed and thinking, *maybe this guy isn't the best doctor in Chicago. Maybe I should get someone else to look at it.*

But Fox reassured me, saying I'd be as good as new in no time. In a week or so, he sent me home again with still another ration of painkillers and sleeping pills. For the next month, I lay in bed with my leg propped on four pillows and watched Marlo Thomas on afternoon reruns of *That Girl.* I watched her so much I think I fell in love with her. I began drinking whiskey and smoking cigarettes. I stopped shaving. The only way I could control the pain was with the Percodans and the whiskey and the sleeping pills and the cigarettes. It was a bad combination. I stayed awake twenty-one hours a day, never leaving the bedroom. I think I started to go a little crazy. Nikki and Rick would come in and visit with me, but Helen's mother, who was there to help out, would chase them out. I guess she didn't want her grandchildren to see their father in such a sorry state.

After a few weeks, Fox took the cast off and I finally began the long rehabilitation process. I had some Universal exercise equipment in my basement and I worked out every day, building up my legs, which had atrophied during the twelve-week siege of two operations. The pain in my groin was finally gone and I began to wean myself off the pills.

In June, I got in my truck and drove left-footed some 1,700 miles down to Florida. We'd bought a place on Marco Island, a new development on the Gulf Coast, and Helen wanted some things taken down there. The ocean was like a warm bath full of salt. The buoyancy allowed me to exercise my legs in new ways. Every morning I used the Gulf as my personal gym. I would stand in the water and run in place. I started by going in up to my chest. As I got stronger, I stood in less and less water until finally I was out of the water completely and running along the beach. Then I swam and exercised some more during the day. As I gained strength and mobility, I began to feel better about the future—and things seemed generally brighter. Maybe Fox had done a good job after all. But still one problem remained: I couldn't do half a deep-knee bend if my life depended on it. The joint was stiff and it didn't seem to be loosening up.

In mid-July, I returned to Chicago Heights. While I waited for training camp to start, I worked out every day with Marty Schottenheimer, doing agility drills in the field out behind my house. When I reported to Rensselaer, I still couldn't bend my leg. I asked Fox about it on my first visit to his office. "Doc, I'm worried that I won't be able to hurdle a guy when he comes in low." Needles pulled a fatalistic expression. "Well, Dick," he said. "You'll just have to change your style of play."

This was not what I wanted to hear, and Fox's stock started to drop again. Then I remembered a technique that some of the older players had talked about. It was called breaking the adhesions, and it sounded to me like something that might free up my knee. I asked Fox about it. "Can you do that?" He said he could and would if I wanted it. It was a simple process and wouldn't lay me up even for a night. But he didn't think it would help. I asked if there was even the slightest chance it might work. He shrugged and said, "Maybe." I said, "Let's do it then." We made a date for the next Tuesday and I drove into Chicago with a friend. They knocked me out with some sodium pentathol and while I floated with Dorothy somewhere over Kansas, my fearless surgeon did his thing.

After Fox was done with me and I was still unconscious on the table in the recovery room, my friend walked in and saw a rabbi praying over me. He thought I was getting an emergency dose of last rites. "God *damn!*" he yelled. "You killed him!" I wasn't dead, of course. I guess the rabbi saw me lying there and decided to pray over me, just in case I needed it.

When I got back to training camp and discovered that I still couldn't bend the knee, I began to wonder what the hell had happened. Maybe the knee was still infected or maybe the ligaments had been attached the wrong way. Nobody told me then and it remains a mystery to this day. The official explanation for the "complication" after the first surgery was given years later by Dr. Fox. He said I had an allergic reaction to catgut, an old-fashioned suture material that most surgeons had stopped using. Maybe that stringlike thing I pulled out of my knee when I broke the boil at home was catgut.

But offensive guard Howard Mudd, whose knee had been operated on about the same time, provided a different slant on the matter. Through the rumor mill, he had heard that Fox's operations on me "didn't do a damn thing except cause an infection—and he didn't do much the second time either." Of course, I couldn't get any doctor to come forward with this information later on.

Dooley let me exercise and practice at my own speed. He did this on the theory that I knew more about how my knee was doing than he did. In this sense, Dooley was a good coach. Howard Mudd was not so fortunate. Assistant coach Jim Ringo insisted that he practice every minute of every day. By the middle of the exhibition season, his knee was wrecked. They gave him a check for $5,000, patted him on the back, and said, "Nice to have known you." I still see Howard Mudd occasionally. He says the rebuilt knee he eventually needed doesn't bother him all that much.

When we opened 1971 season at Soldier Field against the Steelers, I had already started to do what Fox had suggested: change my style of play. Instead of hurdling low blockers to get to the ball carrier, I fended them off with my hands and stepped aside or turned my body to take the hit anywhere but the knee. This new technique slowed me down by perhaps a second on average and limited my range by as much as seven or eight yards in any direction. It also forced me to think differently. Instead of going all out at the running back or passer or receiver, I had to worry about myself first. In other words,

Going in for the kill.
WILLIAM H. BIELSKIS

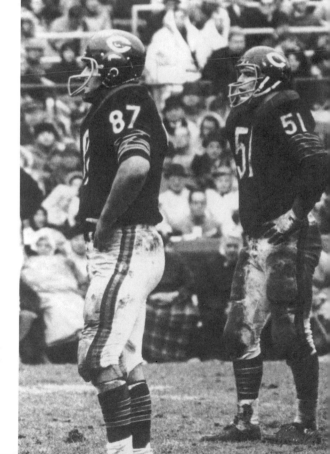

With my good friend Ed
O'Bradovich during a muddy
game at Wrigley Field.
WILLIAM H. BIELSKIS

Listening to the coaches the day before a game. In front of me are Rudy Bukich and Stan Jones. PHOTO BY BILL EPPRIDGE/LIFE MAGAZINE, © TIME INC.

In pursuit of a 49er. That's Howard Mudd on the left, a great offensive guard who later played for the Bears. PHOTO BY BILL EPPRIDGE/LIFE MAGAZINE, © TIME INC.

Shooting the gap on a run. That's Bart Starr handing
off to Paul Hornung. PHOTO BY BILL EPPRIDGE/
LIFE MAGAZINE, © TIME INC.

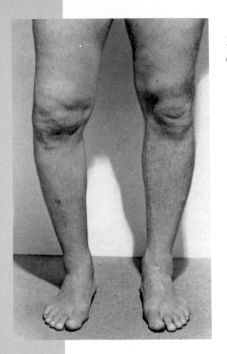

My knees before my last season.
COURTESY OF MEDEX CORPORATION

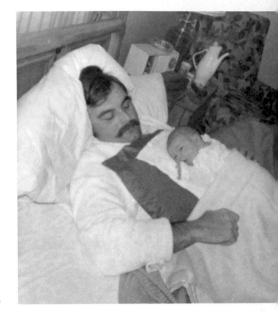

Recuperating from surgery
with my son Matt. BUTKUS
FAMILY PHOTO

A reunion at the University of Illinois. UNIVERSITY OF ILLINOIS

With Rick Richards (left) and Rick Bertetto, the two Ricks, at the party before number 51 was retired. PHOTO BY GERARDO D. JIMENEZ

At the same party with Jay McGrevey, Mayor Richard Daley, and Paul Hornung. PHOTO BY GERARDO D. JIMENEZ

Fishing with Vern Buol. BUTKUS FAMILY PHOTO

With Acuma Pueblo Governor Ron Shutiva holding the Abe Lincoln cane, which is handed down to each new governor of th[e] tribe. DAVE POWLESS

With Gale Sayers. PHOTO BY GERARDO D. JIMENEZ

With Helen at my induction into the Rose Bowl Hall of Fame. RAY POURCHOT

The Big 50, at the Butkus
Awards in Orlando,
Florida. BUTKUS FAMILY
PHOTO

The Butkus family now.
PHOTO BY BILL SMITH

With my sons, Rick and
Matt. FATHER EDD ANTHONY

With Pat Sajak on *Wheel of Fortune*. I won $29,50 for the Serra Retreat House, a Franciscan charity. BRIAN LOCKWOOD/ SLENZAK PHOTO

My first film, *A Man Called Onion*, a forgettable "spaghetti Western," starring Marty Balsam and Sterling Hayden, filmed in Spain. The beard is false because they didn't want anyone to recognize me. BUTKUS FAMILY PHOTO

I had to think before acting. I hated having to do that because it cut down on my efficiency.

But I adapted. That day in our new home stadium—with a packed house watching—I messed up Pittsburgh's young quarterback Terry Bradshaw pretty good by sacking him once and intercepting him twice. But our offense was sputtering and we found ourselves behind, 15–3, with less than four minutes left in the game. As some of the fans began to leave, O'Bradovich smacked one of their runners really hard and the ball popped loose. Linebacker Ross Brupbacher picked it up and ran 30 yards into the end zone. We made the extra point and now the score was 15–10. The fans who had left their seats were standing and waiting to see whether we could get the ball back one more time. With less than a minute left and Pittsburgh on their own twenty-seven, I read the play right and—forgetting to watch out for my knee—blitzed into the backfield, ripping the ball loose from fullback Warren Bankston. OB recovered it on the Steelers' eighteen. Three plays later, backup quarterback Kent Nix threw one in for a touchdown. We won, 17–15.

The next week we came up with some more late-game heroics, knocking off the Minnesota Vikings in Minneapolis, 20–17. This time the offense did a few things right. Nix again relieved Concannon in the second half and threw two touchdown passes to Dick Gordon late in the fourth quarter. A new season, a new stadium, and two quick victories. We were doing great—if you didn't look too closely.

We had won four straight going back to last season—including our final home win against Green Bay and our season closer at New Orleans—and Dooley was on top of the world. But some of us weren't: I know I was hurting and so was Gale Sayers. I remember sitting on the sidelines and watching the greatest runner I ever saw struggle to get up at the end of a play. While my heart hurt for him, my mind focused briefly on the possibility of my own demise as a force on the field.

My knee got bent the wrong way at some point in the Vikings game. All I remember about it is limping in the fourth quarter. The beat reporters started asking questions in their postgame stories and in press conferences. Dr. Fox held his own confab with the writers the next Wednesday and insisted that my knee was in great shape. "You guys," he said to them, "always get all tight. This is a rough game. Things like this should be expected. There's nothing at all wrong with his operative knee."

Don Pierson wrote in the *Chicago Tribune:* "Even if the knee were worse, it is doubtful Butkus could be kept out of a lineup. So it probably doesn't make much difference how he feels."

Meanwhile, I was feeling plenty—and it mattered. The pain and the swelling were increasing every week. I still couldn't bend the knee fully, so I reported early every game day to have my leg taped from the ankle to the upper thigh in a slightly bent position. I hobbled like a war veteran, but the fixed angle allowed me to move better.

Over the next three games, the knee held up and I played well, making a total of forty unassisted tackles. The defense played strong, but we won only one of those games, beating the Saints at home, 35–14. In that game, we looked like champions. Gale made a brief appearance, his season debut, and picked up 27 yards and two first downs on seven carries, which was encouraging. But what really made my day was watching my roomie Doug Buffone run the ball. Doug was lined up as a blocking back on a fake punt play. Doug scooped up the bad snap on the second bounce like a shortstop and wandered for 19 yards downfield. I laughed a long time at that.

The two losses came on the road—to the Rams, 17–3, and 49ers, 13–0. Against the Rams, I recovered a fumble and intercepted two of Roman Gabriel's passes. But it didn't matter because the offense was terrible. Nix threw four interceptions. I recovered another fumble against the 49ers, but again Nix could not capitalize. Gale was on the sidelines, so we had no true running threat. Cyril Pender and Don Shy were good, hardworking ball carriers, but together they were not half of a healthy Gale. Between the Rams and the 49ers, we scored a total of 3 points. Our defense gave up a very respectable 30 points, despite being on the field 64 percent of the time. Those losses were hard on us, but we felt we still had a chance at the playoffs if we could just get the offense moving again.

F ox kept my knee going with multiple shots of hydrocortisone. I no longer practiced between games. It was clear to everyone that my knee was in trouble. But at no time—not once!—did any member of the Bears' organization suggest a program I might follow or offer so much as a word of encouragement. Sometimes I couldn't even stand up on Monday mornings. I had to crawl to the bathroom. Helen didn't know what to say or do. Neither did I. I knew it hurt her to see me in such distress. I stayed quiet and worked out in the basement, trying different techniques to strengthen the knee. Leg extensions would have helped, but back then no one knew the benefits of proper weight training. If I could get through 1971, maybe the knee would improve during the off-season. I was living on maybes now.

But as low as my spirits sank, what happened to Chuck Hughes made me realize how unimportant a knee was in the scheme of things. Hughes was a pretty good receiver for the Lions. He only had average speed, but he ran good routes and caught a lot of passes as a result of hard work and toughness. It happened at Tiger Stadium. For a change, we had the lead, 28–23, late in the fourth period.

But the Lions were deep in their own territory. With 1:12 left, quarterback Greg Landry threw a pass over the middle to tight end Charlie Sanders. I had a good angle on him and I hit him so hard that the ball bounced out of his hands and he seemed to go up instead of down. Now it was third down and Landry came again with the same play, but this time I was not quite there. It didn't matter because Sanders thought I was closer and flinched just as the ball arrived. Incomplete. I stood there clapping because I knew we had the game now. Just one more play and it would be over. Landry then threw a Hail Mary and I dropped back on coverage. The prayer was not answered: The ball fell incomplete.

I turned around for some reason and saw Chuck Hughes walking toward me with a strange look on his face. Then his eyes rolled up and he crumpled to the ground. I ran over to him and frantically waved to the refs and called for our trainers. He was very still and his face had turned blue. The trainers got there and started pounding his chest. I didn't see any response. They carried him off the field. Then Landry threw another pass that was knocked down by Bob Jeter and we ran out the clock.

In the dressing room, we all said a prayer for Chuck, who had been taken to the hospital. Then Dooley opened the doors to the press. Cornerback Jeter and free safety Garry Lyle had made the last hit on Chuck when he caught a 32-yard pass from Landry to set up the two passes to Sanders. "I hit him high around the shoulder," said Lyle, "and Jeter hit him low. I don't think we hit his head."

We were all shaken. OB said he felt sick and left. Then we all left. Later that night, we learned that Chuck was dead.

The next day six of us went to the church services: Bears VP Ed McCaskey, Willie Holman, Jim Cadile, Dick Gordon, Bob Wallace, and me. We had a big rivalry with Detroit then and it felt strange to be with guys for whom I had generated so much dislike. Although the most interesting defensive-offensive matchup was probably between me and Lion center Ed Flanagan, the Detroit fans and writers always compared me to their middle linebacker Mike Lucci. Retired Detroit middle linebacker Joe Schmidt was now their coach and he had been promoting Lucci to the press as being at least my equal, which I'm sure it made Lucci uncomfortable. Schmidt's remarks just made me play harder, although I never needed any additional motivation when we played the Lions. I hated them.

Anyway, there we were, Flanagan, Schmidt, Lucci, and me, all kneeling together in church and paying our respects to Chuck Hughes, and I thought, *Wow, what a way to go!* I mean, putting the grief of the family aside, dying out there on the field was not such a bad way to finish up. I assumed Chuck loved to play football as much as I did and that thought helped me get through some of the bullshit that followed.

Someone in the end zone with a telephoto lens had taken a picture of me just as Hughes fell to the turf. It appeared the next day in one of the Detroit newspapers, and I was surprised to see myself standing almost on top of Hughes with my hands on my hips. The truth was that I was at least 20 yards from Chuck when he went down. But the angle of the camera and the distortion caused by the long lens dramatically altered reality. Except for the relative few who were at the game to see the play firsthand, the city of Detroit and the rest of the country viewed the incident via that photograph and got the distinct impression that was I standing over Chuck like a victorious gladiator.

A few days later, I received a letter with no return address. The envelope was addressed to DICK BUTKUS: MURDERER. Inside the text was short and to the point.

> Well, Butkus, you finally did it.

It was unsigned, of course.

Another letter came the next day. It was from a Lions fan, and it said:

> I used to think you were really out to hurt people. But when I saw you leaning over Chuck Hughes and waving and screaming for medical help, I saw another side of you. Thanks for trying, Dick.

Hell, I always tried. That's the idea, isn't it—to try?

I believe the first letter could only have been written in Detroit. For years, the Lions front office had been claiming that I was a liability to the league. In their eyes, I was a dirty player. Head coach Schmidt and owner Bill Ford even insisted that I tried to hurt players. I could almost forgive Ford because he didn't really know anything about playing the game. But there was no excuse for Schmidt. He was a great linebacker, a Hall of Famer, and he knew that a linebacker's primary responsibility was to knock the other guy on his ass as convincingly as possible.

General manager Russ Thomas claimed he had told Ed McCaskey, Halas's son-in-law, that I should be banned from the NFL. Flanagan accused me of using abusive language. Well, my goodness gracious, that was true enough. I'll admit to that. On the field, I was as tough and mean as I could make myself. Intimidation was a major part of my game. But I knew what I was doing every millisecond of every play—and never did I hit someone with the intention of doing permanent injury. ''Permanent'' is the operative word.

The bad blood between me and the Lions really started a few years earlier when I tackled running back Mel Farr high and tried to rip the ball free. A TV camera caught me in the act of cocking my right arm and it looked like I was karate-chopping Mel. Not true. Hell, the referee was standing right there and he didn't call anything. If fact, that year I was only penalized once for 15 yards.

I did hit as hard as I could, however. And to do it on every play, I used whatever mental trick was available as a motivator. One Sunday at Wrigley before a game with Detroit, I was snapping for the punters—doing my Early Bird chores—when Halas walked up.

''Hey, kid,'' he said from behind his sunglasses. ''Did you hear what Flanagan said about you?''

I looked up at the Old Man.

''What do you mean, Coach?''

Halas looked away. ''I'd get that son of a bitch for what he said.''

Then he strode off across the field.

Well, maybe I wanted to believe Flanagan had said something or maybe I didn't want to think the Old Man was pulling my leg. So I decided to ''get the son of a bitch,'' even if he didn't say anything. Throughout the game, I concentrated on Flanagan, hitting him as often and as hard as I could, even when there was no apparent reason for it. Then on punt plays, I would back up about five yards and time things so that I would be moving across the line of scrimmage like a minivan when he snapped the ball.

Anyway, we were getting beat pretty good. Late in the fourth quarter, Detroit had the ball and was running out the clock. With about twenty seconds left, I called a timeout.

When Flanagan heard the whistle, I had to laugh at the look on his face.

Everybody on the defensive unit got upset.

"What the hell are you doing?" said O'Bradovich. Then everybody chimed in. "Come on, Dick. We're beat. It's over. Let's get out of here."

"Bullshit," I said. " I want another crack at Flanagan. So just shut up. I'm going to get him one more time."

I just couldn't let the clock run out. I wanted one more play, one more chance. My message was simple. I was saying: *Hey, Flanagan! So maybe your team beat us today. But I am going to get you one more time. Maybe when we play each other again, you just might remember this crazy bastard across the line from you. Maybe you'll make a mistake that will help us win. Wouldn't that be nice for the good guys?*

Try to explain this to most of today's players. Bud Grant must be spinning in his grave at what is going on today in the NFL. Even in my time Grant was considered a hard-ass. As coach of the Minnesota Vikings, he instilled in his players the kind of outlook that I most admire. At the end of a game, the Vikings—win or lose—would head straight for the locker room. There was no standing around with members of the opposing team, holding hands and slapping butts and asking about the wife and kids.

Grant understood something that all the great coaches understood. It's a lot easier to play hard against someone you don't like or know. Players today believe they can be friends all week off the field and then go to war for sixty minutes on Sunday. Well, maybe they can do it. I sure couldn't. To me, the opposition was an enemy who wanted to hurt me and keep me from doing the thing I loved most in the world. Bud Grant, Vince Lombardi, George Halas, Don Shula, Tom Landry, and yes, George Allen—they all knew that football at its best must be played with regulated anger.

Mike Ditka said shortly after he took over as coach of the New Orleans Saints, "Football is a nasty game, and you have to be nasty to play it well. Butkus was as nasty as they come. It was like he set himself on an island and said to everyone, 'Okay, take it away from me if you can.' Nobody ever did, and I'll tell you something. Nobody ever will. He was the best."

Although my anger could be towering, it never crossed the line into irrationality. Yet because of the "tough guy" image I carried, there were those who thought I was just one step away from being a serial killer. But the better players knew what I was doing. Ditka knew and so did OB and Atkins and Bill George and Buffone and Lilly and Nitschke and Sam Huff and Jim Brown and Tingelhoff and Sayers. Ditka once asked Gale who was the toughest defender he ever faced. This was down at training camp in Rensselaer. They were sitting on the sidelines watching some drills, and Gale pointed to the field. Ditka was a little surprised.

"Who?" he said.

"He's right out there," said Gale. "Number 51."

Gale told Ditka, who told me, that wherever he went I would be there. Ditka continued, "Gale said he'd cut left, then right, and you would be waiting, and then of course the hit was always memorable."

After the tragedy of Chuck's death in Detroit, our next game was at home against Dallas. It will be remembered by Bears fans primarily for its weirdness. Coach Tom Landry must not have felt the Cowboys could effectively run the ball against us, so he went to the air—but he did it with a twist. He alternated quarterbacks Roger Staubach and Craig Morton on almost every play and between them they ran up 342 yards on 27 completions in 47 attempts. We didn't know who was in there half the time. All told, the Cowboys gained 481 yards to our 194. But they could only get the ball into the end zone twice, partly because our defense kept taking the ball away from them. We forced seven turnovers—and stole the game, 23–19.

With half the season behind us, we were 5–2 and sitting in second place right behind the 6–1 Vikings. Could we keep this run alive? Only if the powers above kept putting in the fix. The next week we played the cellar-dwelling Packers and lost, 17–14, after coming back in the fourth quarter with two lightning scores. With six minutes left, Bobby Douglass hit George Farmer with a 30-yard pass for a touchdown. On the Packers' next possession, they had their backs against the goal line when I stripped the ball from running back Dave Hampton. Douglass took in from the one. In a matter of two minutes, we had tied the game. Just when it seemed as though fortune was smiling on us, Hampton took the kickoff and ran it back 62 yards. With the clock ticking the game away, Lou Michaels kicked a 22-yard field goal and we all went home.

The next weekend our luck returned. It was against the Redskins and their new coach, George Allen. George had left the Rams and joined the Capitol Gang during the off-season. The Rams' players, I'm told, constantly complained about the long meetings and practices. So George had moved on.

We were down 15–9 late in the fourth period when Cyril Pinder broke one for 40 yards and tied the game. All we needed was an extra point, and Buffone and I checked in as blocking backs for Percival. I had picked up a gash over my eye a few plays earlier and I must have been a sight with the blood and all. We set ourselves as Bobby Douglass, who would hold for Percival, called signals. The snap was high, forcing Bobby to jump for the ball. As Douglass scrambled to his left, I thought, *Here we go again.* I drifted into a vacant corner of the end zone and began waving my arms. Bobby spotted me and lofted one just as he got hit. I made an over-the-shoulder catch and fell to the ground. Or was it? One of the officials had thrown a yellow flag. Still on my back on the AstroTurf, I threw the ball in the air and jumped to my feet. I leaned over the official and told him very convincingly that I had indeed checked into the game on offense, which is required by the rules. I must have looked pretty scary with the blood streaming down my face. The official quietly retrieved the flag and signaled the successful conversion, which was only one point in those days. We had won another squeaker, 16–15.

Dooley was crediting these miraculous outcomes to his special off-field coaching technique. In order to better prepare Bobby Douglass for upcoming games, he decided to move into the quarterback's bachelor apartment. This extracurricular bivouac by Dooley gave the Chicago press a lot to write about. The reference "odd couple"—taken from the popular movie starring Jack Lemmon and Walter Matthau—was made repeatedly, but as long as the Bears won, no one seemed to think anything was particularly odd about it—and certainly there wasn't. Nine games into the season, we were in second place, a game behind the Vikings—and that's all that seemed to matter.

Then we turned colder than Lake Michigan in February. No amount of special quarterback coaching could alter the facts that we had no viable running game without Gale Sayers and All-Pro receiver Dick Gordon couldn't catch every Bobby Douglass pass. Once the rest of the league figured us out, we had no options, and the ride down was swift and embarrassing. We lost the last five games, scoring a total of 29 points while giving up 126. In three of those games—against the Detroit Lions, the Miami Dolphins, and the Denver Broncos—we scored a grand total of 9 points. Over that stretch, the defense spent an average of forty-one minutes on the field. We just got worn down.

By now, Dooley was insisting he was "as good a coach as anyone in the NFL." No one bothered to disagree with him. The mood in the locker room was dark. My knee was swollen. Halas, they say, was also inflamed. Rumors were flying that Dooley was a lame duck. It was 1969 all over again. The losing was getting very old.

Our thirteenth game was at Green Bay. We lost, 31–10, but I will always remember that December day. Ray Nitschke was honored, and I watched the best I ever saw stand there and cry like a baby, and I loved him for it—because this game of football is about nothing if not emotion.

Our backs were to the goal and I had been kicked in the head the play before, and now the Packers were on the one yard line and I was standing in the defensive huddle feeling just fine about everything. I was looking in the stands and up at the sky and they tell me I was smiling. OB was yelling at me to call the defense, so finally I just said, "Oh hell, guys, do whatever you want. What's the difference? It's such a beautiful day. Let's just have some fun."

"What the *fuck?*" screamed OB. "Dick, for Christ's sake, call something, *anything!*"

So I called a safety blitz, which is an insane call under the circumstances and Starr waltzed in for the score. The next day when we looked at the film, I was lined up at the back of the end zone, behind the safety, on the play. I didn't remember it at all.

My head cleared up after the extra point had made it 31–10.

Mercifully, the season ended away from home the following Sunday. The Vikings beat us, 27–10, in Minneapolis.

Cooper Rollow, sports editor and bard of the Bears' fortunes, drew on Charles Dickens to describe the season: " 'It was the best of times, it was the worst of times. It was the spring of hope, it was the winter of despair.' "

I was just happy to have survived the season.

The same could not be said for Jim Dooley. Citing Dooley's four-year record and saying, "It speaks for itself," Papa Halas had seen enough. A week after our loss to the Vikings, he fired Coach Dooley, saying it has been an "agonizing decision." Papa didn't like to fire people, but he disliked losing even more.

A few days later, I stopped by the front office to pick up the last batch of my mail before heading for the Pro Bowl. I was still fuming about the lousy season we'd just finished, and I poked my head into the Old Man's office and saw him sitting behind his desk. After a minimum of small talk, I accused him of not being serious enough about putting a winner on the field. I asked him how he could let such a thing happen to the Bears.

"Look, Coach," I said, "who's in the Super Bowl?"

He opened his mouth to say something, but no words came out.

"That's right. Dallas and Miami, two fucking expansion teams."

The Old Man sat there and all the air seemed to go out of him. Then he nodded and admitted that he had made a mistake with Dooley, that he should not have appointed him head coach. He said he was going to rectify the situation.

"Who's getting the job?" I asked.

"Don't worry, kid," he said. "I will make the announcement at the appropriate time."

Two weeks later, Halas proved to me he had no real interest in fresh, independent talent. Instead of looking outside, he again promoted from within. He announced Abe Gibron, the offensive coach, as the new head coach of the Bears. Big and full of fun, Abe at least would bring some laughs to the game. But we needed more than laughter.

At the press conference, someone asked Halas if he had considered coming back himself. The old warhorse responded in form. "Well, I'll tell you, several months ago I got to see the movie *Patton* for the first time. I sat there and the adrenaline really started to flow. What a great Bear coach General Patton would have made. Then for just a flicker I thought I would come back."

The Old Man was talking about a lost era, when coaches and generals called the shots and men obeyed and victories were won because of it. And for a second he thought just maybe he could bring it back, that he could step out onto the sidelines and it would be the 1940s again, when Patton's tank divisions were kicking ass in North Africa and Europe and the Bears were doing the same back home under Halas.

But as he said at the press conference, "The flicker passed."

As a brand-new NFL head coach, Abe Gibron knew that you couldn't win big games without talent, but by the time our exhibition season ended, a number of key Bears went down with injuries. The biggest loss was Gale Sayers, our star running back. In our last preseason game against St. Louis, I watched Gale run onto the field with the offense. He'd had three operations over the last two seasons and had played briefly in just two games. We all knew there wasn't much left in his legs. Yet we hoped for a miracle.

It was not to be. Gale carried the ball three times, dropping it twice. A few days later, on September 10, 1972, he thanked the city of Chicago, his teammates, George Halas, and even the press. Finally he thanked the game of football. Then he was gone, slipping away from the limelight with the same finesse he displayed when he had two good knees and a football tucked in his arm. But Gale will never be forgotten in Chicago or in any other NFL town where he played. He was a Bear for seven seasons, but he only played in five, from 1965 through 1969. I doubt there is another runner in history who did as much in so short a time—and with so little help.

Gale's exit from the game heightened my own fears of an early retirement. Now, of course, I look back and see that neither Gale nor I had anything to worry about. Gale owns a very successful computer software company and I have done pretty well. But back then we didn't have a clue what was in store for us outside the lines—and the thought of finding out before we were ready was scary.

We were pitiful in our opening game against Atlanta, giving up three touchdowns by halftime in a game we eventually lost, 37–21. The Falcons were rated as mediocre, but we made them look like Super Bowl contenders. We put up stiffer resistance in the second half, but it was too little, too late. I recovered a fumble a few minutes into the third period, and Bobby Douglass made it count by firing a pass to Earl Thomas, who juggled the ball for five yards before hauling it in for a touchdown. There was one bright spot in the loss. Fullback Jim Harrison, out of Missouri, gained 113 yards. A Bear running back hadn't hit the 100-yard mark in a game since Gale did it three times in 1969.

Ed O'Bradovich had retired over the summer and now he was writing a weekly column for the *Chicago Tribune*. In his assessment of our first game, OB wrote: ''All I can say is thank God for Dick Butkus. It was so evident to me why Butkus is first-team All-Pro and Nobis isn't. When there is a hole in the line, there is Butkus filling it, making the tackle on the line of scrimmage. Tommy Nobis backpedals three or four yards and then makes the tackle. Both can do the job, but who would you want in the middle?''

It was nice of Ed to say that, but we really stunk up the field against Atlanta. We didn't execute well on the defensive side, especially deep in our own territory. Because if we had, the Falcons wouldn't have scored 37 points. No one can explain away 37 points.

We were better the next week against the Rams. But not good enough to win—we tied them, 13–13. The defense played great. We only let the Rams cross midfield three times. Quarterback Pete Beathard only produced two first downs in the same series once in that game. I don't think we blew a single coverage. Unlike the previous week, we were exploding off the ball. I was in on fifteen tackles and recovered a fumble. The rest of the guys had good days, too. After the game, Bear safety Garry Lyle said, "You guys must have been doing everything right, because nobody got through."

With less than a minute to go and the score tied, the Rams stood on our thirty-eight. It was fourth down. I saw their kicker, Dave Ray, run onto the field. I watched him closely. I thought I saw some tension in the way he moved. Maybe it was in his eyes. Anyway, I called timeout just as they broke the huddle. I think I bothered Ray. He seemed annoyed. A few minutes later, the ball was snapped and he missed the attempt. The tie was preserved. The next day OB remarked in the *Tribune* "That's one of the reasons Butkus is one of the greatest. He plays every angle, physical and mental, and he played a super game yesterday. Ross Brupbacher and Doug Buffone also did fine jobs on their sides as linebackers, each coming up with key stops."

I think the three of us were as a good a linebacking crew as there was at that time. Brupbacher was excellent and Buffone was more than that. Doug was one of the best outside linebackers Chicago—or any team—ever had. We created an awful lot of mayhem together.

The next Sunday we faced the Detroit Lions, our old nemesis. It was our third straight home game. In the minds of the sportswriters, there was an added twist. *Stop Action*, a small book I had written that covered one week in my football life in 1971, had recently been published. I called the Lions "jerks" in the book. They *were* jerks—but they were also very *good* jerks in 1972. Anyway, the press made a big deal out of this before the game.

That day the Lions were especially good. Except for one series in the fourth quarter, quarterback Greg Landry directed them to a touchdown or a field goal on every possession. We managed to put some points on the board, too. Jim Harrison picked up 91 yards on the ground and Douglass made some nice passes. But it was not nearly enough as the Lions won easily, 38–24.

The next day *Chicago Tribune* writer George Langford wrote about the postgame scene in the locker room: "Butkus at first chose not to talk at all. After a league-record shower of more than thirty minutes, the All-Pro was asked what effect his book might have had on the results. 'The book?' he snapped. 'The book didn't beat us, Landry did. You guys [newsmen] started all this stuff. You saw the game. Don't ask me no questions.' " I wouldn't change a word of what I said—except maybe "no" to "any." Abe Gibron meanwhile had lost his famous sense of humor. In a telling outburst that must have gotten Commissioner Rozelle's attention, Gibron laid blame on the officials, calling them "gutless, incompetent and playing favorites." If that didn't get him in trouble with the league, he went to accuse the officials of "controlling the outcome of games the last three weeks."

Then, just as it seemed as though the season was beyond saving, our fortunes turned around, but not before we lost a heartbreaker up in Green Bay. Cooper Rollow, the Bears' press box bard, led his account of that game in the *Chicago Tribune* with another gem from the literary past. "These are the times that try Abe Gibron's soul." Not only Abe's, Rollow might have added. The team was just as disappointed. We played tough and smart on both sides of the ball, but luck made us losers.

Toward the end of the first half, receiver Dave Davis of the Packers ran a deep pattern down the left sideline. Davis and Bear cornerback Joe Taylor leaped and touched the ball simultaneously and it was batted toward Packer Jon Staggers, who made a terrific catch at the three yard line and ran into the end zone, putting the home team ahead, 17–3. We fought back effectively in the second half, scoring two touchdowns while stuffing the Packers' running game. I made fullback John Brockington my personal assignment. But Scott Hunter, Green Bay's young quarterback, was cold fire out there, hitting on 15 passes for 240 yards. With less than a minute to go in the fourth quarter, Hunter made three perfect passes to set up Chester Marcol's field goal, which split the uprights with thirty seconds left, giving the Packers a 20–17 victory.

We were winless in four games. But what I hated even more than our standing in the cellar was the 108 points we'd given up. With Gibron agitated and everyone focused, we went to Cleveland and cleaned the Browns' clock, 17–0. We did it with an unlikely cast. Our talented defensive end Willie Holman had been lost for the season with a torn Achilles tendon, and we started the game with three rookie linemen—Jim Osborne, Bill Line, Larry Horton—playing in front of me. They were gung-ho, each feeling he could beat his man. So I told them to go for it, and damned if they didn't do the job. Meanwhile, Douglass had a great game, passing for one touchdown and running for another on a 57-yard naked bootleg. Afterward, even the Old Man was smiling as he reminisced about the Bears' first win in 1920, back when they were the Decatur Staleys in the APFA and they beat the Moline Tractors, 20–0. Someone asked him when the last shutout was. "Eight years ago," he said, sourly. "When Dick was a rookie."

We kept going, winning the next week over Minnesota, 13–10, at Soldier Field. "We just played football," said Abe Gibron, who acted like a new man after the game. It was a Monday night game, and a cold drizzle was falling all night long. It was a runner's game, and Jim Harrison went to work, gaining 104 yards. We were great in the first half, displaying a down-and-dirty ball-control strategy that resulted in our running forty-one plays to the Vikings' nine. By the middle of the fourth quarter, we were tied, 10–10. Then I guessed right. "Old Reliable Dick Butkus," wrote Cooper Rollow, "the blood and flesh of the Bear defense, intercepted Fran Tarkenton's pass meant for tight end John Beasley and returned it 14 yards to midfield." Three plays later, Percival booted a 20-yard field goal that won the game, 13–10, and moved us out of last place and Abe Gibron out of his personal hell.

Next came the St. Louis Cardinals, and Abe Gibron the magic man pulled out the stops in this game, using Bobby Douglass as a runner, pulling a reverse on a kickoff return—which resulted in a 91-yard touchdown—and employing a shift out of a shotgun formation. The result was 27 points on the board against a tough defense. In the first half, we put up 17 points on three explosive drives that took all of nineteen, forty-eight, and fifty-six seconds. The defense was stingy again, allowing the Cardinals just 10 points. As OB said the next day, "The defense has continually turned the ball over to the offense in good position all season, but in the past the offense hasn't been able to take advantage."

Now, thanks to Abe's creativity and Bobby's growing confidence, the offense was delivering the goods. The 27–10 victory was our third consecutive victory and we were 3–3–1 on the season, just a game and a half behind the Lions, who led the Central Division. Our heads were spinning from the quick turnaround.

As Gibron's strange schizoid debut continued to unfold, Dr. Fox began giving me shots before every game and draining the knee whenever there was a buildup of fluid. You might wonder why I didn't consult other doctors. I can only say that at the time I believed Fox was doing everything possible for my knee. Like many of my generation, I was brought up to believe in the word of doctors, employers, cops, and priests. I still believe in most priests.

This was the last year of a three-year contract and I was afraid I would be thrown on the trash heap like Howard Mudd. As much as I still believed in Fox, I began to wonder if there was someone out there who could keep my knee from blowing apart. A lot of people had advice. One night I found myself being led up the back stairs of a run-down building of an alley in Gary, Indiana, to the office of a Chinese doctor who practiced acupuncture. Back then the technique was frowned on by the American medical community. I tried acupuncture for quite a while. It didn't help my knee any except to lessen the pain for a little while.

Around midseason, a friend named Sam Miller introduced me to a woman named Gladys. She believed that we all have the power to heal ourselves. She told me that she had been born clubfooted and had eventually healed herself. She called her technique mind dynamics and she taught a class in it on weekends. After listening to her for a while, I decided that Gladys might be able to help me. I had always believed that I had a sixth sense when I played football. If this woman had something like that and if it would help my knee, I was all for it.

Sam convinced Gladys to hold a special class in a local motel on weeknights. There were four of us: Joe Elias, his wife Jane, Helen, and me. That first night Gladys had us close our eyes and imagine each color of the rainbow until we could actually see it. This was supposed to put our minds in the alpha state, a childlike trance that allows us to roam our imaginations. Then she helped us imagine our workshops—a place where each of us would meet the person who would watch over us in our times of need. At the appointed time, I closed my eyes and recalled the workshop I had made in my mind. I was shocked to see my father walk through the door. I never thought of him as my protector. But there he was, smiling at me.

If Joe and I thought this stuff was a little weird, Helen and Jane thought it was just great. The next night we were taught how to "read" an individual's physical health. Once we had lifted ourselves into the alpha level, we would beam up the individual we wanted to check out. If the person was sick, there would be a glow—Gladys called it an aura—coming from the afflicted area.

I was so tired after one practice that I fell asleep at the class and didn't wake up until it was over. On the way home, I asked Helen what had happened. She told me that she saw my buddy Rick Richards when she reached her alpha level. She told me that Rick had a growth on the back of his head and that he had to warn the barber about it whenever he went to get a haircut. This was news to me. Helen also said that Rick had a severe jock rash. At this point, I wanted to take her to the nearest emergency ward, but she laughed and told me to calm down—and we drove home to Chicago Heights.

I wasn't through the door a minute before I was dialing Rick's house. I didn't expect to get him because he worked different shifts at a steel mill and I never knew when he'd be home. But he answered. I said, "I've got two questions." He said, "Shoot." First I asked him about the growth on his head. Damned if he didn't confirm it, saying he'd had it for years.

This was interesting enough, but it could easily be explained. Helen may have learned of the bump years before.

Then I asked him about his jock rash.

"How do you know I have a jock rash?" Rick said.

"Helen saw it."

"What the hell do you mean, 'Helen saw it'?"

"She saw it, and now she's healing it," I said, feeling slightly unreal. Then I heard myself say, "It'll be gone in a little while."

When I tried to explain mind dynamics to Rick, he all but hung up in my ear. Must have been too much for him. I know it was too much for me.

That Sunday we played the Lions in Detroit. On Saturday night, Helen got herself onto the alpha level and saw the scoreboard at Tiger Stadium after the next day's game. She told me it showed the Lions' final score as 14. But she couldn't make out the Bears' score. We lost, 14–0. If Helen had been able to peek farther into the future, she would have seen disaster for the Bears. In the remaining six games, we only managed to beat the lowly Eagles, 21–12, at Soldier Field. We lost to the 49ers, the Packers, the Bengals, the Vikings, and the Raiders.

We could put up a good fight, even win a battle or two, but we just didn't have the troops to win the war. We needed the kind of stability that comes with top-quality talent. Our offense was faulty at best. We had no real ground game without Gale and our pass completion percentage was the lowest in the NFL. We just couldn't seem to sustain a drive on offense. As the season progressed, all those extra minutes out on the field wore down the defense. But we were talented and proud. Somehow we kept our points-allowed-per-game average under 20. Despite the pain and the swelling in my knee, I played reasonably well, although my average of a dozen un-

assisted tackles per game dropped slightly. I'd lost some mobility, but I could still read a play and call the right defense
and I could still hit.

Against Green Bay at Soldier Field, I knocked quarterback
Scott Hunter out of the game. Hunter recalled the hit. "It was
third down and three and I was scrambling to my left. I
looked up and one of our receivers was chicken-fighting with
one of the Bears' cornerbacks. I kept my eye on him, but I
thought I could make the first down myself. I couldn't make
it going out of bounds, so I turned upfield and I looked to my
right and here came that big black jersey. I put my head down
and the next thing I knew I was sitting on the sidelines with
smelling salts under my nose. After the game, Butkus came
over to me and said, 'You need to get out of bounds.' "

1972 had been our sixth losing season in the last eight
years. Neither patchwork trades by Halas nor quick fixes by
Fox were helping either patient. But they kept putting me out
there week after week, and each Monday I would struggle out
of bed like an old man and wait for the pain to subside and
the strength to return. On Sunday mornings, a couple of
pounds of tape would be wrapped tightly around my right
leg and I would go out onto that damned AstroTurf and play
myself into another week of misery.

Why did I do it? I can't really answer that. I loved to play
so damn much that even when it hurt I couldn't stop on my
own. If the Bears' management, if Halas or Gibron or Fox or
Mugs had told me to sit one out, I would have groused and
done what I was told. Instead they said, "Go out there, Dick,"
and I went out there. They said, "We love you, Dick," and I
believed them. But the pain was sending me a different message. Nothing, not even love, was supposed to hurt this
much.

"How's the knee?"

Halas sat behind his desk, his eyes on me.

"Pretty good," I said. "It gives me a little trouble now and then, but that's to be expected. Fox seems to thinks it's holding up."

"Good," said Halas. "Glad to hear it because we need you out there, kid."

Then we started to negotiate. I had a figure in mind, a figure that was put there by Keating. It seemed high to me, but I certainly wasn't opposed to it. So when the Old Man asked me what I was looking for, I looked him dead in the eye and gave him the figure.

He started working his lips, just like I knew he would.

When I said I wanted it for five years, Halas shook his head and said that the first number was too much and that the second was too long. I asked if I could use the phone. He said, "sure." I went down the hall to the empty office and called Keating—so he could tell me my next move. After half a dozen of these timeouts, there still had not been any movement. I decided to play on my own. I leaned back in my chair and began to reminisce. I talked about what it meant to me to be a Chicago Bear. How the idea of playing for him had filled my dreams when I was a kid. As I talked, I could see Halas softening. He was being drawn into the thing that mattered most to him: the spirit and tradition of the team. Then I talked about the last few years when we had to go without him on the field and how I missed his presence and how hard I had tried. Then, when I thought he was well primed, I said, "Coach, you give me what I want and I guarantee you we will win the championship. I'll *get* you that title by myself if I have to."

Christ, I was almost bawling.

The Old Man sat there for a moment, his head down, his

teeth no longer clicking. He looked as though he was asleep, but I suspect he was daydreaming about those wonderful years when the Bears were indomitable.

Then he slowly raised his head and looked at me.

"God *damn*," he whispered. "That's a great attitude, kid."

He gave me the money: $115,000 per for five years. It was exactly the figure Keating hoped we'd get, and it was one of the largest contracts any Bear player had ever negotiated.

Halas was famous for cutting his players down at contract time. A guy like Ed Sprinkle would have a Pro Bowl year and the Old Man would tell him that he stunk up the field and he should forget about a raise. But he gave me what I wanted, didn't even try to bargain me down. Was he that easily influenced by sentiments?

But there is another side to this that still puzzles me. Why didn't Halas have me take a physical or at least have my knee checked before he agreed a negotiate a long-term contract? The only reasonable answer is that he believed my knee would hold up. If that's true, then it doesn't follow that he could have been getting the right information. Dr. Fox was the sole voice on the state of my knee. For eight years, he had been examining it—poking, probing, injecting, and X-raying. He'd even operated on it, cutting into it not once but twice. Despite everything, he must have felt it was okay.

⸻

On July 13, I signed five one-year contracts for a total of $575,000, a lot of money. I don't believe any other defensive player in the NFL was making that much then. I felt like I was on top of the world.

The nightmare began a few days later. I had reported to training camp at Rensselaer the night of July 17 feeling pretty good. But the next morning my knee couldn't stand the pressure when I tried to cut to my left. That was the first time I realized that my knee was not working right. There had always been pain, but now I could see that the knee had buckled dramatically to the outside. The angle was so pronounced that I could almost set a dime on it. I showed it to Fox. His answer was the same as ever: more hydrocortisone.

During the exhibition season, it became increasingly difficult for me to play and Gibron decided not to test the knee too heavily in games of no consequence. In our first preseason match against Green Bay, I sat down after the first half. I stayed out of parts of other exhibition games as well. This was new. I'd missed only one game in eight years, and the newspaper writers knew it. They began to ask questions. "What is wrong with you? How are the knees?" Even my teammates were curious. Everyone could see I was limping badly. My knee hurt with every step I took. Fox didn't seem to have any answers. So I made a point to consult other surgeons. I started making appointments with doctors all over the country.

Meanwhile, we had gone undefeated in the preseason. We had just one more game at Washington before opening the regular season against Dallas at home. I started the game, but I had to leave after the first series. We lost, 17–3. The next day and for the rest of the week the sports pages of the *Tribune* and the *Daily News* were filled with speculation about my knee and whether I would start against the Cowboys. The writers scrambled to find a new angle on my knee.

Everyone around me closed ranks and denied there was a problem. Regarding my early exit from the Redskins game, Gibron told the *Tribune:* "Butkus had a small problem, nothing serious." But the *Daily News* ran a different story. It said my knee was "possibly blown beyond repair" and that my future had "all but run out." The *News* then reported accurately that I was on a national talent search for a surgeon who might be able to salvage my knee. The next day the *Tribune* countered by saying the *Daily News* had greatly exaggerated the condition of my knee and my "demise" as a player. It also said the search for a savior surgeon was not true. To back up its claim, the *Tribune* quoted Gibron ("I don't know where they get all that junk"), Halas ("Another ridiculous story"), and even Helen ("He's been playing with pain for years. It's no different now").

The only individual not directly quoted was the man who presumably knew the truth: Dr. Theodore Fox. When the reporters called his office, his nurse said he was too busy to answer questions. She added what I thought was a telling phrase: "He doesn't want to be quoted." As the week wore on, the reporters were all over me. All I said was "Haven't I always been there?" Then I referred them to my roommate and unofficial mouthpiece, Doug Buffone. Trying to keep a straight face, Doug said, "My client does not want to comment further until after the court case." Little did we know then how prophetic those words would be.

On the day before the Dallas game, Cooper Rollow wrote an advance article in the *Tribune* that heralded the start of a new season and the first Bears game to be televised live in the metropolitan area in many years. Congress had successfully prodded the NFL to lift its local blackout policy if the game had been sold out. This was never a problem in Chicago. A sold-out Soldier Field was the rule, even in the worst years.

The next day I limped out on that crummy synthetic grass that was laid over cement and played as hard I could under a strong late-summer sun. Although our defense played well, we could not overcome six fumbles made by the offense, and we lost, 20–17. I made ten solo tackles, assisted on five more, and intercepted one of Roger Staubach's passes. But my knee was talking to me all game long, warning me not to expect this kind of support much longer. After the game, it was swollen more than ever.

In the locker room, the reporters gathered around. One asked me, "How do you think you played?" "How do *you* think I played?" I snarled at him. "I wish I could have intercepted ten passes and made fifty tackles. I'm just out there trying. Now it's your turn to write whatever you want and I'm sure you will." Another writer asked me, "Is the pain any worse than it has been in previous years?" Rather than lie outright, I said, "You're not supposed to think about pain. You're supposed to think about the opponent." Then came the inevitable follow-up question: "Do you think you will be able to play all season?" "Hey," I said in a rising voice, "I might go outside and get hit by a truck. Just write what you think. Just don't put me away so early. It's my career. Let me worry about it." Then I called over to Buffone to hurry up so we could get out of there. Right about then, Gibron came out of his office and gave the press hell about the miserable week they had put us all through. "I read all that crap you wrote about Butkus quitting," he said. "Well, I just hope you got your fucking eyes opened."

The next day the *Tribune* covered my performance almost as thoroughly as it did the game. Cowboy coaches and players were interviewed. Among them were offensive guards John Niland and Blaine Nye, the two Cowboys who were assigned to block me. "It looked like he was having trouble moving," said Niland. "But even when he's hurt, he's ten times better than anyone else. On pass coverage, he was having trouble getting back. He used to move first and then read defenses, but now he reads the defense first, then moves to save steps. But he's still strong, still anticipates well, is a great motivator and leader, and the only way to control him is with cut blocks, even up the middle.'' Nye agreed: ''Either Butkus can still move pretty good or I had my shoelaces tied together.''

Coach Tom Landry's assessment was typically kind: ''Butkus has slowed down. But he's going to play as long as he can get there, and as long as Butkus has two legs, he's going to get there.''

Perhaps the most accurate and telling evaluation of my ability came from my Dallas counterpart, the great middle linebacker Lee Roy Jordan. ''He used to take care of the middle and both sides. Now he just takes care of the middle and gets outside when he can. You can see his leg is not well. It doesn't look like it will ever get better.''

There it was, the unvarnished truth about Dick Butkus according to Lee Roy Jordan—one banged-up linebacker about another. When I read Jordan's quote, I felt in my gut that he was probably right. *Maybe it's really over.* The thought was like a knife in my stomach. Before I would admit it to anyone, I had to convince myself—and the only way to do that was to get the facts from the best medical minds in the country. Not one but several. I was through relying on one man's opinion.

In the weeks that followed, I hopped a jet at O'Hare each Friday to keep an appointment with an orthopedic surgeon somewhere in the country. One week I was in Los Angeles being examined by Dr. Rosenthal, and the next I was with a doctor at Johns Hopkins Medical Center in Baltimore. I went to Atlanta and saw Dr. Alman, and on to the University of Florida in Gainesville to see the head of orthopedics. All the diagnoses were similar. Each suggested I undergo a complicated operation called a tibial-osteotomy, which involved removing a piece of the shin bone. Not only were all the surgeons in agreement about the necessity for the operation, they all said that once the surgery was done, I could never play football again.

Meanwhile, I was playing football. We lost the next game to the Vikings, 22–13, at Soldier Field. My old adversary Mick Tingelhoff, the Vikings' seven-time All-Pro center, said he thought I played as good as ever and maybe I did okay from tackle to tackle. But I wasn't able to adjust quickly. Rookie running back Chuck Foreman got past me for a long run. I was much slower now. I knew where I had to be on every play, but I couldn't get there fast enough. Watching myself on the game films, hopping and skipping and lunging, I understood why I was constantly being ridiculed by the opposition. "Hey, Butkus, you fucking cripple! Get out of the game!"

Not all the barbs came from the enemy. Some of the Bears were bitching about my not practicing. Their discontent was fueled by the speculation about the size of my new contract. I'd been through this sort of thing before, back in my rookie year for example. But for some reason, the backbiting got to me. Maybe it was because I so strongly suspected that I might never be able to go out on the field again and show them that I was worth every dollar of whatever they thought I was getting.

My temper grew shorter as the pain in my knee increased. We played the Broncos in Denver's Mile High Stadium and won, 33–14. It was a rough-and-tumble game, the kind I used to enjoy. The Broncos tried to be the Bears and they paid the price, getting hit with a number of holding penalties they'd been getting away with all season. I'd spotted the holds in the game films, and I kept reminding the officials of it until they started to make the calls. The Broncos didn't score a point until the victory was out of their reach in the fourth quarter.

Although our defense played well, I was unable to appreciate it. The pain in the knee was reaching the point where I could hardly walk, much less play. To make matters worse, I pulled something in my groin and got a deep cut on the back of my right hand. But we'd won and I was still standing on two feet—and just as Landry had said, I was "getting there" most of the time.

Then we went to New Orleans and lost, 21–16. We stunk up the field against the worst team in the NFL. If it weren't for their quarterback Archie Manning, they would have belonged in the Continental League. But we were worse. We let a five-foot-five, 165-pound running back named Howard Stevens bounce through us for two touchdowns. I would have devoured him even a year earlier.

I said as much the next day when I was the Monday morning quarterback as the Playboy Club in Chicago. When someone asked me if Stevens had been running through our legs, I quipped, "Could have been. I never saw the little shit. I don't know if they put him in there to embarrass us or what."

Then the writers started asking the inevitable questions about Bobby Douglass. He usually caught most of the blame for the Bears' poor offense. "Look," I said, "the coaches send the plays in and Bobby's got to run them, so why blame Bobby? If he is so bad, why doesn't Abe make a change? He's the coach. Of course, Abe says that would be putting too much pressure on a rookie—putting Gary Huff in there. But that's how Joe Namath got started. That's how Jim Plunkett got started. That's how Dan Pastorini and Bert Jones got started." Then I mused about what might have been if we had had the first draft pick four years earlier. "What if we'd won the coin toss with Pittsburgh after that 1969 season when we both were 1–13? They got Terry Bradshaw. Well, I dunno. Bradshaw's no genius either."

If we were embarrassed by the Saints, then I don't know how to describe what happened the next Sunday in Atlanta. We scored first, grinding out a touchdown with nine minutes of heavy ground work. Then Mirro Roder's extra-point attempt was blocked, and that was it for the day. Neither our offense nor defense was heard from again that day. The final score was 46–6. Atlanta coach Norm Van Brocklin sent three hit men after me on every play. He had no reason to do it—his team was rolling over us. But he kept sending them. At some point when our offense had the ball for a few plays, I yelled at Abe: "What the fuck am I doing in this game? I can hardly walk." But he didn't seem to hear me—and out I went again. My frustration reached a breaking point in the third quarter when Falcon tight end Jim Mitchell tried to cut-block me across the knees. I threw a kick at him with my good leg.

A little later, my knee collapsed. I was in pursuit of running back Dave Hampton when I felt it go. I limped off the field. No one said a word to me, so I walked to the end of the bench and sat alone for the rest of the game. No trainer or coach or player came down to see me. I sat and fumed.

In the trainers' room after the game, I was beside myself. One of the trainers told me to see Fox. I said, "Fuck Fox." Then Needles showed his face in the training room and waved to me to get my usual injection. "Hey!" I yelled at him. "Why do I need a shot anyway? I don't need a shot. I need a tibial-osteotomy. You know what that is, Doc?" He looked at me and didn't say anything. For the first time in almost nine years, I refused to take a shot.

Meanwhile, a few yards away in the locker room, Gibron was threatening to shake up the team. He would have something to announce the next day. Then the press turned their attention to me: "Why did you take yourself out of the game? Was it the knee?" I didn't answer. I'd heard Gibron tell them

I was bumped from the game because I had aggravated the groin injury I'd sustained in Denver. I said I would have something to announce in a week or so. One reporter even asked "Exactly when do you plan to make the announcement? What day? What time?" So I snapped at him: "When I'm ready! Do me a favor for once, will you?"

The next day back in Chicago I visited Fox in his office. I'd calmed down a little by then. Needles X-rayed my knee and threw the negative up on a back-lit screen and explained in a clear and informed manner how a tibial-osteotomy was done. He went into great detail, using a ruler and pointer to show how the operation would be done. I was somewhat impressed; at least he knew the procedure. Then he said, "You'll be the first guy to play with one of these. You know why? Because I won't put any staples in there."

Although six of the best knee surgeons in the world had informed me that once I had the operation, I could never play again, Fox had disagreed. He was going to do the operation himself and leave out the two staples, which he said weren't necessary. He was going to show the medical world how it should be done. Hearing all this, I concluded that Fox didn't give a flying fuck about my knee after football and I decided that he wasn't going to use what was left of my knee to make his mark.

Throughout the week, the papers kept up the drumbeat. "Is Butkus through? If so, when will he announce his retirement?" That Sunday we lost our fifth game to the New England Patriots, 13–10. They beat us in the waning moments on a fluke touchdown pass by Jim Plunkett. The only positive note was our defense. Rookie defensive tackle Wally Chambers made twelve unassisted tackles. I was just lucky to make the game. The knee was screaming by then, and my sense of isolation was growing stronger by the day.

After the game, the press asked me how I felt about the

statement by George Halas that had appeared in the *Tribune* on Saturday. I said, "I haven't looked at a paper in weeks." Someone just happened to have the paper and quoted the Old Man: " 'We know that Dick Butkus is hurting, but we also know that he is a proud man and true competitor whose problems seem to vary in direct proportion to the showing of the team as a whole.' "

So now he is calling me a quitter, I thought to myself. *As the Bears go, so goes Butkus. Is that what he's saying?* I got angry and said, "Well, he's the father of football. I guess he's right. But I doubt I'd be doing cartwheels right now it we had won today."

The next day I was handed a copy of the Saturday article at the Playboy Club's Monday morning quarterback lunch. I read it through. Halas had brought up our meeting on July 13 when I told him I'd give him a championship if he gave me the contract I wanted. I couldn't believe he would repeat what we said in private. He was always swearing me to secrecy as to how much he paid me. Now, to suite his purposes, he had broken that confidence. Then he drove a needle into me that Dr. Fox might have admired. "That was the Dick Butkus I signed in July—and I know he is still that Dick Butkus with the heart of a winner."

I put the paper down on the table and answered the hurtful words. "In July, I believed I could bring a championship to Chicago and Mr. Halas." Then I expressed publicly what I had been thinking for two months. "But I can't perform as I used to. You see what I do in practice. Nothing—I do nothing! I go to a game cold. I read the game plan. I can't be a leader that way. No one can. Sunday's just not enough. So you can take that article Mr. Halas wrote and shove it. This is *not* July 13."

I sat down and began eating my lunch. I couldn't get my

mind off what Halas had said. *Doesn't he understand what is happening to me? He coached for forty years. He even played the game. He knows what happens to a football player's knees. Is he saying what I think he is saying?* I didn't want to believe it, but the meaning of his words suddenly was unavoidable. The Old Man was saying that I was lying down on the job. As much as the knee hurt, those words hurt much more.

Toward the end of the lunch, the host turned things over to the reporters. Pads and pencils came out and questions flew. In light of my earlier remarks, one reporter asked, "Do you think you should be playing at all?" "I've got some doubts about it," I said. "The other players see me standing around during practice and that's not good for morale. Opposing players call me a cripple and tell me to get out of the league. I can't take my kids anywhere in public because of the negative stuff that gets thrown my way. I'm hopping around on the field like I've got a wooden leg, and all the time you guys are asking me if this is my last year. Hell, I don't know if I can make it to next week."

But I was there the next week when we beat the Houston Oilers, 35–14. I scored our first touchdown by recovering quarterback Dan Pastorini's fumble in the end zone. When the ball was snapped, I thought Chambers may have moved a little early, so when I picked up Pastorini's fumble I yelled, "Touchdown! Touchdown!" at the officials. I was acting so crazy that they looked at each other. Then one of them threw his hands up to signal the TD. Then tight end Mack Alston started screaming, "Offsides! Offsides!" But it was too late. I walked off the field laughing and feeling better than I had in weeks.

Alston and I went at it the whole game. He constantly complained to the referees that I was putting late hits on his teammates. In the second half, I intercepted a pass meant for

Alston. Instead of running with the ball, I took a couple of steps backward and shook the ball at him. "Come and get it, you asshole!" He just shook his head. After the game, Alston told some writers that he thought I'd gone around the bend. Several other Oilers joined him in a chorus of complaints, the most ridiculous being that I had so intimidated the officials that they wouldn't make a call against me. I guess some people think any excuse is better than none when you lose.

Between games I was doing all I could to stay in shape and keep my knee from losing what little strength it still had. At night I slept with three heating pads. Arthur Jones had shown me a set of strength-building exercises he called negative lifting. Arthur found that you can build strength faster by lowering the weight rather than lifting the weight. The equipment would soon go on the market under the brand name Nautilus—and soon after that it would revolutionize the world of physical conditioning.

The next week we beat Green Bay, 31–17. I played better than I had in weeks, making twelve solo tackles and assisting on six others. More than the statistics, however, was the unrecorded fact that I got into the backfield often and terrorized Scott Hunter. The result was that he completed just 3 of 14 passes. But my rejuvenation was short-lived. Toward the end of the game, the knee that had felt so much stronger at first was hurting me more than ever.

Bobby Douglass was fun to watch that day at Lambeau Field. At six-foot-three and 240 pounds, he was more of a fullback than a quarterback and he used his strength and agility to great effect against a team that was almost as demoralized as we were. He ran for 100 yards and four touchdowns. He even passed well—connecting on 10 of 15 attempts. So we gave Bobby the game ball. For the rest of his career, Bobby would remain an enigma. His potential was equally great in either direction. On one play, he could make your jaw drop with his ability to execute while in motion. But thirty seconds later, he would do something so silly that you'd want to laugh or cry—or kill him. In a way, Bobby was a perfect metaphor for the 1973 Bears: talented but flawed.

Throughout the week, my knee did not improve. No matter how diligently I applied the heating pads and ice and worked out with Jones's exercises in my cellar, it just wouldn't respond. The swelling and the pain remained high and the bow out to the side was even more pronounced than it had been at the beginning of the season. We would be in Kansas City on Monday night, November 12, and Howard Cosell and the ABC cameras would be there to capture the game for all of America.

We hadn't played Kansas City since the exhibition season of 1967 when we were unfortunate enough to be the first NFL team the Chiefs met after losing to the Packers in Super Bowl I. Lombardi had said on national television after that game that a number of NFL teams could have beaten the Chiefs that year. Kansas City coach Hank Stram answered Vince's assessment in a convincing manner, beating us 67–0. It was the most one-sided defeat in Bears history. Now we hoped to return the favor.

The field was AstroTurf. It hurt just to walk on it. But I played the first half, hopping around back there with my arms flying out to the sides like a man on invisible crutches. The Chiefs ran a lot of sweeps, which made it difficult for me to get outside to the ball carrier. Jan Stenerud kicked four field goals and their huge defense kept Bobby Douglass at bay. Then quarterback Mike Livingston connected with Otis Taylor on a 24-yard pass. Suddenly the Chiefs had amassed 19 points, their biggest offensive output of the season, and the game was out of reach.

Down on the field, I heard calls of "Cripple!" and "Gimp!" while up in the broadcast booth, Don Meredith was admiring my courage and questioning my intelligence for being out there, and Howard Cosell was speaking of the "imminent demise of the greatest single force since Cyclops." After the game, my emotions hit rock bottom. I told Doug Buffone that I thought it was over for me. The pain had hit a new high, but again I refused to take a shot from Fox.

That week Ed Keating wrote a letter to Mugs, suggesting that since the Bears were out of the playoff hunt, it would not hurt if I were to go to the Mayo Clinic and get a complete checkup of the knee and perhaps even undergo an operation. This, reasoned Keating, would enable the knee more time to heal before training camp next July. Mugs wrote back that a trip to the Mayo Clinic was "out of the question." In the letter, he said that if anyone was going to operate on me it was Fox, who was "the best knee surgeon in the country." If, wrote Mugs, I elected to have anyone else perform the operation, then my contract would be "null and void." In the last paragraph, Mugs delivered what I guessed was the new house policy on me: "Besides all that, Mr. Keating, Dick's pain threshold has been lowered for some reason."

Meanwhile, Abe was describing my condition to the press as "arthritic knees." Sure, there was some arthritis in there, but the pain and weakness was due to destroyed ligaments and an absence of cartilage. Where once my knee was a Mack truck, it was now a bloated Volkswagen with wheels missing. To this day, I do not know if Abe—or even Halas—knew the condition of my knee.

When Abe announced to the press that I would not be suiting up for the Lions game, he added, "And it's a damn shame because he graded out 93 percent on his performance Monday. He had eleven tackles and four assists. He has the greatest desire anybody ever had." When a reporter asked whether I would return to action in 1973, Gibron looked horrified. "Oh no. Just for next week's game." Then he added, "Well, we'll see." It was only the second game in nine seasons that I did not play. The first was on December 6, 1969, against the 49ers in San Francisco—when my mobility was drastically cut by what Fox called a "sprained knee." Whether it was actually a sprain or something else I'll never know. But it was the beginning of the pain. Since then I'd played in fifty-three straight league games, and the knee hurt in every one.

On Wednesday, Cooper Rollow wrote in the *Tribune:* "It has been a sad spectacle in recent weeks to watch Butkus, pro football's onetime premier linebacker, struggling to make tackles five yards deep into the secondary, tackles he once made on or behind the line of scrimmage." If it was sad for Coop, it was like slow death for me. Then it got worse that Sunday in Soldier Field when I stood in civvies and watched my team lose to the Lions, 30–7.

The next day at the Playboy Club's Monday morning quarterback lunch I talked in relative detail for the first time about my knee. From the dais, I told the press that I had been getting lots of mail with home remedies for arthritis. Then I spread my hands out and held them up. "It's not arthritis," I said. "Not much more than 20 percent of the problem anyway. I've got something wrong with the bone, with the joint really. I haven't said much about it before because I didn't consider it anybody's business. I'll find out more about the knee very soon." When someone asked if I anticipated surgery, I shrugged and said, "Maybe."

Another reporter had somehow gotten wind of some recent conversations I'd had with Gale Sayers. He asked me what we had talked about. I told him the truth. Gale had urged me to consider doing something else with my life. Who else had more personal knowledge about bad knees? "He's limping at thirty," I said. "What's it going to be like for Gale later? What's it going to be like for me?" In the stillness that followed, I said, "No use throwing all the coins in right now. Maybe, if I have the operation, I'll be playing next year. Who knows? A little later, someone asked, "What position do you think the Bears should go for in the upcoming draft?"

"Linebacker," I said.

In the following weeks, I got the cold shoulder from everybody in the front office and on the team, every coach and trainer and player (except Doug Buffone). Our next game was in Minneapolis and the only person I spoke to while we lost, 31–19, was this guy dressed up as a real Viking, with horns coming out of his helmet. I guess I had horns too, or at least that was how I was being characterized by Halas and Mugs.

Keating called me that night when I got home to Chicago Heights. He said that he had read Mugs's letter several times and he had the feeling that something was up. He warned me to be very careful what I said and to whom I said it. When I asked him what he meant exactly, Keating just said it was a feeling, a hunch. I pressed him a little more, and he said, "I think they're setting you up."

"Why?" I said.

"They owe you a lot of money, Dick. They don't like to pay players a lot of money, even when they're playing. But they especially don't like to pay when they aren't playing."

"But I have a contract that says they have to pay me," I said.

"That's right, you do," said Keating.

"So . . ."

"So just be careful."

Sure enough, Abe called me into his office that week and said, "Well, are you ready to go against the Rams this Sunday?"

"Abe," I said, "don't you get it? It's over. I'm done. Look at me, Abe! I'm the walking wounded here, and don't give me that crap about my being better with one leg than anyone else with two."

Abe sat there as if *he* was wounded. I guess in a way he was. Here it was late November, just a couple of months since he had predicted great things for the Bears, and like Dooley before him he now sat in his own embarrassment, worrying about his job. In the past nine years, everyone had come and gone: Ditka, Sayers, O'Bradovich, Atkins. Everyone except Butkus, and now he too was saying, "It is over."

"Well, goddamn it, Dick. Why not?"

"Because I can't play anymore, Abe. I'm sorry."

Then we talked for a while, just the two of us, and I said I hoped to be able to have the operation right after the season and just maybe there was a chance that I would be able to play somewhere other than linebacker. Abe said he would take me at any position. All he wanted was my desire. He said that it made everyone play better, that it made him coach better. I pointed out that I had played offensive center in college. Maybe I could do that for a little while. Abe said that would be fine.

That Sunday I stood on the sidelines in Soldier Field and watched the Rams beat us, 26–0. The next day at the Playboy Club I announced I was going to the Mayo Clinic. If Halas wouldn't pay for the trip, I would pay for it myself.

The Mayo Clinic was my last hope for a miracle. I flew to Rochester, Minnesota, feeling very lonely, a Bear in name only. For the first time in years, I didn't feel as though I belonged. I remember reciting the rosary to myself as the twin-prop plane coasted onto the icy runway. *Please, God, don't let this happen.*

Dr. William H. Bickle ran all the same tests that had been run on the knee by the six orthopedic surgeons that I had already visited in the last three months. And like all the others, he said I needed the operation, noting that while my body was that of a thirty-year-old, my knee rightfully belonged to a seventy-year-old. He also said the knee might have to be rebuilt by the time I was fifty, and I thought of all the Howard Mudds who had come running into the league with high hopes only to go out on crutches.

We went to Detroit and lost, 40–7. Then we came home and played the final game of the season against the Packers, losing again, 21–0. I stood alone out there on the field and watched the last Chicago fan disappear from the stands. We'd gone 3–11 on the season, losing the last six games. I wondered whether I might have made a difference. The grounds keepers were already at work, clearing the field of benches and first-down chains and yard markers. At first I was saddened by the likelihood that I would never play again, and images welled up of that College All-Star Game on that sweltering summer night in 1965 when Gale and I stood for the first time in Soldier Field and felt the raw power of postcollegiate stardom. But another, more recent image intruded, of a one-legged man trying to be the player he once was. I limped the hell out there, not bothering to stop by the locker room.

C H A P T E R

11

*"W*e are going to have some problems here."

Ed Keating was on the phone from Cleveland, bringing me up to date on the latest exchange of letters and phone calls between him and the Bears' hierarchy. It was January 1974 and by now the Old Man had taken over the negotiations, leaving less volatile matters for his son Mugs to handle. The hot point of the argument centered on the operation and who would do it. Halas, of course, wanted Fox to wield the knife, while I insisted it be one of the recognized orthopedic surgeons I had visited.

Halas responded by saying I was certainly free to have a surgeon of my choice perform the operation on my knee, but he took the position that in the event that I was unable to perform on the field, my contract would be voided.

Meanwhile, I had gotten a call from George Allen, the head coach of the Washington Redskins. He told me he wanted to acquire my services from Chicago. I related to Allen the recent history of my knee, including what every surgeon had said: Once it was operated on, I could no longer play football. Allen, God bless him, didn't hesitate. "Dick, I want my guy down here to take a look at that knee."

So I flew to Washington, D.C., using an assumed name. Dr. Palumbo examined the knee with Allen looking on. After an hour or so, Dr. Palumbo said that he concurred with the other doctors. Much of the knee had deteriorated. I needed to get the operation.

Allen looked at him, then at me. "Okay, so much for that," he said. "But can he be ready for the playoffs next season?"

Dr. Palumbo shrugged. "Well, he could be."

The thought excited me and I was ready to believe that maybe I could come back. Sure, all the other doctors had said I would never play after the operation, but maybe I'd surprise them. It would be worth it to just play for Allen again. I had instantaneous visions of beating Chicago and the next day's headline: ALLEN AND BUTKUS—BAD NEWS FOR THE BEARS.

"I want one more doctor to look at you," said Allen. "He's in Oklahoma City."

Under my alias, I went to Oklahoma City to see Dr. Don O'Donahue. He'd performed an operation on Redskin quarterback Sonny Jurgensen that had never been tried before. It was a major success and kept Jurgensen playing for several more years. For the umpteenth time, my knee was X-rayed and O'Donahue carefully examined the photos. "Dick" he finally said, taking off his glasses. "There's a chance that if you continue to play even after surgery, we'll have to fuse your leg stiff. My hope is that you don't do that. The risk is too high. The consequences are too severe. We should do the tibial-osteotomy as soon as you are able."

I went back to my hotel room and realized that my playing life was over. There would be no miracle surgery. God was not going to intervene. I didn't pound the table or start crying. I knew I had exhausted every possibility. For the last five years, I had done everything I could to keep going, including acupuncture, mind dynamics, and slathering horse linament—DSMO—over the knee.

I stared at nothing for a while, feeling myself unwind as though I'd just played a long, hard game. Then suddenly I felt hungry, remembering that I hadn't eaten since morning. I picked up the phone and dialed room service. When a woman answered and called me by my alias—"My I help you, Mr. Connelly?—it seemed fitting. Who was I now?

————

Earlier that month I had moved my family to De Land, Florida, far from the postseason noise in Chicago. Now all that was left was to tell George Allen that I would not be playing for the Redskins—or any other NFL team. I did this by phone when I got back to Florida. Allen was disappointed, but he understood. "Watch out for Halas" were Allen's last words before wishing me luck.

I think Helen was relieved that the injuries were behind me. In a way, so was I. I'd had it with the doctors and the soul searching and the snipes in the press.

It was just a little thirty-acre place that we called the farm, but we all loved it. We settled in easily, enrolling Rick and Nikki in the local Catholic school. All I wanted was to forget the past year. But before I could start thinking about my new life, Halas called from Chicago. We discussed the operation. He still wanted Fox to do it. I told him I wanted to choose the surgeon. He repeated his position that anyone but Fox did the job. I would be in violation of my contract if I couldn't play again after the operation. Then he said, "There's a possibility of a trade with the Redskins."

"I'm not going anywhere," I said. "I signed a contract with the Bears and I'm finishing with the Bears."

"Well," Halas said. "Just remember, if you have that knee operated on by any doctor other than Fox and you can't play afterward, then you don't get paid by me."

"That's bullshit!" I yelled over the phone. "I broke my ass for you for nine seasons and this is the way you repay me? Is this your attitude—now that my leg is all used up? Is this the way it's going to end?" Halas mumbled something unintelligible.

Then he said, "You don't have to be pugilistic about it. You'd better get a lawyer."

After I hung up, I called Ed Keating and asked him what "pugilistic" meant. Without asking me why I wanted to know, he said, "It refers to a combative attitude. Like a prize-fighter or the way you played football." Halas knew about being pugilistic. He was the most pugilistic person I ever met in my life.

Maybe I didn't know what "pugilistic" meant, but I sure as hell knew what getting a lawyer was all about. When I told Keating what the Old Man had said, he told me we would need a Chicago lawyer with guts and know-how. He had already picked out the guy and he wanted me to go to Chicago and meet him. A few days later, I sat in the office of James A. Dooley, no relation to the Bears' former coach.

Dooley looked like Ben Franklin—shiny bald on top with a ring of snowy hair, and he wore those little gold-rimmed glasses perched on the end of his nose. His desk was large and it was piled high with papers and briefs. Sometimes he would take notes, but usually he sat at his desk with his head down and his eyes closed. Half the time, I thought I was talking to a sleeping man. But he was listening.

After Keating and I spoke to him, Dooley said he would

take the case, adding that his fee would be one third of any settlement. I told him that all I wanted was the money due to me according to the contract.

Dooley nodded and replied, "I suppose you would like to know what your chances are."

"That would be nice," said Keating.

Dooley smiled. "Well, they would be poor to lousy, except for one thing." He held up one of the five contracts I'd signed and pointed to a single paragraph. "This—paragraph nineteen."

I took the contract and read the paragraph. It stated that regardless of whatever else had been said in the contract about my ability to play effectively for the Bears, they must honor their pledge to pay me my full salary whether or not I even suited up. This was the very same paragraph that Arthur Morse had inserted into my original five-year agreement back in 1965. I handed the contract to Keating and looked at Dooley.

He was shaking his head. "I don't know how they ever let that clause go through. But they did, and it binds them legally to the agreement. There is only one hitch."

Keating had finished reading the clause. "I'll bet I know. The five separate contracts Dick signed."

Dooley nodded.

Keating shook his head. "I knew I should not have let that happen. It's my fault."

Dooley explained that any judge worthy of his robe would rule in our favor, regarding the five contracts as one since the agreement spanned five years and was made at the same time and spirit.

"My job, gentlemen," he said, "is to make sure we get a fair judge."

"How do you do that?" I asked. I knew that Halas's influence in Chicago was second only to Mayor Daley's.

"That's my job, Dick," he said. "Don't worry. This case is ours to lose—and I don't lose."

We shook hands. Then he told me that one of the Bears' lawyers, Don Reuben, also represented the *Chicago Tribune*, which meant that I would not receive much favorable publicity from that paper. It turned out that he was right and wrong. Although the *Tribune* slammed me pretty hard on occasion, there were also some very evenhanded stories written about what one reporter would later call "the Butkus–Halas Affair."

I returned to De Land feeling pretty good, despite the pain in my knee. The Bears had paid me for 1973, and although no checks were forthcoming in 1974, I was confident that Dooley would emerge victorious in our case against Halas. Dooley hoped that Halas and his lawyers would see the futility in fighting our claim and settle out of court. But he warned me I should be prepared for a long battle because he knew Halas was a fighter.

Beginning in early May, Dooley and Reuben began slugging it out. Hardly a day went by when there wasn't a story about the latest exchange in the Butkus–Halas war. Surprisingly enough, a few *Tribune* writers gave our side a fair shake, considering the Bears' close association to the *Tribune*. I guess newspapermen have never liked lawyers. In this case, they had to decide whether Halas's lawyer or mine had a better story to tell. Every day I would get calls from city newsrooms and TV stations around the country, requesting interviews. I turned them all down.

After perhaps two weeks of hearing about the case from a thousand miles away, Dooley called me up to Chicago for a press conference. I was not thrilled with the idea of going back, but Jim convinced me that it would help our cause if the press and the TV people got a chance to talk to me in

person. He said that some writers had been critical of my re-
clusive behavior during this time and that it would be a good
gesture to meet with them. So I picked a date late in the
month that would allow me to go through New York to receive an award I'd won.

At the press conference, I apologized for not being accessi-
ble in recent months. "I want to explain to you how difficult
the last season was for me," I told him. "Especially the last
five games. It was a bad time for me and there were things I
didn't want to discuss. I felt horrible about the whole thing.
But I'm here now, so fire away."

Then I answered every question. The next day Cooper
Rollow raked me over the coals in the *Tribune* for being surly
to the press throughout my career. But he seemed to imply
that Halas was a liar and a manipulator, suggesting that he
had conned the press for years. Finally he asked Halas why
he hadn't done something about my knee the previous year.
"Why wait until now, Papa?" wrote Rollow. "Did it slip your
mind or maybe you hadn't noticed Dick was limping?"

In the same edition, Halas was quoted as saying that he
not only wanted me to have the operation but he hoped I
would have a few more years left to play. "How can ANYONE
say that this man will never play football again?" Halas
asked.

In a column next to Rollow's, *Tribune* writer Rick Talley
called Halas's statements "hogwash" and brought up the
point that six leading knee surgeons had concluded that my
playing days were over. My favorite line was the one that
said Halas was "kicking dirt" on the facts. Then Talley listed
the facts as he knew them. I will always be grateful to a Chicago press that gave me a fair shake, even though I never
came to trust them during my playing days.

A few days later, I flew to New York City to accept the

George A. Halas Award as the most courageous NFL football player of the 1973 season. The nation's sportswriters had decided that I deserved the award. Mr. Halas was not on hand to present the award bearing his name.

Back in De Land, I began training at Arthur Jones's Nautilus headquarters in Lake Helen, about a twenty-minute drive from the farm. I had met Arthur during the previous summer when he had demonstrated his new strength-building equipment. I believe that if I hadn't been working out on his machines all that summer, I would not have made it through the first nine games of 1973. I was in the best shape of my life—except of course for my knee. If Arthur Jones had entered my life six years earlier, I think I would have played a dozen years in the pros instead of just nine.

Arthur eventually put me on salary at his clinic. There was much irony in this, since my knee was hurting more than ever and I soon had to stop working out. Even though Halas had agreed to my having the operation—if Fox did it—I was reluctant to have it done until the suit against the Bears was settled. I thought the case would be resolved in a matter of weeks, but as months dragged by, the pain in my knee increased. Arthur urged me to get the knee fixed anyway. I fell into a long depression and I became a real annoyance to Helen and the kids. I was irritable much of the time and I was drinking too much. Even my brother Ronnie was on my back, asking me why the hell I was creating so many problems for myself and everyone else around me.

When it became too difficult to work out, I called James Dooley and asked him if it would hurt our case if I got the operation. He told me to go ahead and do it. Then I asked him if I would have to go to Dr. Fox as Halas had said. "Hell no. Whoever you like, Dick. It's your knee and no one can tell you who should operate on it."

I don't know why I hadn't done something sooner. Maybe I was still afraid that Halas would somehow be able to use it against me. I guess part of me was still in the clutches of the Old Man. At one time I would have done anything for him, and that kind of loyalty doesn't fade quickly.

I called the doctor in Baltimore. I had liked him when he examined me in the fall of 1973. But when I told him I wanted him to perform the operation, he said, "Dick, you should have your team doctor do the operation." While he extolled Fox's virtues as a surgeon, I felt like he was pulling the wool over my eyes. I called several other surgeons, including one in Los Angeles and another in New York, and got the same answers. What was happening? Had someone reached out and turned these doctors against me?

I still don't know the answer. There was, however, one surgeon that Halas never knew I consulted. Dr. Don O'Donahue in Oklahoma City. I had met him on the suggestion of George Allen after my clandestine trip to see if I could play for the Redskins. I called O'Donahue and he said, "Get up here as soon as you can. The longer you wait, the worse it will get."

I cleared up some business and flew to Oklahoma City on May 29, 1974, and that evening as I was getting prepped for the operation that was scheduled for the next morning, I watched the six o'clock television news with the sound off. Suddenly I saw my picture flash on the screen. I figured it had to have something to do with my fight with Halas if the local news considered it important enough to air. I hardly ate dinner, thinking about it and wondering.

When the eleven o'clock news came on, I learned that Dooley had filed suit for $1.6 million against the Bears for breach of contract. Among the charges Dooley leveled was negligence: that the Bears knowingly allowed me to play, even though they knew they were doing irreparable damage to the knee. As I lay there that night waiting for the operation, I wondered just what lay ahead in my new life. *Will my knee be okay? How long will the lawsuit take? What is going to happen to me and my family, now that coaching seems to be out of the question?* I never got so much as a query—much less an outright offer—from any NFL team. Did Halas prevent any offers from coming my way? Was I blacklisted throughout the NFL? He certainly had enough influence in the league to do so.

I never found out. But if Halas had prevented me from coaching at the pro level, I would've been the last to know. A few years later, I was on a plane with Arizona coach Tony Mason and he told me a story about his college days when he was going out with a different beautiful girl every night. Tony said, "I was no Robert Redford back then, but everyone thought these girls were always so busy—except me. I had to call *them*, Dick." Maybe that was why I was not a coach somewhere. But I would think that some college or NFL coach would've thought to call me.

I'm convinced about one thing: Halas never expected that I would actually sue the Bears. As far as I knew, no player had ever actually filed suit against the Old Man—although a number had threatened to over the years. The wise old fox tried to backpedal when he realized how serious we were. He offered me an ambassador role in the event I wasn't able to play. I laughed at that. Did that mean I would crisscross Chicago and spread goodwill about the Bears after they had treated me like a outcast? No thank you. All my goodwill toward that team was depleted, drawn from me like the strength in my right knee. For nine seasons, I showed up and played in pain because I was taught that you earn your way in this world. But there is another philosophy that says that if you are the employer of a faithful worker, then you honor your commitments to him. In my view, Halas had not done that. His offer was too little, too late.

When he learned of my operation, Halas made a big point out of the fact that the Bears had paid for it. In *Halas on Halas*, he made it seem as though he had taken the money out of his pocket. Hell, the contract called for the Bears to pay for any medical procedure that was required as a result of my playing football. But that fact never made it into the *Tribune* stories. As Halas manipulated the press more and more, people believed that I was a faker and an opportunist. Behind closed doors, however, Dooley was beating the Bears over the head with the truth.

"Well, boys," Dooley would say to Reuben and his assistants as he held up the contract, "it doesn't say anything here about a goodwill ambassador. You could have had him as a coach—and Dick would have loved that—but you see, Mr. Halas, you struck that paragraph from the contract. Why did you do that, Mr. Halas? Well, it's no matter. What we have here is a player's contract with a binding no-cut clause and my client needs to get paid."

Dooley asked me to recall—in as much detail as possible—the examinations by Dr. Fox. When I had done that, Dooley wanted depositions from other players, coaches, or trainers. So I began searching for someone who would corroborate my statements. I knew there was no sense in asking a trainer or coach; they were all on the side of the man who signed their paychecks. This infuriated me. Why couldn't they see that if the Bears would do this to me, then what the hell did they think would happen to them if suddenly they couldn't produce on the field?

Our only option was to find a former player or two who had been shafted by the Bears' management. We didn't have to look very far: Howard Mudd was ready to talk about the less than marvelous way in which he was treated when his knee failed during training camp in 1971. Another ex-player who spoke up was Bill Staley. Regarded as a wacko-hippie type, Staley backed me up when a lot of self-proclaimed tough guys were unavailable. He'd had a few good years with the Bears before his knee caved in and Needles operated on it. In our conversations, he did not speak highly of Dr. Theodore Fox.

If Mudd or Staley or I had injured our knees while working on a construction site, we would have been receiving long-term disability checks for the rest of our lives. Yet here we were, playing a sport that breeds injury and they expected us to clean out our lockers and go quietly when they couldn't use us anymore. That's what happened to Mudd and Staley, but these two men came through for me in a way that some people who called themselves friends never did.

At the top of the list of those who stood by me when it felt as though the whole world was against me was Jay Mc-Greevy. I met Jay when I was a rookie. I liked his quiet, unassuming manner. Jay owned a company called Remco Federal. He would enlist star players from the Chicago Blackhawks hockey team and the Bears to help promote the products he sold. He paid us to make appearances at various stores that sold his KitchenAid products. The money was gravy, but I did it because Jay was a nice guy.

He qualified as such by passing my acid test. One sweltering weekday afternoon in July the two of us were driving downtown in the Loop. We came to the corner of State and Madison and a cop was directing the traffic. He signaled us to stop. When Jay brought the car to a halt, I had the impulse to play a practical joke. I reached over and turned off the engine, took the keys out of the ignition, and threw them out the window. Then I slipped down as far as I could so that I was barely visible as I peeked over the dashboard. When the cop motioned us through the intersection, Jay sat there yelling at me. "Dick, for crissakes. Now what am I going to do?"

Horns were blaring from a couple of dozen backed-up cars whose drivers were anxious to get home from work and have a cool drink. The cop came over and leaned in the window on Jay's side and said, "What's going on here?"

"I dropped my keys out the window by mistake," said Jay, who was nonplussed.

The cop looked at Jay for a long moment, then nodded. "I see. Would you mind getting out of the car and finding them, so the city of Chicago can resume its daily functions?"

Jay jumped out of the car and started looking for his keys. Now the cop looked questioningly at me. I shrugged and said, "I dunno what to tell you, officer. The guy is a little unpredictable. Sometimes he does crazy things."

"Well, you better watch him, Dick," he said, smiling. "That guy could get into a lot of trouble."

"I will, officer."

Jay got back in the car with the keys and we drove off. I think I laughed for about half an hour as Jay mumbled obscenities.

Another bit of abuse usually came on Tuesdays when Ed McCaskey distributed the paychecks. Jay always needed extra tickets for his clients. If we had any, we would gladly give them to him. But we wouldn't make it easy. He'd come into the locker room after practice to pick them up, and we'd be in the big shower. He'd poke his head into steamy chamber, and one of us would say, "Here you go, Jay," and toss the tickets into the gutter. Cursing us for our childish behavior, Jay would scramble to snatch the tickets before they disappeared down the open drain, getting himself drenched in the process.

Ditka and OB were always major accomplices in our little "make McGreevy pay" tricks. But he took it well and he was such a friendly guy that there wasn't anything we wouldn't do for him.

During the lawsuit, Jay was my closest friend. We are still very close. Never did he question my decision to sue the Bears. Whatever I needed, whether it was advice or just company, Jay has always been there. When I was in De Land, he called me often. Whenever I was in Chicago, I stayed at his home in Hinsdale—and still do to this day. Jay got to know my moods better than anyone except maybe Helen.

He remembers things from that time that I have forgotten. For example, he recalls one hot summer day in 1974 when he had to go out of town for the day. He says it was 8 A.M. and I was sitting in the screened-in porch at the back of his house, reading something from Shakespeare (yes, believe it or not, Dick Butkus was reading Shakespeare). I was doing a lot of reading in those days in an effort to improve myself for whatever career I chose to pursue.

"Are you going to be all right by yourself?" Jay asked.

"Of course," I said.

Jay didn't come back until 10 P.M. He claims that I was still sitting on the porch, reading the bard. That I had stayed on the porch all day on such a hot afternoon was remarkable to Jay. But it wasn't to me. For months, I had been paralyzed, caught in the gap between football and another shapeless life.

I had played myself in the TV movie *Brian's Song* and had made a number of commercials and there was something about it all that I liked, something that seemed to free me up in the same way football had. I even liked the Monday morning quarterback lunches at the Playboy Club. I was able to get outside myself and perform the role of the public figure known as Dick Butkus.

My public and private sides are different, yet in some ways they are the same. When I am asked to perform publicly, I have always been able to speak more easily and with a greater articulation than I can when I am alone with just a few friends. However, my "public side" is usually consistent with my private thoughts and values.

According to McGreevy, I spoke very little during the long-drawn-out legal battle. On deposition days when I was in Chicago, Jay and I would sometimes drive to a construction site where they were razing an old building and watch the big wrecking ball knock walls down. I honestly don't remember this, but I'm sure Jay is right. The fact is I do like to watch buildings being torn down. It's a linebacker's way to get his mind off other things, I guess.

Another man whose encouragement mattered a great deal to me at the time was James Dooley. As my lawyer, he was somewhat obligated to boost my spirits during working hours. But Jim went well beyond the call of duty. More than most, he knew not only the facts of the case but also what was in my heart. We became good friends in the months the case dragged on. Each weekend he came down to Florida to his place in Bell Harbor and we would get together.

I remember when Dooley was being asked to run for the Illinois State Supreme Court. One day while we were having lunch somewhere in Chicago, Dooley was amazed at the number of people that came to our table to thank me for playing hard and to wish me luck in my battle against the Bears. I guess he didn't realize how many people in Chicago had real affection for me. When Dooley decided to run for the bench, he asked me to lend a hand. I would go to various mills and factories to hand out brochures and talk to the workers about voting for him. I knew I was backing a good guy because most people liked him—and they voted him to the Illinois Supreme Court.

But the bitter taste from the Bears remained. Whether or not we won the case, something deep inside me had been crushed. There was a popular theory at the time that Halas fought me to show other players that no one—not even Dick Butkus—was going to push him around.

While TV contracts were bringing millions of dollars to team owners, players' salaries were also soaring. New promotional and marketing opportunities were transforming top players into national icons every bit as popular as movie actors and rock singers. The word "superstar" was born because the original word "star" lost its meaning in the new galaxy of entertainment sports. It all meant more dollars—a lot more dollars—and Halas must have felt that if it hadn't been for him, none of it would have happened.

Certainly Halas deserved to prosper. The question was how much and at whose expense? Players were no longer field hands to be bought or sold. They were becoming two-legged money machines with lawyers, agents, accountants, and investment brokers in tow. Now the players had a union. All of this must have had an unsettling effect on the Old Man, who was looking on a bright financial future for his children and his team. But at seventy-eight it wasn't his future. So he made a stand, not only for himself but for all the owners. He was going to show all those cocky players how it was done. He was going to deal with me as he did so many other players, no-cut contract or not. Halas thought that he could beat me up in the press, just as he had done to Virgil Carter, Dick Gordon, George Allen, and so many others who dared to raise their voices against him. Halas could charm or intimidate, depending on what was needed to achieve his ends.

But he eventually learned that he couldn't intimidate me. What Halas hadn't counted on was the extent of my popularity in Chicago. The average Bears fan appreciated how I played the game more than anything the Old Man had to say about me. Those fans knew that no one had ever played the game harder or loved it more. They knew I wasn't faking the injury to my knee. They had watched me play for nine years—and they knew somehow that the threshold of pain had become too great in 1973.

The biggest barrier to the settlement was, as Dooley had said at the beginning, finding the right judge. The suit bounced from judge to judge, mainly because Halas's lawyer Don Reuben couldn't find one that he would approve. Finally Reuben found a judge who was satisfactory to both parties— Judge Robert Cherry. I was relieved when Dooley called to tell me that the case could go to court.

But in his first ruling, Judge Cherry decided against Halas on a key motion—and suddenly he wasn't so acceptable to Reuben, who insisted that a new judge be found because Cherry had once been the partner of Arthur Morse, who had negotiated my first contract with the Bears. Reuben contended that Cherry's former relationship with Morse had prejudiced him. When Cherry refused to disqualify himself, Reuben took the matter to Chief Judge John Boyle, who promptly turned him down.

On the heels of this defeat, the *Chicago Tribune*, with all the major events in the world to editorialize about, decided that Judge Cherry was worthy of six inches of opinion space. After explaining why Judge Cherry may have been in conflict, the editorial said: "We wonder if the time hasn't come for Judge Cherry to gracefully turn matters over to another judge."

At about this time, Len O'Connor, the city's leading television commentator also took an interest in Judge Cherry, who eventually stepped down from the case, even though the Illinois Supreme Court had supported his decisions. Then

Mike Royko, the nationally syndicated columnist and the most outspoken journalistic voice in Chicago, let his readers know about "the Butkus–Halas Affair":

> Now, I'm not going to quarrel with the right of the *Trib* or O'Connor to editorialize about any subject they choose. But since they brought up the question about conflict of interest, which is an interesting one, I wonder why they omitted the truly interesting facts from their opinion-swaying editorials.
>
> For instance, the *Tribune* did not mention that Halas's attorney is one Don Reuben.
>
> I'm sure the *Tribune* knows who Don Reuben is.
>
> Don Reuben is the *Tribune*'s lawyer, and one of the most powerful men in the vast *Tribune* organization.
>
> Nor did Len O'Connor mention that this very same Don Reuben is his close friend and news source. Or that O'Connor dedicated his excellent book on Mayor Daley to Don Reuben. Or that Don Reuben has been an attorney on occasion for O'Connor.
>
> And it wasn't mentioned that Reuben is the attorney for Channel 9, the *Tribune*-owned TV station, on which O'Connor delivered his commentary on Judge Cherry's possible conflict of interest.
>
> Now, I'm not saying that Reuben, the powerful *Trib* lawyer, had anything to do with that *Trib* editorial.
>
> And I'm not saying that Reuben, O'Connor's friend and source, had anything to do with O'Connor's commentary.
>
> All I want to say is—Judge Cherry, meet Mr. Pot and Mr. Kettle.

Royko's column appeared on October 10, 1975. It signaled a sea change for city opinion as more voices began to be heard in the case. For one thing, Halas had never been revered by the mass of Bears fans, some of whom began to write letters in my favor.

With the facts of the case tilting my way and public opinion running against him, Halas finally decided to cut his losses. He instructed Reuben to make a deal with Dooley. On September 13, 1976, two and a half years after we filed suit and three years after the start of my last season, the Bears agreed to pay me $600,000. At about the same time I sued the Bears, I also sued Dr. Fox and four other doctors, as well as the hospital that treated me. As part of my settlement with the Bears, I agreed to drop the suit against the doctors and the hospital.

As I sat in Dooley's office after the settlement conference, I wondered what the case had all been about. The answer, of course, was money. A few hours earlier, I listened to Halas's attorneys laugh at the weakness of their case, and now I asked Dooley what their fees amounted to. He ran some numbers in his head and said: "Probably $100,000."

I said, "Well, that's not all that bad, I guess, for two and a half years' work."

"What?" said Dooley, looking up from some papers he had been reading. "No, Dick. That was just for the last month."

For Halas, the lawsuit had never been just about me. It had been about all the players who would be injured in the future. If he could keep me from winning in court, there would be no precedent upon which to base future lawsuits.

All he had to do was pay me $115,000 for each of the four years that remained on my contracts. Instead he spent millions trying to put me in my place. He did the same thing to George Allen in 1966. I didn't get it then and I don't get it now.

They say it's just business. But calling it "business" doesn't excuse Halas's behavior. Even today, I hear people in Chicago say, "That's Dick Butkus. He sued the Bears."

A few days later, I was back in De Land. I went into my bank and told the manager Jimmy Ford that I wanted to make a deposit. He looked at the check and turned pale. It was a lot of money for Jimmy Ford and Dick Butkus of De Land, Florida, but apparently just a drop in the bucket for George Halas.

*W*ith the long, hard battle behind me, I rested in De Land and looked into a hazy future. I had always planned to stay in football as a coach. But the lawsuit had probably nullified any chance of that. So if it wasn't going to be football, what would it be? One thing I knew: I wanted to do something new. I vowed to myself that I would learn something useful so I could make an honest living outside of football.

While this was happening, I decided that I would tend to the cows and horses on my thirty acres of paradise in De Land. The ranch was subdivided into pastures of long grasses that were dotted with huge spreading oaks. It certainly wasn't Chicago, but I loved it.

I remember dropping Nikki and Rick off at their first day of school in January 1974. I was feeling guilty because I had uprooted them from their friends and cousins in Chicago. But they were young and I knew they would make new friends in Florida. I was not so sure I would adjust.

I still felt hurt by Halas's actions. In many ways, it was like having your family turn on you. As I watched Nikki and Rick walk off to a brand-new school, I felt as though the ground on which I once stood had been cut away. For the first time in my life, I was without the support of a football family and I was scared.

A few weeks later, I got a call from ABC's *Monday Night Football.* Don Meredith would be leaving the network to go to NBC and Howard Cosell had suggested that I be interviewed for the job. I found myself in Roone Arledge's Manhattan office at 1330 Avenue of the Americas, discussing a new career less than two months after ending my last season as a player. Everyone, including Roone, who as president of ABC Sports had the final say, seemed genuinely happy with the prospect of my joining Howard and Frank Gifford on the biggest show in American sports.

But when my contract dispute with the Bears came up, Roone explained that many NFL people and some viewers might question my objectivity if it was known that I was involved in a legal wrangle with the Bears. We ended the discussion amicably and I went home to De Land.

After my knee operation at the end of May, I got a call from someone at the University of Illinois who offered me the analyst's job on radio broadcasts of Illini games. I said I was definitely interested. But I still had to get through the late spring and summer. I was wearing a full cast from the knee operation and working out on Arthur Jones's Nautilus equipment.

Arthur and I drew closer and closer during the months following my exit from football. As he explained the business to me, I began to gain interest in strength training. Arthur was a brilliant man, perhaps the smartest individual I have ever known. His theories on bodybuilding changed the training methods for athletes around the world.

In June, I got a call from a producer at ABC's *American Sportsman* who asked me if I'd be interested in doing a television show on sailfishing off Costa Rica. The producer was the same Pat Smith who has been helping me write this book. When I asked if I could bring a friend, Pat said sure. A few days later, Jerry Mucha, a friend from the South Side who had been visiting me in De Land, and I took off for San José, Costa Rica.

I had been under a lot of stress since my battle with the Bears and I guess I was an accident waiting to happen. I was still wearing the cast from the operation and I was drinking pretty heavily. Jerry and I stocked up in the duty-free liquor store in Miami and took off with Pat and his crew. Also aboard the Laxa Airlines 707 was Stu Apt, an internationally known angler when he wasn't flying Pan Am 747s to and from South America.

Jerry and I started drinking bloody Marys and by the time we landed at Guatemala City, Guatemala, to unload some cargo, we were fried. Jerry, who liked to assume various personalities when he was on a toot, was playing the role of a spoiled rich kid whose father owned oil wells in Venezuela. The stewardesses were especially fond of the blue-eyed oil scion. I was playing myself as best I could.

At Guatemala City Airport, we tossed down a few more drinks at the bar while Jerry told an American woman that he was an engineer for a German precious metals consortium. He got so deep into the bullshit that we barely got back to the plane before it took off for San José. Once in the air, Jerry got the stewardess all flustered by asking her when we would land in Caracas. When she explained that we were not going to Caracas, Jerry insisted the pilot change course and drop him in Venezuela where his father's chauffeur was waiting for him.

That night in San José, Pat Smith joined us and we drank and gambled in the hotel casino until dawn when superangler

Stu Apt appeared fresh from a night's sleep. Stu was not amused. I suppose I should have understood that this trip was important to Stu—the national exposure he would get on ABC would be good for his career. But it just didn't occur to me.

That morning we flew to the Pacific side of Costa Rica in a chartered World War II relic known as a C-47. It was held together with bailing wire and piloted by a wacked-out cowboy. At first I didn't think much about it, but when I noticed that Stu was nervous, my heart started to beat a little faster. After a very shaky approach over mountains and jungle, we landed in a farmer's field that was dotted with goats and cattle.

After half an hour of waiting in the middle of nowhere, some vehicles appeared and we were taken to a place called Playa del Coco on the Golfo de Papagayo. The Pacific Ocean was a beautiful blue. Parrots talked in the trees and pelicans soared lazily over the crashing surf. The breeze was soft, the air balmy, and Jerry and I decided we had arrived in heaven.

But Pat and Stu were not happy. A fifty-foot Norseman, a top-of-the-line sportfisherman, was supposed to ferry us out to another ship anchored somewhere at sea. But there was no Norseman within sight.

So while Jerry and I sat on the beach and shared a bottle of rum—Jerry was telling the camera and sound crew that his father invented the Bic lighter—Pat and Stu stood helplessly at the water's edge and stared at the horizon. About three hours later, a blip appeared. About a half an hour after that, we finally saw the Norseman rocking easily beyond the breakers. There was no dock on the beach, which made it difficult to board, considering the fact that we had lots of expensive and highly perishable camera gear. So everyone but Jerry and me—I was still hobbled by the cast—waded out through the surf to the boat with sixty cases of camera equipment on their heads. The captain, an old salty character by the name of George Seeman, then announced that he was out of gas.

This put Pat into a rage, now convinced this trip was jinxed. He calmed down when Seeman said he knew of a place nearby where they could buy some gas. But he'd need our help. While we motored south along the coast, passing dense and glistening jungle coves, Jerry and I drank most of the skipper's hooch and finished off an entire platter of sandwiches we found in the fridge.

We pulled into a cove and dropped anchor about a hundred yards from shore. Then Seeman's first mate, Carlos, and Jerry dove overboard and swam to the beach. They climbed a hill and disappeared into the jungle. I looked up at Seeman, who was standing on the bridge about ten feet above, and said, "Hey, George! what's going on?" Seeman ignored me, probably because he was mad at us for drinking his booze and eating his sandwiches.

After a few minutes, we heard some banging and saw the jungle move. Two fifty-five-gallon drums seemed to pop onto the beach, followed by a disheveled Jerry and Carlos. They rolled the drums into the surf and swam them out to a diving platform at the stern of the boat. The task now was for Jerry and Carlos to hoist the drums onto the diving board so that we could haul them onto the deck with block and tackle. Although Jerry and Carlos were strong, they could not get the drums onto the diving board. While they struggled with the drums, I noticed that hundreds of small greenish eels were swimming all around them. I asked Seeman what they were.

"Sea snakes," said Seeman.

"Sea snakes?" I said. "Are they dangerous?"

"Most powerful venom known to man. One bite and you're dead," snarled Seeman. "But they're not usually aggressive."

So I yelled to Jerry, "Hey, those little eels are called sea snakes! One nip and you go home in a box!"

Jerry found new strength and practically threw the drums onto the platform. Then he was out of the water like a porpoise. Carlos followed at a leisurely pace, laughing his head off. The trip got even crazier after that. We got lost in a rainstorm on the way back to Coco Beach and when we finally reached the mother ship, which looked like it was built in the 1920s, I was so tired that I fell asleep without eating, a first for me. But I didn't sleep through the night because a fire broke out in the engine room. While everyone battled the blaze, Jerry snapped pictures of the action with my camera.

Anyway, we caught a lot of sailfish and I enjoyed it very much. In the end, Stu and Pat were happy, too. They got a good show and Pat asked me to do the narration when the piece was edited. A week later, Jerry and I were back in De Land and while we were putting together a photo album of the trip to send to Pat Smith, I got a call from Ed Keating. He said that the Miller Brewing Company was gearing up a whole new ad campaign involving a number of famous athletes and that it could lead to a long-term involvement for me if the campaign was successful. Keating said the agency wanted to know if I was interested.

I had just spent a week in front of the cameras and I found that I liked it—much to my surprise. Over the years, I had done some local commercials while playing for the Bears. I felt confident that I could do a decent job for Miller Lite. It was also honest income. This acting thing seemed to suit me and I wondered just how far I could take it.

So began a fourteen-year relationship with Miller Lite. In my first commercial, I portrayed a bowler known as Mister Sensitive. With former Giant lineman Rosey Brown as my teammate, I threw a bowling ball down an alley so fast that I made the pins shatter while a waitress holding a tray with bottles of Miller Lite looked on in amazement.

After the commercial appeared on national television, Ed called to say the Miller folks were delighted with the results. He said he could almost guarantee more work from Miller. I asked him how many commercials would be involved. Ed thought it might be as many as two a year. Well, that was fine, but I still needed to do something with myself for the other 359 days in the year. But it was a start.

Arthur Jones was keeping me busy a lot of the time in Florida. Part of my job was to work on football training films for high school and college coaches, emphasizing the training techniques Arthur had developed with his Nautilus machines. He also produced similar training films on basketball, using Hubie Brown and Al McGuire. I also did testimonial films on each piece of Nautilus equipment, demonstrating how they should be used. I did all the voiceovers for those films. Arthur wrote the scripts and coached me on my delivery.

Arthur and I traveled everywhere together. When we went to conventions or expositions around the country, Arthur would fly one of his planes while I drove one of the equipment trucks, hauling the strength-building machines. Then I would help unload the machines and set them up in the convention hall. I would also man the booth and sign autographs. One thing about Arthur: There was only one star to his operation, and it wasn't me.

Which was just fine as far as I was concerned. I was there to learn, and I learned a lot from him. His knowledge of business, of strength building, and of life in general was impressive. I had come fresh from a life that had made few demands off the field, so I was eager to learn everything Arthur had to teach me.

When I first met Arthur, he had me work out on his machines under his direction. Months later, he called me a "hundred percenter." I asked him what he meant by that. Arthur said, "You're an all-out guy. What you did on my machines was impressive. Most guys quit. Only the hundred percenters keep going like you did."

Arthur had filmed my knee operation. Somewhere in July 1974, I sat down to watch the edited version. It was all new to me because I was unconscious while Dr. Donahue operated. He removed the back half of the kneecap with a medical saw, then he sculpted the edges with a hammer and chisel.

Dr. Donahue's work has held up for well over twenty years. The most he could guarantee me was three or four years before I would need an artificial knee. Part of the reason for my knee's longevity is the Nautilus equipment that Arthur developed. So just as all the other men in my life—Bernie O'Brien, Pete Elliott, Bill Taylor, and for a while George Halas—had helped me through the difficult stages of my life, Arthur helped me work through the hardest stage of all: leaving football.

That fall I did the radio commentary for a number of Illinois games. I was very green and made lots of mistakes, but I enjoyed it and I learned a lot. Then in November, I got a call from Zev Braun, a Hollywood producer who used to work out with Gale Sayers. He asked me if I wanted to go to Spain to appear in a movie. I told Zev I had no real acting experience, but he said he knew that and thought I'd be pretty good in the role he had in mind.

A week later, I landed in Madrid. Sterling Hayden and Marty Balsam were also in the movie. It was a forgettable "spaghetti Western" called *The Onion Man*—about a Popeye-like character played by Italian star Franko Nero, who took a bite out of an onion instead of eating spinach to get his strength. I was one of the bad guys. They gave me a false beard to wear, because only two Americans could appear in the film and they didn't want people to know it was me. I didn't think it was necessary, but what did I know? This was my first movie. So every morning I sat for an hour in makeup while someone pasted a beard on my face. People said I looked like Ernest Hemingway.

Because the movie was all in Italian, there was no English version of the script available, which made it more difficult. I had always relied on being prepared, knowing the plays before I got to the field. Every morning I arrived on the set and was given my lines a few minutes before I was to say them. With no time to rehearse, I would go out there and perform, but I got through okay. Marty Balsam helped me a lot. He taught me how to relax. He said that if I was a flop, nobody would know because no one would see the movie anyway.

Christmas came in the middle of the shoot and Zev Braun took me to Rome for the holiday. He introduced me to Italian movie magnate Carlo Ponti, husband of Sophia Loren and one of the coproducers of the *The Onion Man*. Ponti was sitting in a screening room, reviewing scenes from a movie starring Marcello Mastroianni. I had to laugh as Zev told Ponti what a good actor I was, while up on the screen was one of the best ever. But Ponti was very nice about it and he encouraged me to stay with it. Zev and I hit it off. He was from Chicago and a big Bears fan. He told me I had good screen presence and urged me to take acting lessons and pursue a career in the business.

I suppose I decided to be an actor because the profession bears similarities to football. Both involve performances in front of an audience and they both demand mental and physical training. An actor can throw himself into a character he's playing, just like a football player can throw himself into the action on the field. But perhaps the similarity that mattered most—at least for me—is that good acting is largely about teamwork. Actors play off each other as do football players. It is the teamwork of a cast that draws me to acting. I love being on a set with actors and directors and the crew. Especially the crew.

But the rewards of acting did not come as easily to me as they did in football. For the next six years, I led a bicoastal existence while I tried to break into show business. During that time, I must have had half a dozen agents and I made many trips to Los Angeles to do readings for television and feature film parts. The answers I usually got were: "Thanks for coming, Dick. Gee, I loved to watch you play for the Bears. You were great. Hey, by the way, can I get an autograph for my kid?" Or they told me how impressed they were with my reading, and if it were up to them, they'd sign me up for a part in a heartbeat. But usually the role had already been promised to some big star who hadn't accepted as yet. Or, even worse, they'd wink and say, "Great job, Dick—your agent will be hearing from us." But I got enough parts to keep me on the hook.

I approached my new field of endeavor like a rookie at preseason camp, full of determination and desire to please, but that eventually wore off. Nowadays I'm very careful about doing readings. I ask questions first and depending on the answers, I do the reading or not.

As my acting career took on a larger proportion of my life, a curious thing began to happen. Instead of fading as I might expect it to, my football reputation seemed to grow beyond Chicago and spread to people who had never seen me play in a game—or for that matter watched much football. Certainly the commercials helped, especially the ones for Miller Lite—

and so did my occasional appearances on television shows. Children seemed to know who I was. But something else was happening, something that is still inexplicable to me. Almost from the first season after my retirement, the name Butkus carried more weight than it did even when I played.

Although the process started out pretty slowly, looking back on it all these years later, it seemed as though it happened overnight. Sportscasters and writers started to invoke my name as a synonym for aggression and toughness, and the name Butkus was being used increasingly by everybody from standup comics to major feature film actors. In the 1976 film *Rocky*, Sylvestor Stallone called his bulldog Butkus. Years later on *Saturday Night Live*, a recurring skit depicted three beer-drinking Chicagoans toasting a picture of me above the bar.

The stories of my exploits on the field began to grow and take on a life of their own. Friends of mine would ask about things that occurred during my playing days, things that seemed absolutely preposterous . . .

———

The year is 1969. The prospects were not pleasant for the defense. We've lost our first exhibition game to the Redskins, and now we are in the visitor's locker room, getting ready to play the Miami Dolphins. Not only will we have to put up with the best one-two-three combo of running backs in the NFL, but we will have to do it in Florida's fierce summer heat. You could sail a boat on the humidity. With the sun hitting the grass, the temperature at field level must be over 100 degrees. So when someone suggests that we make it a short afternoon, I'm among the first co-conspirators.

The party gets going early in the first quarter when someone on the line smacks a Dolphin lineman in the chops and a donnybrook breaks out. Bodies fly as both teams empty the benches. It is such a marvelous spectacle that I forget for a moment why I'm out there. I'm intent on watching guys hold their own.

Suddenly I hear: "You're out of the game, Butkus!"

"Who, me?"

I'm astonished. I haven't done a thing except maybe direct a little traffic, point some people in the right direction. Nevertheless, I turn and start walking off the field. Then Dooley almost ruins the whole thing by appealing to the official on my behalf. The official's response is something that I will never forget. He said I *bit* his finger. Now, I ask you, would I do such a thing?

To set the record straight, I never bit the hand of an official in a game against the Dolphins, although the story has been written countless times and today is accepted as fact. When someone asks me about that, it doesn't matter that I say it didn't happen. I can explain until I'm blue in the face, but they won't believe me. It's nuts. If I bit him, I'd say so. Another story that never happened describes me complaining to an official about some perceived infraction. The official finally gets tired of listening to me and says, "Dick, if you don't shut up, I'm going to bite your head off." To which I am supposed to have replied, "Well, if you do that, you will have more brains in your stomach than in your head." That's pretty funny, but I didn't say it—even though I wish I had.

This garbage has mixed with the true accounts of my football life, and it has all grown into this larger-than-life reputation I have no control over. Now I am constantly being referred to as a "legend," even though I wonder if I warrant such a title. Webster's New Unabridged Dictionary defines legend as a story coming down from the past, especially one popularly regarded as historical but not verifiable. When I think about it that way, with all those false stories about me floating around, I guess I qualify after all.

⸻

Fame wears two faces. It protects me, but it also hounds me. In some ways, it prevents me from living a normal life, but at the same time it brings me handsome fees for doing things my father would never have called "work."

Fame is also untrustworthy. One day it's your best friend, smiling encouragement and patting you on the back, then without so much as a nod it leaves you in the dark, wondering about its true nature. The truth is, fame is neither friend nor foe. Fame is a fraud. If you buy into it too heavily, it will ultimately steal everything you have, and I'm not talking about so much money or possessions as I am about a sense of yourself.

I can understand a child or even a grown-up fan being thrilled to get an autograph of his or her favorite athlete or celebrity, but what are the motivations of those people who seem to spend their lives seeking the signatures of the famous and infamous? These are people who don't discriminate. They would ask Charles Manson for his autograph if they could get to him. Maybe it's a piece of history for them. But I have to tell you, it embarrasses me a little when anyone asks me for my autograph. I don't know why, but it does, even after signing thousands of them. Maybe it has to do with that blue-collar ethic, the one about not getting above yourself and putting on airs. Sometimes the autograph hounds can be spooky. They hover on the periphery, waiting with paper and pen. At other times, especially when I'm eating in a restaurant, it can be enraging. Dozens of times, I have been approached in the men's rooms of the world at the most inconvenient moment.

But truthfully, I don't actually mind signing autographs

at the proper time and place. I spend many hours every month signing photographs of me as a player. But I do that in the comfort of my own home, and at a time convenient to me, and I often do it for nothing. I don't even mind signing autographs at a sports event or any public place when I am clearly not in a hurry or otherwise occupied.

All I ask is that people be polite and a little thoughtful. I resent having a piece of paper shoved under my nose just as I am bringing a forkful of food to my mouth. And being told, "Hey, Butkus—sign this." That sort of thing can really piss me off, and often I say so at the time.

As to the remark "Well, Dick, when they stop asking you for your autograph, you'll feel differently," I say, "Hey, I might like it."

On Super Bowl Sunday, 1979, I was sitting alone in my condo on Marco Island when I got a call from a gentleman who informed me that I had just been unanimously voted into the NFL Hall of Fame in my first year of eligibility. I put the phone down and sat there staring out the window. I don't think I ever felt more at peace in my life. It had all happened for me. Somewhere in my mind, the half-formed image of a little boy emerged. Did I really think all this would happen? Or did I want it so badly that the idea of it not happening was intolerable.

That August I traveled to Canton, Ohio, and received the warmest, most heartfelt tribute that any football player could ever receive.

It was from Pete Elliott, my coach at the University of Illinois. "The first play I ever saw Dick Butkus make was against a bootleg pass—the hardest play a linebacker has to cover. He was a freshman and he had not practiced yet with the team. Dick took two steps to his right, stopped, turned and ran stride for stride with the end crossing the middle— and intercepted the pass." Pete laughed a little at the memory. "It was immediately evident to me that Dick was a superior football player. But it didn't take a coach to see that. Anyone who ever saw Dick Butkus play knew it immediately. His tackling was devastating, his instincts were absolutely unbelievable. But the thing that sets him apart from every other athlete I have ever known is his great, great intensity. Dick Butkus played all out, all the time, every game, every practice. He is the yardstick for all linebackers for all time."

After the applause settled down, I thanked Pete, Bernie O'Brien, and Bill Taylor. I expressed my concern for George Halas, who was getting out of the hospital later that day after an attack of phlebitis. I thanked members of the Bears' organization who had been helpful to me: George Allen, the Old Man, Abe Gibron, Joe Fortunato, Don Schinnick, Bill George, and others. Then I looked out at the crowd and thanked my family. I began with my mother, and although I stumbled a little, I was okay. The apple caught in my throat when I mentioned my father, who had passed away in 1973. I barely got through my sisters and brothers. Then I thanked my kids for their patience and understanding and lost it altogether when I spoke of Helen. Then I wound it up by saying to her, "So thank you for being my biggest fan and . . . my best friend."

It was done now. It was a little like dying and being born at the same time. Johnny Unitas, Yale Lary, and Ron Mix were also inducted that day. As we stood around the podium after the ceremony, Ed McCaskey arrived. He hurried up to me and said, "Sorry, Dick, I was delayed."

Still carrying resentment at what I perceived as an intentional slight by the Bears, I sarcastically apologized to Ed for keeping him from his day at the racetrack. It wasn't fair of me to have said it. But at the time I figured Ed was one of the people who urged Papa to fight me on the contract. If I had been thinking a little more rationally, I would have realized that Ed was not one of Papa's favorites. In Halas's eyes, Ed was the husband of his daughter Virginia—no more, no less. Over the years, I have come to believe that Ed had nothing to do with it. Now I think of Ed McCaskey as a friend.

In 1986, I went back to the University of Illinois. Attorney Fred Richman prevailed upon the powers at my alma mater to retire my number. The only other retired football number belonged to Red Grange, and the honor of seeing my college number, 50, in the showcase in the field house lobby will be with me until the day I die. It was a quiet affair, as I had requested. We went down to Champaign–Urbana for a weekend and watched Illinois get creamed by Nebraska to open another losing season for the team. I remember taking some perverse pleasure in Pete Elliott being there. It had been years since Pete and I had been back at Illinois together since he and Bill Taylor had been so badly treated after winning a Rose Bowl for the school. Again, the experience felt like a healing of old wounds.

Then, on Halloween Eve in 1994, the Bears retired my pro number, 51, and Gale's number 40. It had been a long time coming—more than twenty years—for Gale and me. In 1987, during the season of the players' strike, the Chicago newspapers were pushing for our numbers to be retired, since it was announced that Walter Payton's number would be retired at the end of the season. Ed McCaskey came up to me in the visitors' locker room after a game with the Eagles in Philadelphia. I had just broadcast the game on WGN. After some small talk, Ed explained that it would be difficult to retire my number because so many Bears numbers had already been retired. He said they'd run out of the numbers for the new guys in the coming years.

But in 1994, the Bears finally decided to do it. It was an ABC Monday night game against the Packers, and Gale and I shared the spotlight, just as we had so many times a generation ago. It was classic Chicago weather, forty degrees and rain lashing in from nearby Lake Michigan. Helen and the kids were there, along with my brothers and sisters and their spouses, the two Ricks, Steve Thomas, Jay, and several other friends who had stuck by me during my long good-bye. While I stood in the rain and watched the ceremony on the field, I was thinking about the night before at the Tuscany's Restaurant on Taylor Street. Jay McGreevy had arranged a dinner for perhaps fifty people, including Ed and Virginia Mc-Caskey, Paul Hornung, Mayor Daley, Gale Sayers and his wife, and my family and friends. I will remember that evening for the rest of my life. When we started walking toward the mike, I stepped into a quagmire and nearly lost one of my shoes. I looked out at the crowd and was surprised to see so many people had stayed. The rain was coming down hard and the Bears were getting pounded by the Packers and it seemed to me those folks would have been better off at home or in a warm restaurant with drinks in hand. But they'd stayed, God bless them, and because of that I felt warm inside. Then I said a few words and left. It was short and sweet, partly because I wanted to keep it brief and partly because I had to get back upstairs to the WGN booth to broadcast the game. Funny thing about the weather that night. Sunday and Tuesday were clear and in the seventies. It was as if that storm had visited Chicago just for Gale and me.

Important as they were, those three events were not all that was going on in my post-playing life. While living in De Land, I was able to change my outlook in several important ways. I

learned to open up my life not only to greater spiritual rewards but to others who wished me well. The process of personal renewal began in the months before my victorious suit
against Halas and the Bears. I have already said that I was
difficult to live with during that time. As the months passed,
the pain of withdrawal from the game intensified, leaving me
with a sense of powerlessness.

With the help of Helen and some friends, I looked into the
Crusillio movement of the Catholic Church. Helen had been a
member since my playing days back in Chicago. She was always baking cakes and pies and going off to meetings. I had
no idea what she was doing, but I did know that her faith and
optimism was something that I wanted for myself. Although
I can't go into detail about my initiation into the movement,
believe me when I tell you that never before in my life have I
felt such an emotional release. It's hard uncompromising
work, but the result was that I not only felt closer to God but
my capacity for love had multiplied.

As I became more involved, I helped spread the movement
throughout Florida prisons. In Raiford, a maximum security
penitentiary, I met Murph the Surf, who had stolen the Star
of India, a spectacular jewel, from the Metropolitan Museum
of Art in New York City. At that time, Murph was serving
two concurrent ninety-nine-year stretches for murder. Well-
spoken and wearing the shiniest shoes in the joint, his manner and persona seemed to belong in a country club. I liked
him personally and I admired his commitment. The last time
I heard from him, Murph was working outside the prison
system, spreading the ministry. Eventually, I studied to be a
deacon, going to Orlando on weekends. What I learned will
stay with me the rest of my life, acting as an effective coun-
terbalance to the temptations of fame.

Meanwhile, the Miller commercials were a big hit. They

involved a whole gang of well-known actors, writers, and athletes. Bubba Smith and I teamed up as a couple of ex-football players who were looking for a new life. In a series of very funny, well-written commercials, we played golf, tennis, and polo. We went to the opera dressed in tuxedos and hoped they sang it in English next time. The thirty-second spots were seen all over the country, and the playback from friends and associates was impressive. Everyone seemed to like them.

Every fall all the Miller players would get together and make a Christmas commercial: stand-up comedian Rodney Dangerfield, the NHL's Bernie "Boom Boom" Geoffrion, novelist Mickey Spillane, baseball's Billy Martin, billiards champion Steve Mizerak, basketball's Tommy Heinsohn, and baseball broadcaster Bob Uecker. We had great times together, and I guess it showed in the commercial. We were all coachable, but nobody was any better than Bubba and me, at least that's what we thought. In the hands of directors Bob Giraldi and Steve Horn, we all found it easy to do our jobs. I think I caught the acting bug by doing those Miller commercials.

I had done a few other acting jobs, including a six-week shoot for a TV movie called *SuperDome*. David Janssen was the lead. The cast also included Ken Howard, who went on to star in the CBS series *White Shadow*, and Tom Selleck, who would become a star in another successful CBS series called *Magnum, P.I.* We had a great time. Selleck and Howard were good guys. Janssen was also a good guy and a great actor. I watched him perform and damned if I could tell when he was doing it, which is the ultimate compliment for an actor.

During a day's shooting, there was nonstop kidding around. Selleck, who had played some football, joined me in telling the actors the wrong way to slip their thigh pads into their football pants, thus creating extreme discomfort in the groin area when they put them on.

I played guest roles in a number of TV series early on in my acting career: *Wonder Woman, Bronk*, and *Simon & Simon*. I liked the experience, but still hadn't committed myself to the profession. One day I got a call from an agent named Tim Karg. He asked me if I wanted to do a *Magnum, P.I.* episode. The show had become a hit. I said sure and went off to Hawaii. It occurred to me on that set, with the winter breezes rattling the palm fronds, that this acting thing might be a very pleasant way to earn money. It was Christmas later that week, so at a party one night, I noticed that the director was with a spiffy-looking blonde at the table.

I walked up to him and said, "Hey, one of the AD's just got a call from the doctor in L.A. Your wife came through the operation in flying colors, so don't worry about a thing. She's just fine."

The director laughed a little, but it was clear that I had embarrassed him. He vowed, "I'll get you for that, Butkus." The next day on the set I was informed that my character had been changed overnight and that now I had no lines. Selleck said he was sorry about the character switch, indicating with a shrug that there was nothing he could do about it. I told him not to worry. I certainly wasn't. I got the same money whether I said anything or not.

Over the years, I've heard nothing but good things about Selleck. One Christmas he gave Porsches to the supporting actors in the series, and someone once told me that he actually stayed on the series an extra season so that his buddies could have one more payday before he moved on to feature films.

The experience in Hawaii only increased my determination to succeed in the acting business. The next morning Tim Karg met me in L.A. and we discussed how I might get more work. Karg asked me if I would consider moving to L.A. I told him that if that was necessary, I would do it. Within a couple of weeks, Karg had me up for a recurring role in an upcoming series. I read for the part, and when I didn't hear anything for several days I said the hell with it and flew home to De Land. I no sooner unpacked my bags when Karg called me and said that I had a reading for NBC at 8 A.M. the next day.

So back I went on the midnight flight out of Orlando with a two-hour stopover in Atlanta, arriving at LAX at 3 A.M., West Coast time. A few hours later, I read for the network executives and landed the part. It was that easy. I did the pilot. Immediately after that gig, I landed another part. It was in *Rich Man, Poor Man*, an ABC miniseries that launched Nick Nolte into stardom. Nolte was friendly and very helpful. I found that actors and football players are alike in at least one way. If they are really good at what they do, they are usually pretty nice people.

Now I was hungry for work, so I accepted just about every offer that came my way. I was looking for quantity, not quality, on the theory that the more roles I played, the better I would get. Virtually all the parts were either ''jocks'' or ''heavies''—but that was okay. I was there to learn and the money was good. By now I had moved out to L.A. and was living by myself in a second-rate motel. It wasn't long before I realized that I needed a West Coast manager, someone on the spot who knew the ins and outs of the entertainment business. Then I was told I would need a publicist, a theatrical agent, and a commercial agent. All would take a little piece of my income for marketing a little piece of my ass. But I was told it was worth it.

My West Coast manager turned out to be Sy Katz. I liked Sy immediately, but I had to do something that was very un-comfortable before I hired him. I had to cut Ed Keating loose. When I called Keating at his office in Cleveland to explain that

I needed a manager who specialized in show business, he didn't want to hear it—and our parting was not on the best of terms. In fact, we didn't speak to each other for years. Then one day Ed called out of the blue and told me that his son, a U.S. Marine, had been seriously wounded in a freak accident at Camp Pendleton.

The tragedy brought us back together, and a few years later—in 1996—Ed himself died of cancer. I was proud to be among his all-star team of pallbearers that included baseball men Dennis Eckersley, Frank Robinson, and George Hendrick. Ed's death helped close the door on a part of my life that had been equal parts high and low drama. I am glad he called that day to share his grief over what had happened to his son. By doing so, he allowed me to be there for him in the way he had been there for me at the bitter end of my playing days.

Years before Ed's passing, in the late 1970s, I had tried with some success to mend another broken fence from the past. In October 1979, I was staying at Jay McGreevy's house in Chicago when I noticed a stack of books in one of the downstairs rooms. There were 100 copies of *Halas by Halas*, the Old Man's recently published autobiography. Jay had bought the books as Christmas gifts for some of his customers. It just happened that I was about to attend a function that Halas was also scheduled to attend. On an impulse, I appropriated one of Jay's copies and took it to the dinner. That night I slipped the book under the Old Man's nose and opened it to the front flyleaf. He looked up at me and smiled, his eyes warm like they used to be.

"How are ya, kid?" he said.

"I'm fine, Coach."

"Good," he said.

Then he took out an old-fashioned fountain pen and signed my copy of his book. In blue Waterman's ink, it reads:

To Dick Butkus.
The greatest player in the history of the Bears.
You had that old *zipperoo.*

I wonder why he couldn't have said that to me when I played for him. Maybe he thought such an admission would put him at a disadvantage or maybe he just couldn't bring himself to say it face-to-face. Maybe it had to take a lot of time and a little pain for both of us to realize that we loved each other and that football was the medium of that love. Calling me the greatest Bear was as good a tap on the helmet as I ever received from anybody. It was right up there with Bernie O'Brien's comments about me to the press half a lifetime ago.

I wish that Halas was still here so I could return the favor:

To Coach:
The greatest Bear of them all.
Hooray for Halas!

The Old Man died in 1983. He was eighty-eight.

In 1983, I rented a beachfront house in Malibu from a comedien-turned-producer named Howard Morris. Hard as the move may have been on the kids, it was especially difficult for Helen. We had brought our widowed mothers to De Land and set them up in apartments, and now, just as things were settling down, Helen had to readjust to my wanderings.

We had all grown to like De Land. The kids had found new friends, of course, and Helen never has trouble in that department. She believes in happy endings but knows that sacrifice is the price of that ticket. Just as I could never have made it through my earlier years without my mother, I could not be who I am or do what I do without Helen nearby.

But Malibu was hard to dislike. With the Pacific rolling to within a few yards of our porch, whales and porpoises migrating in the distance, and movie stars jogging with their dogs along the beach, it seemed that we had found the American dreamscape. It wasn't perfect, though. Far from it. But we liked it then—and we do now.

While Helen got the kids in school and got involved with a church parish in nearby Pacific Palisades, I got down to the full-time business of being an actor. Karg hustled at first and helped me get parts in TV series and feature films. Also helping me were the Miller Lite spots, which were being run year-round on national TV. They were such a big hit in the industry that as soon as Karg would mention them to the casting director, I would get a chance to read for the part. Those commercials were great door-openers not only for acting parts but for other commercials. Offers flowed, but I turned down a lot of them. To date, I have made well over 200 TV appearances—and the offers keep coming.

But I had set my sights on a career in television and feature films, and I worked toward that end with every ounce of my available energies. I obsessed on a role, just as I would obsess on an upcoming game. The difference was that the profession of acting does not involve the same level of intensity. The waiting around was awful. When I finally would get a part, I'd almost overprepare myself. I was having trouble finding the right level of enthusiasm for acting. Karg suggested I take some acting classes. It seemed like a good idea. When I wasn't "working," I'd still have a way to become a better actor. The classes would be my Fernwood Park.

The first night of class, I met another student during a coffee break. He asked me what I had done and I told him about *Brian's Song* and *Simon & Simon* and a few other things. He thought that was just great.

Then I asked him, "How long have you been studying at the studio?"

"Almost five years," he said.

"Wow, five years," I said. "I guess you like this teacher, huh?"

"He's wonderful," said the student.

"What have you done?" I asked.

"Oh, I haven't done anything yet," he said. "He doesn't think I'm ready."

Not ready?

The words sent shivers through me.

Five years?

Who was this teacher anyway? Sir Laurence Olivier? I was practicing "Drop that gun, you dirty rat!" and this guy was teaching "To be or not to be." As far as I was concerned, it was *not* to be. I finished my coffee and went home to watch the Blackhawks and Rangers on TV.

As it turned out, the offers to appear in episodic roles—playing nonrecurring characters in TV series—kept coming with surprising regularity. I was having a great time. In fact, I couldn't believe I was getting paid for showing up, hitting my marks, and saying my lines. And when I began to hear what some of the actors were being paid, especially those in long-running series, I really got excited. I began studying the better actors. How, for example, did David Janssen do it? The guy was so steady and cool, no matter what was going on around him. The same was true of Rock Hudson in *McMillan and Wife* and Tom Selleck in *Magnum, P.I.* and Linda Carter in *Wonder Woman.*

Linda Carter was something else. She was tall and gorgeous and had a pair of blue lights where her eyes were supposed to be. I played a heavy, some kind of crook, and there was one scene where Wonder Woman turned the truth-seeking power of her eyes on me and I was supposed tell the truth. Well, so there we were, maybe a foot apart, and the director yelled "Action!" I looked into her eyes and nothing came out of my mouth. I couldn't speak. All I could see were those beautiful eyes. I was a zombie.

So the director yelled, "Cut!" I gathered myself and we set up for the second take. "Rolling!" shouted the director of photography. "We've got speed!" said the engineer. "Action!" said the director. And I looked into her eyes and again I was in Goo-Gooland. When something like that happens, it is really hard to keep a straight face. Everybody wants to howl and the laughs usually start slowly and build up. Hell, it must have taken me twelve or thirteen attempts before I could deliver my lines. Linda was hysterical. Everybody was, including the director. I was mostly red-faced.

After playing dozens of parts, I found that the most successful series had two things in common: an actor-friendly climate and good writing. In CBS's *Murder, She Wrote*, for example, Angela Lansbury and the entire crew were one big happy family. For six months a year, the cast, crew, and producers were together twelve hours a day, six days a week—eating, drinking, working, traveling. They got along and the scripts were always fun and written with the actors in mind. The same was true of the *Matlock* series. Andy Griffith was a family all by himself.

As the shooting seasons rolled by and I came no closer to landing a good part on a long running series or feature film, I started to lose faith in the possibilities of an extended acting career. Time and again, I was led to believe that I would either star in a series or in a feature film. There were many close misses, but none closer than the time Bubba and I were given holding money to do a feature called *Blitz* for Orion Pictures. Pat Smith had left ABC to start a production company in New York that eventually failed. He needed work, so he came out to L.A. and set up shop in my house on the beach. I introduced Pat to my agent of the moment, Tom Jennings—I had fired Karg a year earlier—who had introduced him to Mike Medavoy, head of production for Orion. Medavoy and Pat hit it off and Medavoy told Pat he was interested in making a movie with me in it. So Pat and I sat down and wrote a ten-page treatment for a buddy movie to star Bubba and me. Medavoy liked it and hired Pat to write the script. Pat went home to New York and about eight weeks later he sent the first half of the script to Orion. Memos started flying around the studio offices in Century City that they might have a potential hit on their hands. When the second half of the script arrived, they were convinced of it. Medavoy was the driving force behind the project. He told Pat that he thought I had a "John Wayne" quality and that I could be a big star with the right script and the right director.

Irwin Yablans, producer John Carpenter's *Halloween*, was hired to head up the project. Pat came out from New York to do some rewrites. Bubba and I were paid holding fees to ensure that we would be available to make the movie. Tom Jennings had been made one of several executive producers. The script was "costed out" and Medavoy and Yablans started looking for the right director. The picture would be shot that summer in New York City. Meanwhile, Bubba and I had finished our weekly stints as the ground support crew on an ABC series called *Blue Thunder*, and we were waiting for the word.

Then it all blew away. The decision was made to drop the project. The only reason Tom Jennings could determine was that recent receipts for five Orion releases had totaled deep within the red. Pat went on to write for *General Hospital*, Jennings returned to agenting, Bubba brooded, and I fumed. Four careers had stalled at the brink of major success.

An interesting footnote to the *Blitz* affair is that Orion had commissioned another script to be written expressly for Rodney Dangerfield. When the studio executives read the script, they hated it. But Dangerfield had a million-dollar-plus "pay or play" deal, which meant that he would have to be paid whether or not the movie was made. Rather than eat the loss, Medavoy and his colleagues—Bill Bernstein, Eric Plescoe, and Arthur Krim—decided to roll the dice. The movie was *Back to School*. It grossed millions and Orion's financial ills were healed for the moment. So, go figure.

I began a serious reappraisal of my life. I asked myself the big question: Was I really that interested in an acting career? Sure, I enjoyed it. Who wouldn't? Everyone dreams of seeing themselves on the screen—at home or in the movie theater. But did I *need* to do it the way I needed to play football? To answer that question, I had only to recall that night at acting class when I left after the coffee break. Football for me was a way of life. I know some actors who feel that way about their craft, and I had to finally admit that I did not share their passion—and never would.

While I continued to be available for roles, I no longer sat by the phone. I shifted my focus back to the game I love so much. WGN Radio in Chicago offered me the color commentary slot on its broadcasts of Bear games and I accepted. After several seasons, CBS asked me to join Brent Mussberger and Irv Cross on *NFL Today*. Every Saturday from August through the NFL playoffs I got on a plane and headed for New York. Meanwhile, I landed that elusive recurring role. I played a cook in the coffee shop in *My Two Dads* on NBC. Between the jobs, I was bouncing from coast to coast, never feeling as though I was prepared. To be honest, I couldn't stand certain members of the cast on *My Two Dads*. But life wasn't all that great on the weekends either. Irv and Brent were really good guys—I'd known Brent when he wrote for the *Chicago Tribune* at the beginning of my pro career—but I did not particularly enjoy the experience. The whole exercise seemed false somehow. Part of my unease was due to the show's strict format. Everything was planned and rehearsed, and I seldom felt as though I could be myself. It seemed to me that the show's formula was more important to the producers than providing the audience with interesting, insightful analysis. I left after the second season.

By now we had purchased the house overlooking the ocean, the house where I have my koi fish pond. It is a terrific house, with cathedral ceilings, a huge kitchen, and a spacious deck. It is a universe away from 10324 South Lowe.

Soon after we moved into the house in Malibu, Nikki went off to Notre Dame, from which she graduated with honors, and Rick started his career in the feature film business. Matt went to USC, where he played defensive tackle. Eventually, Nikki married a great guy, Francis, from Holland. They now live in Philadelphia, where Francis is getting his MBA at the Wharton School. Rick lives in Venice when he isn't working on a movie somewhere in the world, and just the other day I helped Matt move into his own digs a short run up the coast near his job in Ventura.

What about me? Well, it's been pretty much business as usual. I recently played a guest role on ABC's *Coach* and another on a new NBC series called *The Chicago Suns*. There are a number of commercials on tap, and plenty of charity golf tournaments and card signings—I could do that stuff all the time if I wanted to. Although I haven't been doing any sportscasting lately, it's always possible I'll be back in the booth before too long. Two new ventures are taking up a lot of my time these days. One is a company called Avid Sportswear, makers of top-of-the-line golf clothes. The stuff is absolutely great. My other interest is Bear Paw, Inc., a company owned with Dave Powless, who played with me on the Illini Rose Bowl team and for the New York Giants and the Washington Redskins. Dave is an Oneida and Bear Paw specializes in voluntary employee benefits for those living in North American areas. I've learned a lot about their struggles and how they view the world.

In truth, I would rather travel to a remote reservation in New Mexico than sign autographs for a weekend. To meet these people and get to know them is reward enough. Although they have been kicked around pretty bad, most of them would rather die than let you know how much it hurts. They remind me of the people back in Roseland, always looking for a fair deal, an even chance. The great majority of those Native Americans I have met are fiercely honest, down-to-earth, and hardworking. Many remind me of my father: quiet, soft-spoken, with a eye out for the humorous side of things.

Recently, a coffee table book on the pros called *Football* was published by *Sports Illustrated*. In it was a list of the fifty best NFL players of all time. There were just three players ahead of me, all offensive players: receiver Don Hutson of the Green Bay Packers, quarterback Otto Graham of the Cleveland Browns, and fullback Jim Brown, also of the Browns. What mattered more than my ranking was the inclusion in Peter King's text of a quote attributed to Buffalo Bills public relations director Scott Berchtold, who grew up in the 1960s: ''A lot of kids suddenly wanted to be defensive stars around that time. They wanted to be Dick Butkus.''

The highest compliments I have ever received have been

those little taps on my helmet after I stopped a runner short of the first-down markers or broke up a pass. Like the nod from my father when he came home from work, or a smile from my ma, or a wink from the Old Man as he prowled the sidelines—those private gestures were all the gold I ever needed. They were what I played for then and what I remember now.

The next time you go to an NFL game do yourself a favor and listen to the crowd. Hear them when the quarterback connects on a critical pass play and hear them when a runner breaks into the open for a long gain. Then listen for the sound that comes when a linebacker puts a big hit on a ball carrier at the line of scrimmage.

When you hear that sound, I hope you'll think of me.